MYTH, TRUTH AND LITERATURE

Colin Falck's book has had a widespread influence since it
first appeared in 1989. Hailed as a work that alters the
way we think about literary theory and its institut-
ionalization in America and Britain, it is a philosophically
informed account of the "paradigm-shift" required to
replace structuralism and post-structuralism as modes of
perceiving literature and related culture. Falck now
supplements this second paperback edition with important new material opening up fresh horizons within the
subject.

This controversial book provides a challenge to philosophers and theologians, as well as to anyone concerned
with the fate of literary studies.

Colin Falck was born in London and educated at Christ's
Hospital and Magdalen College, Oxford. He was Lecturer
in Modern Literature at the University of London (Chelsea
College) from 1964 to 1984, and is currently Associate
Professor in English Literature at York College, Pennsylvania. He has taught creative writing in many
institutions. Colin Falck was cofounder and associate
editor of the poetry magazine *The Review*, 1962–72, and
poetry editor of *The New Review*, 1974–78. His pub-
lications include two poetry collections *Backwards Into the
Smoke* and *Memorabilia*, two editions of *Poems Since 1900*
(edited with Ian Hamilton), and centenary *Selected Poems*
of Robinson Jeffers (1987) and Edna St. Vincent Millay
(1992).

MYTH, TRUTH AND LITERATURE

TOWARDS A TRUE POST-MODERNISM

COLIN FALCK

2ND EDITION

CAMBRIDGE UNIVERSITY PRESS

Published by the Press Syndicate of the University of Cambridge
The Pitt Building, Trumpington Street, Cambridge CB2 1RP
40 West 20th Street, New York, NY 10011-4211 USA
10 Stamford Road, Oakleigh, Melbourne 3166, Australia

First published 1989
Reprinted 1991
2nd edition 1994
Reprinted 1995

Printed in Great Britain by
Athenæum Press Ltd, Gateshead, Tyne & Wear

British Library cataloguing in publication data

Falck, Colin
Myth, truth and literature: towards a true post-modernism
I. Literature. Theories
I. Title
801

Library of Congress cataloguing in publication data

Falck, Colin.
Myth, truth and literature: towards a true post-modernism /
Colin Falck. – 2nd ed.
p.   cm.
Includes index.
Originally published: Cambridge [England]; New York: Cambridge
University Press, 1989.
ISBN 0 521 46185 5 (hc). – ISBN 0 521 46751 9 (pb)
I. Myth in literature.   2. Truth in literature.   3. Literature –
Philosophy.   4. Poetry – History and criticism.   5. Postmodernism.
I. Title.
PN56.M94F35   1994
809'.915 – DC20   93-46138   CIP

ISBN 0 521 46185 5 hardback
ISBN 0 521 46751 9 paperback

UP

To Isaiah Berlin

belated harvest

I laboured at a solid foundation, on which permanently to ground my opinions, in the component faculties of the human mind itself.   *S. T. Coleridge*

Literature is, to my mind, the great teaching power of the world, the ultimate creator of all values... [It] must take the responsibility of its power and keep all its freedom.
          W. B. Yeats

Artists are the antennae of the race.   *Ezra Pound*

CONTENTS

PREFACE TO
THE 2ND EDITION

As an academic fashion, the Anglo-American literary post-structuralist movement collapsed with extreme suddenness shortly after
the first publication of this book in 1989. No credit is being claimed
here for that collapse, which (aside from any question of the operation
of a *Zeitgeist*) must be put down at least in part to the greater-than-
usual aesthetic sterility of the movement itself and to its inability to
appeal to any but the most aesthetically insensitive and theoretically
obsessed of readers – a category that recently seems to have included
many graduate students in leading American and British universities.
In preparing this second edition I have allowed the opening chapter
on Saussurian and post-Saussurian literary theory to stand, not
because I believe that theory still to have any real life in it, but
because it seems to me important that the theory itself should not be
allowed to disappear altogether before it has been clearly seen to be
dead on philosophical grounds as well as from a merely fashionable
point of view. Part of the purpose of this new edition is to make such
a state of affairs more likely, and I have added now, as an appendix to
the original text, an essay on the poetic theory of Romanticism which
I hope may suggest some aesthetically non-sterile critical ways in
which we might at last once again begin to move forward.

The theoretical void which has been left by the bankruptcy of post-
structuralist theory is necessarily also a spiritual void. The French-
based literary-cultural theorizing of post-Saussurianism, with its
callow and philosophically incoherent anti-metaphysical posturings,
has tried to disengage literature from its troublesome spiritual
dimension altogether – by simply denying the existence of that

dimension. It has thereby threatened to deprive an entire generation of students and intelligent readers of a part of their spiritual birthright. The replacement of this movement, now more or less universal in (especially American) academic circles, by the theories of "multi-culturalism" threatens to do the same thing all over again. A situation has developed where, as Paul Valéry (facing a different version of the same problem) once wrote,

> [a]s bad luck will have it, there are among those men with no appetite for poetry – who don't understand the need for it and who would never have invented it – quite a number whose job or fate it is to judge it, discourse upon it, stimulate and cultivate the taste for it; in short, to distribute what they don't have. They apply to the task all their intelligence and all their zeal – with alarming consequences.[1]

Because of this situation, students and readers are growing up with no real sense of the spiritual significance of literature and with no invitation to develop their own creative sensibilities in truly literary ways. This near-death of intuitive aesthetic sensibility in the academic world, together with the stifling of critical inquiry by journals with names like *Critical Inquiry*, the dismantling of the traditional literary canon for almost entirely non-literary reasons, and the virtually total supplanting of literary discussion and criticism by cultural-political discussion and criticism in books and articles now written about literature, has meant that there are no longer any places in the world of organized literary education where the value of literature as an open and unprejudiced imaginative enhancement of life can be either acknowledged or cultivated. Yet it is hard to see why the rest of us should have to pay such a high price for this revenge of the uncreative sensibility upon the creative – for this dislike or fear of literature by those who have somehow worked their way into the positions where they are able to shape and to control the judgements that can acceptably be made about literature. An academic English-teaching system that no longer fights the mental fight against the all-embracing technologico-Benthamite spiritual corruptions of our modern world is a teaching system that has lost its soul. It may be time to remind ourselves that some of the greatest traditional critics – Johnson, Coleridge, Arnold, Eliot, Lawrence (to name only the better-known Anglo-Americans) – were those who themselves

---

[1] I am indebted to Frank Kermode for this quotation, which he uses as an epigraph to his *An Appetite for Poetry* (London: Collins, 1989).

created literature, rather than those "who don't understand the need for it and who would never have invented it." Unlike their present-day successors, these traditional critics could occasionally even do philosophy as well. Some of our most important modern ideas about the nature of art, and consequently about the nature of human life itself, were formulated by the poet and playwright Friedrich Schiller in the interstices of his own poetic activity.

Something is now needed which will fill the spiritual vacuum that stands more clearly revealed the more completely the inadequacies of French anti-metaphysical theory are demonstrated. What is needed, for the most part, already exists, and has long been available to us. It is the great tradition of Romantic poetic theory from Vico, through Hamann, Herder, Goethe, and Schiller; from Blake, through Coleridge and Keats, and culminating in the ideas of such literary and aesthetic philosophers of the modern period as Santayana, Collingwood, and Heidegger. The ideas that make up this tradition are unlikely all to be true, since these writers contradict each other quite freely. But there are certain basic contentions that they have in common, which in effect define the theoretical side of Romanticism itself, and which conflict with the ideas of post-Saussurianism – as well as providing the necessary basis for its refutation. These ideas in fact converge with some of the main trends in professional modern philosophy as practiced by professional modern philosophers. My aim in the new Appendix to this edition is to help to re-focus some attention on this rich theoretical realm. The essence of post-Saussurian theory is to reject, or to annihilate, the aesthetic or spiritual dimension of art – and of life – entirely, and thereby to reduce art or literature to something merely cultural or political. The essence of German and English Romantic philosophy is to show why this can never be done. The importance of Friedrich Schiller, to take only one example, is (from this theoretical standpoint) that his ideas are still our best key to understanding the true imaginative and spiritually educational value of art, and therefore its true place within the institutions of human life as such. His ideas are also crucial if we are to hope to rescue the concept of "play" from its present post-structuralist trivialization – with its spin-off effects of further trivializations within the realm of literary production itself. The present book was written out of a conviction that it is time for us to grow up again as critics, and that the increasing hermeticization of literary production, where writers speak mainly (and mainly approvingly) unto other writers, might be arrested through a long-overdue revitalization of practical literary criticism.

The new Appendix to this book is an additional essay, rather heavier in tone than the book's main argument, but which is intended to stand behind that argument and to give it support. Some of the material I have dealt with has already been discussed in such excellent surveys of Romanticism as M. H. Abrams's *The Mirror and the Lamp* and *Natural Supernaturalism*, but my concern here has not been with the history of ideas as such but with the question of which of these ideas are true. The ones I have selected for discussion in this new Appendix seem to me to be ideas which, suitably re-expressed in a modern idiom, might enable us to find a new and healthier comprehension both of the nature of literature itself and also of the actual particular literary texts that we may find ourselves reading or creating.

Readers' and critics' responses to *Myth, Truth and Literature* are still reaching me from many directions, and it seems to me too early as yet to attempt any substantial revision of the book's main argument. My suspicion that theology is now an entirely sterile subject, on the other hand, has been strengthened by the absence of any sensible responses or reviews from that particular quarter. For the most part it seems to me that more religious sense has come out of New Guinea or the jungles of South America in recent decades than out of the combined lucubrations of the world's churches.

In addition to the thanks expressed in my first edition I would like to record my gratitude to Frank Kermode and to Alexis Lykiard for their professional help and advice. I am also indebted to York College, Pennsylvania, for a slight but perceptible reduction in my teaching duties to enable me to wrestle with these and other world-historical matters.

PREFACE TO
THE 1st EDITION

In trying to write a philosophical book about "what poetry is" I have perhaps been more likely to fall into the kinds of intellectual pretension and vacuousness which are sometimes thought to be the defects of continental-European thinking than into the opposite and rather anti-intellectual kinds of defect which are more commonly found in English-speaking literary discussions. My worst fear is that I may somehow have managed to fall into both these kinds of defect at once. It was Coleridge who, before settling into another of his long bouts of philosophical laboring, said "I hope philosophy and poetry will not neutralise each other, and leave me an inert mass." Yet it was Coleridge also who led the way in these matters within the English tradition, and it is from him that we must find a way of going forward if these matters are to be further pursued. Apart from his famous – but soon abandoned – efforts in *Biographia Literaria* and elsewhere to provide a "deduction of the imagination, and with it the principles of production and of genial criticism in the fine arts," there have been few attempts in English to explore the place which poetry or literature occupies in human life or to integrate into one argument the sometimes competing claims of literature, theology, and positive knowledge. Literary critics and reviewers, often incomparably good at their own jobs, tend to rest aggressively on their prejudices when asked to pronounce on what it is that they spend the better part of their working lives doing. Philosophers, when they have concerned themselves with literature at all, have – with certain exceptions to whom I am overwhelmingly indebted – usually concerned themselves only with very specific and rather spiritually undemanding aspects of it.

This situation seems to me not to have been helped by the recent incursions of continental-European – in effect mainly French – varieties of linguistic theory into the English (and particularly into the American) literary tradition. The linguistic theories of Saussure and his successors are undeniably based on a correct recognition that "correspondence," or "thing-and-name," theories of linguistic meaning are philosophically indefensible. But these structuralist and post-structuralist theories seem themselves no less undeniably to be false in so far as they claim that linguistic meanings are a matter only of the relationships which hold between linguistic terms themselves, and that there is therefore, in some (admittedly rather special or arcane) philosophical sense, "nothing outside of the text." The structuralist or post-structuralist tradition of linguistic – and therefore also of literary – meaning in effect *abolishes reality*. To try to talk about literature in the language of structuralist or post-structuralist theory can seem rather like trying to talk about a game of soccer or baseball without ever actually being allowed to mention the ball.

Our most urgent current need in literary theory seems to me to be for a "paradigm-shift" which will enable us to restore the concepts of truth or of vision to our discussions of literature. The aim of the present book is to suggest something of the philosophical basis on which such a kind of paradigm-shift might begin to be made. Literature, the book's argument proposes, in fact gives us our purest and most essential way of grasping reality or truth. Since this is also what religion has traditionally claimed to do, it follows that literature and literary criticism may need to be prepared to embrace, and to subsume, religion and theology if they are to discover or to re-discover their own spiritual meanings. In so far as religions themselves – and in particular Christianity – have increasingly tended to "internalize" or to "de-mythologize" themselves and to abandon their claims to be descriptive forms of truth about the world, a way is in fact conveniently open whereby our spiritual awareness can begin to be "re-mythologized" through the imaginative insights of poetry or literature. The only religious "scriptures" that can now be authentic for us may be the poetry or literature to which our own culture gives us access. Ideas such as these have long been at the edge of the consciousness of poets or critics, as with Matthew Arnold, or even quite central to it, as with Wallace Stevens, but they have only rarely been seriously argued for, and then not for a discouragingly long time. It must follow from these considerations that a truly modern or "post-modernist" literature will be one which takes these existential or spiritual obligations seriously – perhaps alongside, but perhaps also partly displacing, the kind of ludic charm which is the hallmark of most of what currently passes for literary "post-modernism." Through its quintessential activity of finding new ways of inscribing reality for us, poetry or literature is in the business of soul-making, and its method, as John Keats saw, is negative capability.

The argument of the book is in two main stages. The first aims to develop a certain philosophical view of the human situation, and in particular of the nature of human language. The second tries to suggest some of the implications of these general conclusions for the nature of literature and of religion. Throughout both of these stages there is a need for the arguments to be developed with a great deal more rigor and detail, but my present aim has been only to assemble into a single discussion certain important issues which seem to me to belong in a single discussion. I hope very much that others will be able to strengthen some of the argument's links and to provide more rigor than I have been philosophically equipped (or have perhaps in any case had the space) to provide myself. These factors may also help to explain the tendency for the argument to operate on two levels: the main argument, which is perhaps excessively bare and skeletal, and a second level, conducted mostly in the footnotes with which the bare text is rather baroquely encrusted, which suggests ways in which the main argument might be developed more adequately. (Some readers may feel, for example, that I have allowed concepts such as "pre-conscious" or "pre-experiential" to become a catch-all for philosophical problems which have merely been displaced rather than adequately dealt with. There is truth in this; but to explore this region would take another book, or several others, and it might even perhaps be argued that it is in this area of the nature of "the pre-conscious subject" and of the relationships between our pre-conscious and our conscious subjective awarenesses that some of our most important philosophical problems can now be seen to lie.)

As far as intellectual debts are concerned, it must be emphasized that the continual engagement and re-engagement with Kant which is to be found here does not signify a presumption of "refuting" Kant so much as a recognition that it was Kant who, by engaging with some of the most important problems of philosophy, by insisting on the possibility of a priori philosophical argument, and above all by linking the continental-European and the English-speaking philosophical traditions, provides the best platform for the present – however inferior, logically unrigorous, and generally amateurish – argument to take off from and return to. More recently, I must register a debt to P. F. Strawson for his re-presentation of various Kantian issues in a compellingly modern metaphysical way, however much I am unable to measure up to the strictness and the elegance of his dealings with them. My other main philosophical debts have perhaps been to Martin Heidegger, Maurice Merleau-Ponty, George Santayana, and Owen Barfield; these debts are far too general for specific acknowledgement, even if I could begin to trace them, and are to be felt on every page of my discussion.

I would like, finally, to thank the following for reading earlier versions of parts of the text and for making valuable suggestions: Rosemary Ashton, Stuart Hampshire, Iris Murdoch, Richard Rorty, Roger Scruton, Charles Taylor, and Jerry Valberg. Among these I would particularly like to emphasize my gratitude to Iris Murdoch and Charles Taylor for their much-needed help and encouragement at difficult times. Other thanks are due to Perry Anderson, Renford Bambrough, John Bayley, William Cookson, Peter Dews, James Dougherty, Jude P. Dougherty, Denis Dutton, John Fisher, Roger Gard, Warwick Gould, Cleo McNelly, Tom Paulin, Christopher Ricks, M. L. Rosenthal, George Steiner, Stephen Wall, and Julian Wood.

Sections of the book have appeared in slightly different versions in the following journals:

Part of chapter 1, under the title "Saussurian theory and the abolition of reality" in *The Monist*, 69 (1986), 133–45.

A further part of chapter 1, under the title "Structure and intuition" in *Philosophy and Literature*, 9 (1985), 184–97.

Part of chapter 2, under the title "The process of meaning-creation: a transcendental argument" in *The Review of Metaphysics*, 38 (1985), 503–28.

Part of chapter 3, under the title "A defence of poetry" in *The Journal of Aesthetics and Art Criticism*, 44 (1986), 393–403.

Part of chapter 4, under the title "Beyond theory" in *Essays in Criticism*, 36 (1986), 1–10.

A further part of chapter 4, under the title "Fictions and reality" in *Philosophy*, 63 (1988), 363–71.

Part of chapter 5, under the title "The 'identity' of poetry and religion" in *Religion and Literature*, 20, No. 2 (1988), pp. 41–56.

I am grateful to the editors and publishers concerned for their permission to reprint this material.

Acknowledgements are due to all those who have given permission for the quotation of copyright work by other authors. Robert Frost's poem "The Cow in Apple Time" is reprinted by permission of the Estate of Robert Frost, Edward Connery Latham as editor, and Henry Holt and Company, Inc. (New York) and Jonathan Cape Ltd. (London), from *The Poetry of Robert Frost*. Ezra Pound's poem "Shop Girl" is reprinted by permission of New Directions Publishing Corporation (New York) and Faber and Faber Ltd. (London), from *Collected Shorter Poems* of Ezra Pound.

Throughout the text the philosophical "he" or "his" should be taken to mean "he or she" or "his or her" in all cases. Translations in the text which have not been otherwise attributed are my own.

INTRODUCTION:
TWO FACES OF ROMANTICISM

Thus men forgot that All deities reside in the human breast.

BLAKE

What matters in life is life itself and not some other thing
that life leads to.

GOETHE

...sure a poet is a sage;
A humanist, physician to all men.

KEATS

Romanticism, as almost any mention of the Romantic philosophers
and poets is likely to remind us, was a spiritual revolt, a Promethean
conspiracy to steal fire from the gods and to use it to drive them from
their stronghold. The fire was consciousness, and it was mankind
who would be installed in the gods' place. Romanticism looks
forward to Marxism, to psychoanalysis, and to every significant
modern attempt to persuade men to take control of their own
destiny. Man, Feuerbach said, "is the beginning, the middle and the
end of religion."[1] "In man," said Nietzsche, "there is both the creator
and the thing created."[2] Even more than the rather mechanical
atheism which preceded it, Romanticism made possible a realistic
engagement with humanity's problems, because it was with Romanticism that men began to grasp the seriousness of what they were
doing in questioning their long-sacred beliefs – and yet remained
determined to go on doing so. For too much of their history men had
"forgotten" – as Blake claimed to be reminding us – the simple truth
that "All deities reside in the human breast."[3]

But the gods, for Blake, were not dead. They resided in the human

[1] See Ludwig Feuerbach, *The Essence of Christianity*, trans. George Eliot (New York: Harper, 1957), p. xix.
[2] Friedrich Nietzsche, *Beyond Good and Evil*, sec. 225.
[3] William Blake, *The Marriage of Heaven and Hell*, in *Complete Writings*, ed. Geoffrey Keynes (London: Oxford University Press, 1966), p. 153.

breast as they always had done. Like Pascal, Blake knew that there is no salvation for us in mechanistic science and that the heart has reasons of which Reason knows nothing. He also knew that the gods in the human breast are stranger than any yet recorded in scriptures, and that there are devils among them. To know them for what they are, we must hear what they have to say. There is a second face of Romanticism, which looks backwards for its inspiration to religion, and which encourages us not towards mastery but towards submission. "All that is visible clings to the invisible," said Novalis.[4] A time may come, Coleridge hoped, when "passiveness" will attain the dignity of "worthy activity."[5] Keats admired what he called negative capability, "that is, when a man is capable of being in uncertainties, mysteries, doubts, without any irritable reaching after fact and reason."[6] (One must learn, Rilke told one of his correspondents nearly a century later, "to have patience with everything unsolved in one's heart and try to love the questions themselves."[7]) We know by now, life being what it is – and even more importantly, perhaps, what we have made of it – that this second side of Romanticism is also its darker side.

Was it inevitable that these Romantic aspirations should conflict and lead in different directions? There was a time when it seemed not. For Goethe – "that uncrowned king of Romantics," as the English critic Owen Barfield persuasively called him[8] – it was reasonable to suppose that heroism and submissiveness might complement one another, and that they might do so above all through art. Art, Goethe believed, was at the service of life. If art expressed despair, it also enabled men to comprehend despair and to rise above it. Readers of *Werther* were not meant to go away and commit suicide. Keats, at a not entirely different crossroads in England, came round to an essentially similar point of view. The negative capability which he admired was the quality which "went to form a man of achievement," and he added "especially in literature" as though achievement in literature was only a part of what he had in mind.

---

4 Novalis, *Schriften*, vol. 2, ed. R. Samuel (Darmstadt: Wissenschaftliche Buchgesellschaft, 1980), p. 650.
5 Samuel Taylor Coleridge, *Notebooks* vol. 1, ed. Kathleen Coburn (London: Routledge and Kegan Paul, 1957), entry 1834.
6 John Keats, letter to George and Tom Keats of 21 December 1817.
7 Rainer Maria Rilke, letter to Franz-Xaver Kappus of 16 July 1903.
8 Owen Barfield, *Romanticism Comes of Age* (Middletown, Conn.: Wesleyan University Press, 1986), p. 16.

For both Goethe and Keats, remote from each other in so many ways and yet in some ways so strangely comparable, the purpose of art lay in its value for life, while the purpose of life – as Goethe said – was life itself. Art, and a man's talent, might need solitude for their development, but character was formed in society. Life, for Keats, was a "vale of soul-making" in which misfortunes gave us an opportunity to try the resources of our spirit. This seemed to him a "grander system of salvation" than the Christian religion, and one "which does not affront our reason and humanity."[9] Both Goethe and Keats, disgusted by the vulgar superstitions of Christianity, looked forward to a time when art would replace religion altogether as our most original and essential source of spiritual nourishment.

[9] Keats, letter to George and Georgiana Keats of 21 April 1819.

1

SAUSSURIAN THEORY AND THE ABOLITION OF REALITY

> In this condition there may be discoverable under new
> forms certain spiritual illuminations, shining with a
> morality essentialized from experience directly, and not
> from previous precepts or preoccupations. It is as though
> a poem gave the reader as he left it a single, new word,
> never before spoken and impossible to actually enunciate,
> but self-evident as an active principle in the reader's
> consciousness henceforward.
>
> HART CRANE

1

The founder of modern linguistics Ferdinand de Saussure – on whose
insights into the nature of signs and language the greater part of the
French and American literary theory of the past two decades has
rather perilously come to depend – based the main arguments of his
project for a newly scientific study of language on what are in fact a
pair of philosophical axioms. These are: (1) what Saussure called his
"Principle 1," or "*the principle of the arbitrary nature of the sign*";[1] and
(2) what might be called (though Saussure himself did not name or
isolate it as such) "*the principle of the relational nature of all linguistic
meaning.*" In his argument leading up to the statement of "Principle
1" Saussure remarks that

> [s]ome people regard language, when reduced to its elements, as a
> naming-process only – a list of words, each corresponding to the thing

[1] F. de Saussure, *Course in General Linguistics*, ed. Charles Bally and Albert Sechehaye
from notes based on Saussure's lectures of 1906–11, trans. Wade Baskin (London:
Fontana/Collins, 1974), p. 68; italics added.

that it names... This conception is open to criticism at several points. It assumes that ready-made ideas exist before words.

(p. 65)

The truth is rather (Saussure proposes) that the linguistic sign unites "not a thing and a name, but a concept and a sound-image" (p. 66). The real significance of "Principle 1" within Saussurian theory lies not so much in the arbitrariness of the link between the "sound-image" and the "concept" – which Saussure goes on to speak of as the "signifier" and the "signified" (p. 67) – but in the fact that since the notion of a one-to-one correspondence between words and worldly things is "open to criticism" there must be a sense in which our very concepts themselves, along with the sounds which we use to signify them, can be seen as inherently arbitrary rather than as determined in their form by any "natural" or extra-linguistically-given relationship to reality. It is this philosophically radical assertion which provides the basis for the second main Saussurian principle concerning the *relational* nature of all linguistic meaning. Linguistic signs, since they do not have their meanings by virtue of one-to-one correspondence with things in the world (or therefore with the ideas of things which people may have in their minds), must therefore have their meanings by virtue of their relationships with other signs within the linguistic systems of which they form a part. "It is evident," Saussure argues,

> even *a priori*, that a segment of language can never in the final analysis be based on anything except its non-coincidence with the rest. *Arbitrary* and *differential* are two correlative qualities... Everything that has been said up to this point boils down to this: in language ... there are only differences *without positive terms*.

(pp. 118–20)

Perhaps the most profound of the philosophical difficulties which these Saussurian principles are capable of leading us into comes from the fact that what Saussure regarded, at any rate primarily, as a set of regulative principles for the reform of language *studies* – a setting of the linguistic scientists' house in order (together with perhaps a notable "semiological" extension of the size of that house[2] – has been

---

[2] "*A science that studies the life of signs within society* is conceivable... I shall call it semiology... Linguistics is only a part of the general science of semiology" (p. 16).

interpreted by Saussurian theorists as an exhaustive and (give or take certain qualifications) philosophically incontestable account of the essential *nature* of language itself. This never-properly-acknowledged shift of emphasis has made it possible for the most basic of the Saussurian principles – "the principle of the arbitrary nature of the sign" (Saussure claims at one point that "no one disputes the principle of the arbitrary nature of the sign" [p. 68]) – to take on a charisma which it has never been obliged to earn by any properly philosophical argument, and which properly philosophical argument would in fact show to rest on a set of verbal ambiguities which conceal what is at bottom a fairly simple philosophical fallacy. What the fallacy amounts to, in the most naked and un-semiological of terms, is that from the idea that language, or our utilizing of linguistic signs, is not a kind of "naming-process" in the sense of being a baptismal labeling of already-discriminated ideas or objects in the world (so that we should have to presuppose the world to be already discriminated into objects before we ever come to apply our language to it), a transition is made to the idea that the relationship between language and the world is not, and does not need to be thought of as including or comprising, a kind of "naming-process" in any sense whatever. From the idea that words do not have their meanings by virtue of their one-to-one correspondences with items in reality, it is inferred *tout court* that language cannot be held to relate in an intelligible or usefully discussable way with any extra-linguistic dimension or "presence" in reality at all.

2

The function of the linguistic sign, Saussure tells us, is not one of uniting a verbal name with a pre-verbally differentiated item in the world, because – *inter alia* – this would oblige us to assume "that ready-made ideas exist before words." By "ready-made ideas" Saussure evidently enough means "ready-made ideas" of things or objects, rather than the merely fragmentary or not-yet-structured "ideas" of the senses (in the special meaning of "ideas" with which the word was used by empiricist philosophers such as Locke, Berkeley and Hume). It might be as well, perhaps, to get in at the philosophical deep end here and to recall that it was a large part of Kant's enterprise in his *Critique of Pure Reason* to try to work out the implications of this (as he also saw it to be) impossibility of the existence of "ready-made ideas" which are somehow available to us antecedently to our possession of conceptual language. Recognizing that Hume had been right when he pointed out that the conception of human knowledge as based on a mental associating of passively received sensory data leaves us with an insoluble problem about what it is that holds the experiencing or mentally-associating agent himself together, Kant turned Hume's problem around and proposed that perceptual experience of a stable and persisting world can in fact only be possible if there already (in some way independently of the senses) exists a unified and unifying perceiver or consciousness to whom such a perceptual experience of enduring worldly objects can belong or appertain. After much argument Kant concluded that it must be through our exercise of the "logical functions of judgement" that such a unified and unifying consciousness is enabled to come into existence: it is only through our possession of certain *concepts* of "the objects of experience" that we are able to possess the unity of consciousness which is necessary in order for our experience to be experience at all.[3] A more linguistically sophisticated argument to establish the dependence of our capacity for perceptual experience on our possession of publicly-shared concepts was developed later by Wittgenstein, when he showed that the recognition of a perceptual similarity or distinction – and therefore any actual *perception* of anything at all – must depend on the publicly-established "rule" or "rules" which we are following when we make particular discriminations, and that it is only because I belong to a community of concept-using experiencers whose concept-using can (in some sense) be publicly observed that I can ever actually have any experience of my own. For both Kant and Wittgenstein, we can only have the experience – which we indisputably do have – of a world of things and persons (including ourselves) if we are already in possession of conceptual language.[4]

If we were to bring this Kantian or Wittgensteinian line of argument to bear within the Saussurian tradition of linguistic

---

[3] It will be argued below that Kant has here succeeded in identifying some, but not all, of the necessary conditions which underlie our capacity for self-conscious or objective experience.

[4] Both Kant and Wittgenstein are using what Kant called "transcendental" argument: they are asking what must be the case in order for us to be able to have the kind of experience which we in fact do have.

theory, we could say that if the possibility of linguistic signs depended on the possibility of the linking-up of words with "ready-made ideas" of worldly objects, so that some kind of baptismal "naming-process" had to be seen as underlying all the connections between our concepts and the items in the world that they refer to, then it would never have been possible for our conceptual language to have got off the ground in the first place. It would never have been possible for us to have had the necessary experience of things *independently* of language, since our very consciousness as experiencing agents is itself dependent on our possession of concepts. Saussure, evidently taking the conclusions of some such argument for granted, proceeds from this rejection of the (in effect pre-Kantian) notion that "ready-made ideas exist before words" to his own – and for his own purposes more productive – notion that what the linguistic sign does is not to link a word with a ready-made idea but to link a sound-image with a concept. He then goes on to tell us new and revealing things about sound-images and concepts: most importantly that they have their meanings, or linguistic "values," not by virtue of their relationships with things or objects in the world, but by virtue of the relationships in which they stand within the language-systems of which they are constituent units. *But reality itself, meanwhile, has come very near to being forgotten about altogether.* Within the defining terms of Saussurian theory, all possible questions about how our concepts – whether signified by "sound-images" or by other textual signifiers – relate to any term or dimension which lies *outside* language are left with no alternative but to lapse from the argument as undiscussable. (For Kant, at any rate in the *Critique of Pure Reason*, this can scarcely be seen as a problem, since reality "in itself" is defined from the start as being beyond the purview of our conceptual understanding.)[5] It is as though the rejection of a *wrong* answer to such questions proved the questions themselves to be entirely misconceived or illegitimate. Later Saussurian (or "post-Saussurian") theorists have sometimes argued as though any attempt to frame questions about the relationship between conceptual language and a dimension of reality which is exterior to language must be swept aside as evidence of our continued enslavement to outdated metaphysical or ontological

---

[5] This is the doctrine of the human inaccessibility of "things in themselves." P. F. Strawson has spoken rather tartly of Kant's "senseless dogma that our conceptual scheme corresponds at no point with Reality" (*The Bounds of Sense* [London: Methuen, 1966], p. 42).

notions.[6] And yet no convincing argument as to why such meta-physical or ontological notions might be outdated (or as to which of them either are or are not outdated) has ever been put forward. The result has been the creation of a metaphysical or ontological void (or perhaps the seeming legitimization of a metaphysical or ontological void which existed at the heart of our culture already) in which Saussurian theory can guiltlessly disport itself, but in which we are also deprived of any conceptual basis for getting nearer to an understanding of – or (which is where any understanding would have to begin from) even for taking an interest in – the nature of truth.[7]

We can see this more clearly, perhaps, if we look at some of the implications of the commonly followed distinction which was made by Saussure between *langue* (a language's relational system proper) and *parole* (our various particular speech-acts, including all the particular sound-qualities and psychological components which may feature in individual speech-acts but which are nevertheless not a part of the language's relational system). The main philosophical problem to which this distinction gives rise is that the theoretical splitting-apart of *langue* and *parole*, together with the Saussurian tendency to concentrate on the *langue* or system as the most interesting or important-to-study part of language, makes it virtually impossible for our actual *using* – within our living, worldly situations – of language to be recognized as a part of its essential nature rather than as something to be hived off into a different realm for empirical study (a less glamorous realm of psychological accompaniments, "phonology" and noises *per se*, and in general of *behavior*). The effects of this displacement of emphasis from the necessarily situated or embodied nature of language (language being a special part of our situated and embodied human "forms of life" in general)[8] must – whatever the pedagogical usefulness of the distinction for the purposes of linguistic *studies* – in the end be philosophically disas-

---

[6] See in particular Jacques Derrida, *Speech and Phenomena*, trans. David B. Allison (Evanston, Ill.: Northwestern University Press, 1973); also Roland Barthes, *The Pleasure of the Text*, trans. Richard Miller (New York: Hill and Wang, 1975).

[7] At this point it might be best just to register one's *awareness* of some of the recent neo-pragmatist arguments about this last concept. See for example Richard Rorty, *Consequences of Pragmatism* (Minneapolis: University of Minnesota Press, 1982), *passim*.

[8] See Ludwig Wittgenstein, *Philosophical Investigations*, trans. G. E. M. Anscombe (Oxford: Blackwell, 1958), pp. 8–12, and *passim*.

trous. It has been claimed by recent semiological commentators that the result of the Saussurian revolution in linguistic theory has been to give linguistics "a suitable object of study";[9] but if we adhere to the Saussurian distinctions as anything more than academically useful prescriptions we shall in fact find that Saussurian theory has given us a suitable object of study only by giving us an object of study which is incoherently abstracted from the nature of language as a living process and which is therefore without any real philosophical or human significance. (More accurately, we might say: by giving us an object of study which has the same degree, and same kind, of human significance that logic has.) The Saussurian categories make it easy for us to ignore our actual language-using *activity*; and between the relational, or what Saussure calls "synchronic" aspects of language (which are its aspects as a system, complete at any particular present moment), and the historical or behavioral, or what Saussure calls "diachronic" aspects (which are a matter of contingent facts about linguistic changes which occur with the passage of time), the true nature of the language-using process and of its place in human life can very easily be allowed to slip away out of the picture altogether. This may be unimportant if we are concerned only with the proper methods of studying actual language systems, but it cannot be unimportant if we are purporting to argue about the nature of language itself – as a dimension of human existence – and of its way (or ways) of relating to reality.

Since the time of Saussure a great deal of discussion has taken place about the nature of the *langue/parole* (and the synchronic/diachronic) distinction and about which of the components of our actual language-using might be assigned to which category, but none of it has altered the fact that any truly Saussurian theory can in the end only provide us with a "suitable object" of linguistic study which is at the same time an artificial or dead object.[10] The most radical of the reasons for this lies in the fact that in order to create a linguistic object of study on Saussurian principles at all, our necessary nature as embodied or incarnated beings (and more generally, all actual *context*, both physical–biological and cultural–historical) must necessarily be excluded from the discussion as irrelevant. In Saussurian terms, one of the distinctions we are called upon to make

[9] Jonathan Culler, for example, puts it this way in his *Saussure* (New York: Penguin Books, 1977), p. 27.
[10] Derrida's very important departures from Saussure are discussed below.

is between linguistic "values" and linguistic "significations": linguistic "values", or the patterns of relationships between linguistic terms, are what the (synchronic) study of language should properly be concerned with, while linguistic "significations" are a matter of what is referred to by the words we use, or of what is contextually implied when we make use of language within certain particular extra-linguistic situations of utterance.[11] Since linguistics is concerned with "values" rather than with "significations," the way is therefore cleared – as it were by default – for a treatment of language as a disembodied and contextless process which is absolved from any questions of validation in terms of its contextual relationship to the world we use it in. And yet linguistic values (as Saussurian theory of course knows, but as it has no way of acknowledging within its treatment of language as a self-contained relational system) must in fact be continuously modified through the exposure of our concepts to contingency within continuously changing extra-linguistic – which means, at least part of the time, continuously changing physical and perceptual – situations. (At a further remove, they are also continuously modified through the exposure of our concepts to contingency within – in the traditional sense of the word – continuously changing *textual* situations.) The very possibility of language as a system at all, and therefore the very possibility of an object for Saussurian theory to study, depends on the continual modification of our language-systems within the extra-linguistic context of our embodied lives. Our transient perceptions must necessarily depend on our concepts ("seeing" something "as" something is "like an echo of a thought in sight," Wittgenstein tells us [*Philosophical Investigations*, p. 212], in a formulation which echoes Kant's "imagination is a necessary ingredient of perception itself");[12] but our concepts must also, and for the same reasons, depend on our transient perceptions, in so far as our use of concepts to give articulation to not-yet-fully-articulated perceptual situations must provide our language with the only rationale for its development that it can ultimately have. This continual modifiability of language-systems within contingent contexts is an irreducible aspect of the *nature* of language – just as (and for the same reason that) *temporality* is itself an irreducible aspect of the nature of all our experiencing. A

[11] See Saussure, p. 114.
[12] Immanuel Kant, *Critique of Pure Reason*, trans. Norman Kemp Smith (London: Macmillan, 1933), A. 120, n. a.

theory which would ignore this necessity of the human situation is a theory which has ignored a philosophically ineliminable dimension of the realm which it has set out to study.

It may be easier to see the real issues here if we go back yet again to Kant's arguments in the *Critique of Pure Reason*. The main problem which faces the Kantian account of the conditions which underlie our capacity for having perceptual experience of an objectively-existing "external" world is that the Kantian experiencing self, even though it is a concept-using and therefore perhaps philosophically plausible *subject* (as contrasted with the self of Hume and other empiricists which was really no more than a bundle of passively-received ideas or impressions), is nevertheless still not an essentially *embodied* subject, and is therefore open to some of the same objections which can be brought against Descartes's conception (as in his *Cogito*) of the thinking self, or *ego*, as the foundation of all our experiencing.[13] The problem which arises here is that it can only be possible for me to arrive at any concept of "myself" and "my" experience if I can also ascribe experience to others; but if the others to whom I ascribe experience were disembodied consciousnesses (whether of the kind which Descartes imagined, or of any other kind) there would be no way in which they could have any presence for me as "objects" of my experiencing (or therefore be known about by me at all). Under these conditions it would therefore be impossible for us to have the experience – which we all do have – of a shared inter-personal world both of objects and of "objectively" observable people.[14] (The mere "unity of self-consciousness" which Kant offers us [*Critique of Pure Reason*, B. 131–32] does not in fact give us any solution to Hume's problem of the inexplicability of the nature of the self,[15] since without being embodied or located there can be no way for the Kantian self to be a perceiving agent with any identity which

[13] This notwithstanding Kant's argument (B. 407 *et seq*). against the Cartesian idea of a soul-substance or *res cogitans*. The issue here is what Kant *omits* from his account of the necessary conditions which underlie our experiencing, and specifically his omission of the necessity of our embodiedness. Kant's leaving of the "I think" so empty is really the reverse face of the Enlightenment's pursuit of *universal* knowledge, and goes with the centuries-long tradition of such a pursuit which becomes dominant in Western philosophy with Descartes (but which in fact has its origins in Greek philosophy as early as Socrates and Plato).

[14] For an elegant and detailed presentation of this line of argument see Strawson, *Individuals: An Essay in Descriptive Metaphysics* (London: Methuen, 1959), ch. 3, secs. 3–6.

[15] See David Hume, *A Treatise of Human Nature* (New York: Dutton, 1977), p. 319.

endures through time.) A further problem which arises is that it would be impossible for us to have any awareness of ourselves as *experiencers* of the world if we did not also have an awareness – which was more than merely an "observed" awareness – of ourselves as *agents* able to exert an influence in that world. I can know about my bodily movements and my bodily situation in a specially direct way through the active interventions which I am able to make in the world around me. There is no way in which the distinction between myself and that which is not myself could arise for me on the basis of passive observation alone.[16] It is only because we *are* bodies that we are able to perceive bodies (or any "thing" at all), and what holds the bodies which we perceive together *as* bodies is, on the most fundamental level, not the quasi-judgemental application of logical categories but the primitive awareness which we are able to have of them through our own bodies in the course of our bodily interactions with them. This primitive bodily awareness – our ability to come up against discrete, persisting presences that have a bodily continuity separate from our own and from our own agency – must be an awareness which precedes and underlies any conscious awareness of our "selves" and of that which is not ourselves, and must be the basis on which our awareness of an articulated world, and of ourselves as parts of that world, must ultimately depend.

The *body*, we might say, is the realm in which, or through which, we have our contact with, and therefore our awareness of, other consciousnesses – and at the same time, by contrast, our awareness of our own selfhood as well: we cannot see another person only as "external behavior," but must necessarily see his behavior as already inhabited by *mind* or *spirit*.[17] Were this not so, there would be no way – to use the Kantian or "transcendental" turn of argument – for us to have the kind of experience which we do have. In trying to explain how it is that – despite our awareness of a dualism of "inner" and "outer" in human behavior – we are nevertheless able to experience

[16] For some of the implications of this argument see Stuart Hampshire, *Thought and Action* (London: Chatto and Windus, 1959), p. 47ff. For a more extended treatment of the issue see Maurice Merleau-Ponty, *The Phenomenology of Perception*, trans. Colin Smith (London: Routledge and Kegan Paul, 1962), Part I, ch. 1 *et seq.*

[17] Philosophy in this area might be rather easier if we could find a general term which would distinguish this animate bodily realm from the mere – Cartesian or Newtonian – physicality of natural-scientific "bodies," or brute matter. Merleau-Ponty has remarked that this realm, which in French he calls "*chair*," has no name in philosophy as yet. See *Le Visible et l'invisible* (Paris: Gallimard, 1964), p. 183.

ourselves as belonging to a common world of things and persons, we may perhaps find ourselves tempted to rely on a notion of different kinds of "knowledge." (My own actions or behavior, it might be said, are something that I know about by different criteria – we might call them "intentional" – from the criteria – we might call them "observational" – by which I know about other people's actions or behavior.)[18] This invocation of "knowledge" will not give us the explanation we need, however, since I can only have *knowledge* if I already have a conception of myself as distinct from the things that I know, and I can only have a conception of myself if I also have a conception of certain other selves in the world around me[19] – which is the very thing which we are trying to explain. What is really needed to bridge the "inside–outside" dualism of human behavior coherently, but without obliterating the distinction which it seeks to register, is some notion of a process of *sympathy*, or of pre-conscious imitative identification, which takes place below the level of any knowledge or criteria and which is the pre-logical and pre-conscious ground of all our inter-personal experience. It is sympathy, and not knowledge (although our philosophical vocabulary is severely depleted in this area, and we may need a better word than "sympathy" for the concept we are after), which *links* our own experiencing and other people's experiencing into a single world of human apprehension and agency. Before knowledge or conceptuality, in the hierarchy of our awareness, there must be *life*, and the response of life to life.[20] What is needed in the present context is a range of concepts that will characterize those (necessarily semi-articulate) processes of sympathy or identification that lie below the levels of any "subjective" or "objective" awareness and of any kind of logical thinking. (More generally, we need a range of concepts which will characterize our entire engagement with the world around us, or with reality, at the pre-linguistic and pre-conscious levels of our existence.) Rather

---

[18] This is the line taken by Strawson, for example. See *Individuals*, pp. 104 ff.

[19] This has been pointed out by Strawson himself. See *Individuals*, pp. 99–100, 109.

[20] Owen Barfield has characterized as "logomorphism" the Kantian tendency, which he sees as widespread in modern "common-sense" thinking, to project logical modes of thought back into the pre-logical stages (and pre-logical ages) of human consciousness. He remarks that "it does not require a very active fancy to see the Königsberg ghost hovering above, and intertwining itself with the ideas of minds that never even knew Kant's name" (*Poetic Diction* [Middletown, Conn.: Wesleyan University Press, 1973], p. 184). To speak of these pre-conceptual processes in the language of knowledge, as Strawson does, can only be a metaphor which distracts our attention from whatever may really be taking place.

than tying ourselves to the usual vocabulary of "common sense," we need instead to find ways of acknowledging the intuitive, hunch-like, or obscure nature of the apprehensions which we have – or it might be better to say "which take place" – on this primitive level of our embodied awareness (we are *in* the world before we either experience or understand the world), as contrasted with the clear and distinct notion of experience which we have been led to accept as a result of the feed-back of Cartesian and empiricist (and eventually Kantian) ideas into our "common-sense" thinking.[21] The notion of the *emerging* of meaning is almost entirely unmarked in our serious thinking, and tends instead to be confined to the – philosophically disreputable – level of folk-wisdom or religious superstition in the form of such notions as "intuition," "hunch," "presentiment," or "sixth sense." (It was the pursuit of the wholly certain, and the suppression of hunch and intuition, which made Descartes's sceptical philosophy possible and which marked the transition from the common sense of the ancient or medieval world to the common sense of later centuries. But we could in fact only have the kind of clear and distinct perception which this Cartesian tradition seeks if we were unlocated angelic observers detached from any bodily participation in reality.)

Language, which (as Kant and Saussure both recognize) is itself a behavioral and "experiential" pre-condition which enables our full subjectivity and objectivity to become possible, arises out of, and must continue to rest on, this level of pre-linguistic awareness of other presences – both animate and inanimate – which co-exist with us in the world around us. Both consciousness and the thing we are conscious of, instead of (as Kant in fact supposed) coming into the world fully-fledged as "pure" subject and "pure" object, must arise out of, and depend on, a pre-linguistic mode of life which we share with other inhabitants of our world and which is not yet a realm in which subject and object – or awareness and corporeality – have clearly differentiated themselves: this process of sympathy must have something in common with, and itself be a part of, the realm of shared sympathies and antipathies which makes up the mutual awareness and "experience" of biologically complex but not-yet-language-using organisms. The most fundamental behavioral and experiential (we might do better to say "vital") pre-condition which

[21] Kant, for example, seems to imply that an unintelligible perception must be regarded as "a merely subjective play of my fancy" (*Critique of Pure Reason*, B. 247).

allows language *itself* to come about – to arise or evolve out of the merely "lived-in" awareness of animal life, and to create the whole realm of subjectivity and of an objective world – must ultimately (as Kant and Saussure both do *not* recognize) be a process of some kind of *expressive bodily gesture*. It is only if we remain at the level of bodily or animal movement but also *invest it with signification* that it can be possible for us to make the transition towards a discursive conceptual language.[22] Bodily gesture must be our only way of acceding to this world-apprehending state: no verbal sounds alone, and *a fortiori* no written signifiers, could themselves make possible such a transition, since there would be no way for us to know, without an already established background of conceptual language, what the verbal sounds or written signifiers in question were supposed to mean. (Wittgenstein remarks of the Augustinian "correspondence" theory of language-acquisition that "Augustine describes the learning of human language as if the child came into a strange country and did not understand the language of the country; that is, as if it already had a language, only not this one.')[23] This gestural dimension of language can also properly be spoken of as its ontological dimension, since it is the dimension within which our very awareness of the presence of an experienceable reality or world around us arises.

The kind of bodily gesture which is in question here, therefore – and this is crucial for any philosophically coherent criticism of Saussurianism – cannot in its most fundamental form be a matter of gesturing (as the "thing-and-name" correspondence theory would require) at already differentiated items in the world. The process of bodily gesture on which language rests must instead be a process through which *any* awareness – including our most embryonic awareness of ourselves, and our most embryonic awareness that there is a world around us – is originally established. We are concerned here not with the (by Saussure and Wittgenstein properly dismissed) "thing-and-name" model of linguistic gesture, but with an expressive and all-embracing gestural process in which our conceptual language itself must be based (and out of which it must

---

[22] Merleau-Ponty has suggested that the operations of language are "a supreme instance of bodily intentionality" ("Sur la phénoménologie du langage," in *Signes* [Paris: Gallimard, 1960], p. 111). See also below, chapter 2.

[23] *Philosophical Investigations*, pp. 15–16. The philosophical implications with regard to the *true* nature of the birth of language of Wittgenstein's argument against the false, Augustinian or "correspondence" theory, have scarcely begun to be explored as yet.

no doubt originally have crystallized) and on which it must always continue to depend for its rational evolution. (The "relationship between language and reality" which is here in question is precisely a relationship between verbal language itself and a pre-verbal awareness *for which we feel a need to find* a verbal expression.)[24] It is through gesture – in our gestural apprehension of our own powers and agency, and of powers and agencies outside us – that our conceptual language has its true origins and basis: gesture is the first manifestation of our awareness of a *presence* outside us, and it is in gesture that – our humanly conceptualized, but we can know of no other – reality must have its roots in pre-conceptual life.[25] It is a necessity of language, we might say, that it should always be able to "go beyond" by means of a process of new articulation out of the incompletely-articulated awareness that we apply it to whenever we use it in new contexts; and it is an aspect of this necessity that our creative using of language should have its basis, and its continuing rationale, in a process of expressive bodily gesture.[26] From another point of view we could say that the extension or modification of our concepts through their involvement in our articulation of not-previously-experienced perceptual situations (or for that matter through their implication in not-previously-experienced textual situations) must be seen as the contextual and temporal embodiment of a continuous "naming-process."[27] The categories of Saussurian theory, in so far as they are set up in such a way as to prevent us from recognizing these ontological or metaphysical necessities, and in so far as they are conceptually unable to recognize or to deal with the whole extra-linguistic and contextual dimension of human existence, cannot avoid misrepresenting or belying the true nature of conceptual language and of the relationship in which it stands to the world we live in.

[24] Of course, as J. L. Austin, Wittgenstein and others have helped us to see, there is not just "one" relationship between language and reality; but a corollary of this is that there are also "as many" different kinds of pre-linguistic awareness as there are different kinds of language-using.

[25] We are here of course concerned with a metaphysical, rather than with an evolutionary–temporal, kind of priority. It may be metaphorically useful, even so, to speak in temporal- or evolutionary-sounding terms in discussing the "transition" from non-language-using to language-using modes of awareness or experiencing.

[26] See also below, chapter 2.

[27] For Saussure, any "naming-process" on which language might (mistakenly) be thought to depend can only mean "a list of words, each corresponding to the thing that it names" (p. 65).

3

The implications of this line of argument for the main tradition of Saussurian (or as some of its practitioners might prefer to think of it, post-Saussurian) theory ought therefore, it would seem, to be philosophically terminal. We can see how this might be so, perhaps, by considering the single, but particularly central, example of some of the philosophical claims or presuppositions which lie at the heart of the work of Jacques Derrida. Derrida departs from Saussure by (*inter alia*) extending the Saussurian notion of "difference"[28] in such a way as to call in question Saussure's belief – which Derrida takes to be common to the whole of Western philosophy since Plato[29] – in the primacy of the spoken word over every kind of written or (in the ordinary sense of the term) textual language. Saussure mistakenly supposed that the totality of an utterance's meaning was somehow immediately "present" to a speaker's or a hearer's mind, but the truth is rather (Derrida argues) that the meanings of both spoken *and* written language-uses alike depend on the "differences" between the spoken or written linguistic elements which are being directly used and the other elements of the linguistic systems to which (precisely by virtue of their "difference"-based relationships) they belong. Derrida therefore departs from Saussure in rejecting the notion of the Saussurian "signified" altogether: there is no way for us to have a direct apprehension of conceptual meanings, and each "signified" can only be understood as a link in a never-ending chain or network of "signifiers." Rather than there being any full or immediate "presence" of meaning, there must therefore be an endless "deferral" of full meaning; and the two notions of "difference" and "deferral" are combined by Derrida into the notion which he creates through his special spelling of "*différance*" with an "a."[30] Referring to Saussure's argument to the effect that "in language there are only differences *without positive terms*" (Saussure, p. 120), Derrida remarks that

---

[28] For example: "there are only differences *without positive terms*" (Saussure, p. 120).
[29] John Searle has usefully argued that Derrida is wrong in his reading of Western philosophy on this point. See his review of Jonathan Culler, *On Deconstruction*, in *New York Review of Books*, 27 October 1983, pp. 74–78.
[30] See in particular *Speech and Phenomena*, p. 82 *et seq.*, pp. 129–160. See also *Marges de la philosophie* (Paris: Minuit, 1972), pp. 3–29; *Positions*, trans. Alan Bass (University of Chicago Press, 1981), p. 8 *et seq.* and *passim*.

[t]he first consequence to be drawn from this is that the signified concept is never present in itself, in an adequate presence that would refer only to itself. Every concept is necessarily and essentially inscribed in a chain or system, within which it refers to another and to other concepts, by the systematic play of differences.

(*Speech and Phenomena*, p. 140)

In an earlier discussion of Husserl's division (in his *Logical Investigations*) of linguistic meaning into "expression" and "indication," Derrida argues along similar lines against any treatment of language which would abstract its essential meanings from the occasions of its use. For Husserl, he points out,

[i]ndication must be set aside, abstracted, and "reduced" as an extrinsic and empirical phenomenon, even if it is in fact closely related to expression... Husserl's whole enterprise... would be threatened if the *Verflechtung* [sc. intertwining] which couples the indicative sign to expression were absolutely irreducible, if it were in principle inextricable and if indication were essentially internal to the movement of expression rather than being only conjoined to it, however tenaciously.

(*Speech and Phenomena*, p. 27)

This recognition of the essential inseparability of logic and contingency (or of linguistic structure and linguistic event) does not for Derrida entail any recognition of the necessarily embodied or physical nature of the contingent dimension of meaning on which the rationality of our language depends. The whole process of linguistic evolution is for Derrida subsumed under the notion of *différance*, which remains, in effect, a disembodied process or system which simply evolves as it does and which cannot meaningfully be thought of as having any relationship with anything "outside" itself.[31]

As a variation of the notion of *différance*, Derrida has in other contexts offered us the notion of *archi-écriture*, or of what he also sometimes calls a "general text," which is the unified and *différance*-based order of both speech and writing (and of every other kind of textuality) comprehended together as a single system.[32] A necessary truth which this notion of *archi-écriture* or of a "general text" helps

---

[31] An essentially similar view of language can also be derived from the later writings of Wittgenstein.

[32] See *Of Grammatology*, trans. Gayatri Chakravorty Spivak (Baltimore: Johns Hopkins University Press, 1976), pp. lxix, 56–57; *Positions*, pp. 7 et seq., 44.

to obscure is that it would be possible for us to have embodied or physical situations without also having (either spoken or written) texts, but that it would never be possible for us to have (either spoken or written) texts without also having embodied or physical situations. The possibility or impossibility which is in question here is an a priori or metaphysical one, rather than anything to do with merely contingent limitations. Derrida's transformation (*via* the notion of *archi-écriture*) of every kind of language-using into an honorific "text" – which enables him to rely on some of the associations of the word "text" in the ordinary sense and to ignore or to forget about the necessities of physical incarnation – is really a verbal sleight-of-hand which allows him to eliminate the "experiential" dimension from his theoretical picture altogether. Derrida has said consistently, if with rather ostentatious absurdity, that he rejects the very notion of perception itself:

> Perception is precisely a concept, a concept of an intuition or of a given originating from the thing itself, present itself in its meaning, independently from language, from the system of reference. And I believe that perception is interdependent with the concept of origin and of center and consequently whatever strikes at the metaphysics of which I have spoken strikes also at the very concept of perception. I don't believe there is any perception.[11]

Even allowing for the fact that what Derrida is rejecting here is an idea of perception as an awareness of something "present itself in its meaning, independently from language, from the system of reference" (surely an idea which modern philosophers have abandoned, without abandoning the notion of perception itself), he has nonetheless provided us with the basis of an argument which – if we simply run it in the opposite direction – must destroy the foundations of his philosophical position altogether. The Derridean (and ultimately it is perhaps also the Nietzschean) case against what Derrida calls the "metaphysics of presence"[34] must fail, in other words, because it fails to recognize that our sense of "otherness" or "presence" is a prerequisite of our having the kind of experience of a world of things

---

[11] Discussion following "Structure, sign and play" in *The Structuralist Controversy*, ed. Richard Macksey and Eugenio Donato (Baltimore: Johns Hopkins University Press, 1972), p. 272. See also *Speech and Phenomena*, p. 103, where Derrida remarks that "[t]here never was any 'perception.'"

[14] See for example *Writing and Difference*, trans. Alan Bass (London: Routledge and Kegan Paul, 1978), p. 279; *Of Grammatology*, p. 12.

and persons such as we do have, and because it offers us an account of signs and language in which this radically important recognition can find no place. Among the conditions for our being able to have self-conscious experience is that we should be able to be aware of our own existence as intentional agents within (rather than merely as passive observers of) the world through an apprehension of other bodily presences around us with which our own agency interacts. Without such an awareness we could have no awareness of any distinction between ourselves and the things in the world which are not ourselves. To experience such "external" presences or objects consciously we do indeed (as Kant, Saussure, Wittgenstein and Derrida would all concur) require conceptual language. But the very way in which our conceptual language acquires and evolves its meanings must be through its ("imaginative") involvement in the continually shifting bodily contexts of our perceptions as we make experiential sense of the world we inhabit. (The Derridean picture, in its cut-offness from extra-linguistic reality, resembles the Kantian picture in the *Critique of Pure Reason*, and the arguments against both are essentially the same.[35] We can only have concepts at all because we can develop, modify, and ultimately sustain a rationale for those concepts through our apprehension of reality in corporeally-shared extra-linguistic situations.) The Derridean notion of *différance* takes us beyond both Kant and Saussure in its recognition of the essential inseparability of the a priori and the empirical; but the full implications of this recognition – above all that both the a priori and the empirical, and therefore *différance* itself, must be seen as an embodied process – are never acknowledged by Derrida himself.

The point which is at issue here is that our belief in the ontological priority of speech over writing – and of physical incarnation over speech – does not have to depend on any of the erroneous (what Derrida calls "logocentric")[36] theories about fully-experienced "presence" (as for example in the "one-to-one correspondence" theory of linguistic meaning) with which Derrida and some of his followers have tried to link it. This belief therefore remains unimpugned by Saussurian theorizing – but for reasons which no Saussurian theorist has been conceptually in a position to acknowledge. It is only if we are embodied that we can have the experience of

[35] Derrida in effect goes a step further than Kant and leaves reality out of his picture altogether.
[36] See for example *Of Grammatology*, p. 12.

a world of things and people such as we do have; and when once we are embodied we can only have the experience which we have (because we can only have conceptual language at all) through a located gesturing which – after all proper recognition has been given to the *différance*-based nature of linguistic meaning – must necessarily be seen as a "reaching beyond" into an incompletely-articulated extra-linguistic "presence."[37]

4

Saussurian theory's dismissal or disqualification of any kind of "naming-process" as the ground or basis of our linguistic meanings has been unquestioningly accepted by a great many Saussurian or post-Saussurian literary theorists in both the French- and the English-speaking worlds. One can even perhaps discern a note of business-like satisfaction in the writings of certain commentators who seem relieved at last to have found a tool which will rid them at a stroke of the ("Romantic") imagination and all its uncontrollable mysteries, of the spiritual importunities of intuitively experienced meaning, of the claims of the irrational and the unknown upon us, and of the disorderly and unsystematic activities of poets and writers in general. Saussurian theory

> clearly strikes down the most archaic language theory of all, one still occasionally revived by poets ... the apprehension of language as names and naming

writes Fredric Jameson in his early exposition of literary structuralism, *The Prison-House of Language*.[38] But it does not do so; it strikes down (or rather it rejects, since few arguments are provided – but we have been able to suggest the kind of Kantian or Wittgensteinian arguments which might be called for) only the version of the "naming-process" which is the baptismal labeling of some kind of already-differentiated and pre-baptismally identifiable item of the world's contents, such as a dog or a child. It does not strike down the

---

[37] It is on this necessity of – physical, but also cultural – embodiedness that the notion of "hermeneutics," or of the interpretation of expressions uttered from within other, relatively distant, physical or cultural contexts, has its proper foundation. The possibility of understanding, and of misunderstanding, across a physical or cultural "gap" lies at the very basis of our possession of a common world.

[38] Fredric Jameson, *The Prison-House of Language* (Princeton University Press, 1972), p. 30.

more fundamental "naming-process" which must be at work in all our uses of language (which must mean to some degree in *every* use of language) where the words which we already possess are set to work within extra-linguistic contexts within which they have never previously been set to work. There is a sense in which our words – to the extent that they are a gestural or what we might call a "directional" apprehension, rather than a labeling of already-isolated objects or situations – can never signify exactly for us, but must always do a part of their work in the dimension within which they "reach beyond" from the already-understood to the not-yet-understood, or from the already-perceived into the not-yet-perceived. The Saussurian conceptual system (particularly Saussure's distinction between the *langue* of a language's relational system and the *parole* of our actual language-using[39] – and for essentially similar reasons the "grammatology" of Jacques Derrida[40] or the "grammar" or "informal logic" of philosophical neo-pragmatism[41] – leaves no room for any account of how contingency *gets into* the linguistic system: on all of these conceptions of language the duality between relational system and experienced intuition, between "what we just do say" and what we have not yet found a way to express, is broken down altogether. Yet the very process of conceptual language-using can only be given the rationality or direction which it possesses through the entry into it of contingency *via* the transient embodied situations in which it is involved in the course of our ordinary experiencing.

The Saussurian rejection of the linguistic "naming-process" and of any meaning-determining "presence" outside language itself is in fact entirely fallacious. And yet there has grown up on the basis of it the whole internally interdependent sub-structure of post-Saussurian literary theory, including – amongst many others – such doctrines as:

1 That "[a] critic must choose either the tradition of presence or the tradition of 'difference,' for their assumptions about language, about literature, about history, and about the mind cannot be made compatible" (J. Hillis Miller).[42]

[39] See Saussure p. 9 *et seq.*
[40] See *Of Grammatology, passim*; *Positions*, especially pp. 17–36.
[41] See for example Wittgenstein, *Philosophical Investigations*, p. 116.
[42] In *The Quest for Imagination*, ed. O. B. Hardison Jr. (Cleveland: Case Western Reserve University Press, 1971), p. 216.

2 That – beyond the paradox-value of saying so – "all readings [of literary texts] are misreadings" (Harold Bloom,[43] Paul de Man)[44] and that there can only be more or less energetic, interesting, careful, or pleasurable misreadings but never more or less profound, illuminating, or revelatory ones.

3 That texts are interesting for their erotic significance (Roland Barthes)[45] or for their power significance (Michel Foucault)[46] rather than for their truth significance.

4 That there is no clear distinction between the texts of criticism and the texts of literature itself (Geoffrey Hartman,[47] Harold Bloom).[48]

5 That texts are mainly interesting because they are (or to the extent that they are) about *language*, or about *themselves*.[49]

6 That literary "fictions" are the unilateral creations of humanity (Northrop Frye:[50] Frye, through his Aristotelian concern with the institutions of literature, is often a Saussurian *avant la lettre*) or Nietzschean affirmations into an otherwise empty universe.

7 That "[p]oems can only be made out of other poems" (Frye).[51]

8 That "allegory," because it recognizes "the arbitrary nature of the sign,"[52] and not "symbol" is the only authentic mode of literary discourse (de Man).[53]

As against this by now deeply entrenched and interlocking structure of literary-theoretical fallacy, we have no philosophical choice but to insist:

---

[43] See *A Map of Misreading* (New York: Oxford University Press, 1975) and as a recurrent theme in Bloom's other books since *The Anxiety of Influence* (New York: Oxford University Press, 1973).

[44] See "Nietzsche's theory of rhetoric," *Symposium* 28 (1974): 50–51.

[45] See *The Pleasure of the Text*.

[46] See for example *The History of Sexuality*, vol. 1, trans. Robert Hurley (New York: Pantheon, 1978).

[47] See "Monsieur Texte: on Jacques Derrida, his *Glas*," *Georgia Review* 29 (1975): 760.

[48] See for example *Kabbalah and Criticism* (New York: Seabury Press, 1975), pp. 33–34.

[49] See for example Terence Hawkes, *Structuralism and Semiotics* (London: Metheun, 1977), p. 100; but see also much of the actual post-structuralist criticism of recent years.

[50] See in particular the second essay of his *Anatomy of Criticism* (Princeton University Press, 1957).

[51] "Poetry can only be made out of other poems; novels out of other novels. Literature shapes itself, and is not shaped externally" (*Anatomy of Criticism*, p. 97).

[52] Saussure, pp. 67–68.

[53] Paul de Man, "The rhetoric of temporality" in *Interpretation: Theory and Practice*, ed. C. S. Singleton (Baltimore: Johns Hopkins University Press, 1969), pp. 173–209.

1 That language is not a prison-house, or a closed "hermeneutic circle," or a labyrinth with no outlet (the outlet is through our embodied selves and their unbroken inherence in reality).

2 That for a poem to "mean" as well as to "be" does not in any way depend on a "correspondence" theory of language.

3 That the opposition of "referentiality" and "rhetoricality" is an illusory one and is wholly reconciled within the gestural–expressive view of language.

4 That the much-mentioned "aporias,"[54] and the "abyss,"[55] along with the rest of the transcendence-free[56] vocabulary of post-Saussurian literary theory, represent only post-Saussurian theory's uncomprehending encounter with the inherent mystery of all life and all experience.

The necessities of human embodiment which lie at the basis of language (and therefore also of consciousness and of our recognition of the distinction between ourselves and that which is not ourselves), and the "naming-process" which – in every possible form of it – Saussurian theory tries to eliminate from our conception of language, are in the end one and the same thing. Our shared verbal recognition, or grasping, of a linguistic achievement – the recognition that something "has been said" – is identical in principle to, and in the end only a bodily refinement or abstraction out of, our recognition or grasping of the meaning of a bodily gesture. "Listening to a speaker instead of looking at him tends to make us think of speech as essentially a system of sounds," R. G. Collingwood reminds us;

> but it is not; essentially it is a system of gestures made with the lungs and larynx, and the cavities of the mouth and nose ... The language of total bodily gesture is ... the motor side of our total imaginative experience.[57]

However dormant the connections may have become between the "sound-images" (or written signifiers) used and the realities expressed in our various actual languages, some survival of the underlying gestural relationships must continue to be present. Poets in particular – but all of us to the extent that we are poetically alive

54 See for example Jonathan Culler, *On Deconstruction* (London: Routledge and Kegan Paul, 1983), pp. 23ff.

55 For some explanation of this notion see Frank Lentricchia, *After the New Criticism* (University of Chicago Press, 1980), pp. 177ff.

56 See chapter 2 below.

57 R. G. Collingwood, *The Principles of Art* (Oxford: Clarendon Press, 1938), p. 243.

to the language we exist within – may be concerned to re-awaken them. The Saussurian first principle of "the arbitrary nature of the sign" must therefore, for this reason if for no others, be abandoned as philosophically unsalvageable. The Saussurian or post-Saussurian conception of language belies altogether its nature as what might be called embodied or "lived" logic, as well as of course (and conversely) belying the true nature of the "present" and of experienced "presence." If we are to get beyond the philosophical limitations of Saussurianism we need to recognize instead, and to find ways of describing, the entry of contingency into the relational system and the temporal *moving onwards* of language through the process of insight or intuition (which means an apprehension of "felt" qualities – but one which cannot be called subjective since it occurs on a level experientially prior to subjectivity and objectivity) which takes us beyond the meanings we already possess and enables us to use our old words in new extra-linguistic contexts; in other words a process through which the sensed, but not yet articulated, presence of an extra-linguistic reality gets itself (literally) incorporated into our linguistic structures. The Romantic theorists had more to say about this process than any Saussurian theorist has yet said, when (in the spirit of Kant in his *Critique of Aesthetic Judgement*) they understood our creative language-using in terms of a reasoning of the known into the unknown of which we are possessed. This "going beyond," or (since this seems in fact to be the irreplaceable philosophical word for it) human "transcendence," is something which cannot be argued away, but which we can at best – or at worst – only conceal from ourselves – or ourselves from – by taking refuge in inauthentic categories.[58]

5

The Derridean, or more generally post-structuralist, campaign against what Derrida has repeatedly called "the metaphysics of presence" ought most sensibly, perhaps, to be understood as yet

[58] In Heideggerian terms, we could say (*pace* Derrida, who often seems to be ready simply to take what he needs from Heidegger and to throw the rest away) that questions of "*différance*" cannot be pursued in abstraction from questions of Being. The necessities of human incarnation, on the other hand, are not always well handled by Heidegger himself – for example he recognizes no particular significance in gesture – perhaps partly because of the dependence of his notions of spirituality on the Western theological tradition.

another twist in French intellectual history's inability to come to terms with the indefinable: as yet another *revendication* of the *laïque* against the transcendent. (The neo-pragmatist analogy here might perhaps best be understood in terms of an Anglo-Saxon, and generally anti-mystical, "common sense.") "Structuralism" and "post-structuralism" can be easily enough distinguished as stages of a movement (the transition between them can perhaps be traced to Derrida's rejection of the Saussurian "signified" and the substitution for it of an open-ended process of "*différance*") but they at the same time possess in common the Saussurian emphasis on the relational aspects of sign-systems at the expense of any concern with the "experiential" or intuitional apprehension of truth or reality. Without embarking on a full-scale critique or "deconstruction"[59] of Derrida himself, it could fairly enough be claimed that beneath the considerable sophistication and erudition of Derrida's philosophical discussions there lies a rejection of mystery or of transcendence which is almost totally barren of philosophical argument.[60] Derrida may perhaps claim that he does not in fact *deny* extra-linguistic "presence" or reality, but only insists that "there is no presence *before* the semiological difference or outside of it."[61] This, although it looks like an important qualification, is really no more than a concession to common sense, since the Derridean "position" leaves no room for any account of such "presence" (just as – and for some of the same reasons that – it leaves no room for any account of the experiencing subject) and makes it only too easy for less sophisticated theorists than Derrida himself to deny or to forget its existence. (The parallel with the later Wittgenstein and some of his neo-pragmatist followers can seem almost uncannily close at this point.) Derrida's way of sidestepping the necessities of transcendence, we have in effect been told, is his strategy of using the only available language while not subscribing to its premises"[62] – which (since there is a limit to how far we

---

[59] For a sympathetic exposition of this notion see Culler, *On Deconstruction*: "[t]o deconstruct a discourse is to show how it undermines the philosophy it asserts, or the hierarchical oppositions on which it relies, by identifying in the text the rhetorical operations that produce the supposed ground of argument, the key concept or premise" (p. 86). See also Vincent B. Leitch, *Deconstructive Criticism* (New York: Columbia University Press, 1983).

[60] It is where notions of transcendence are directly concerned that Derrida's language is most inclined to become assertive or rhapsodical rather than argumentative. See for example the end of "Structure, sign and play."

[61] See *Speech and Phenomena*, p. 141.

[62] Gayatri Chakravorty Spivak, preface to *Of Grammatology*, p. xviii.

can step outside the language we have our existence within) would seem to invite a reply along rather brutally Johnsonian lines.[63]

The main advance of the later stages of the Saussurian movement over its earlier stages (of the later Roland Barthes,[64] for example, or of Derrida, over their more strictly Saussurian predecessors) is that these more recent practitioners would like us to be able to *enjoy* our truth-free or reality-free condition rather than (in a traditional "onto-theological" manner) simply continuing to worry about it. The post-structuralists have in this respect aligned themselves with Nietzsche: there is no ontological truth, there is only power, or play. No post-structuralist has yet produced an *argument* (and only those who already agree with him are likely to accept the post-structuralist's insistence, like the neo-pragmatist's, that arguments are part of the *old* game, which he no longer wishes to play)[65] as to why "play" is the concept which we most centrally need in this context, rather than (for example) "waiting or listening for inspiration," or "trying to get things right," or "negative capability,"[66] or the more Heideggerian "care" or "concern."[67] None of these truth-related and un-semiological notions in fact presupposes any form of belief in a "pre-existing" reality "eternally present to man's gaze," in something outside us "which will ... step in and save us," or in "truth as correspondence to reality."[68] If we need a theoretical notion of play (and it does go back to Schiller, after all),[69] we need a notion of play which comprehends, or is itself comprehended by, the notion of truth or reality. If it will help us to deflate the over-earnestness (and Derrida would suggest, nostalgia)[70] associated with traditional notions of Being, then we can agree to say that all language is founded in play; but we must then also say that play is itself founded in our

[63] Derrida's "strategy" is in some ways the opposite of what Heidegger is doing when he puts the concept of Being (*Sein*) under erasure (S̶e̶i̶n̶) to signify its *interdependence* with our human nature.
[64] See particularly *The Pleasure of the Text.*
[65] Compare, for example, Wittgenstein's discussions of the nature of philosophy in *Philosophical Investigations.*
[66] See Keats, letter to George and Tom Keats of 21 December 1817.
[67] See Martin Heidegger, *Being and Time*, trans. John Macquarrie and Edward Robinson (Oxford: Basil Blackwell, 1962), pp. 225–73.
[68] See Rorty, *Consequences of Pragmatism*, pp. 93, 150–53, 208.
[69] See Friedrich Schiller, *On the Aesthetic Education of Man: In a Series of Letters*, trans. Elizabeth M. Wilkinson and L. A. Willoughby (Oxford: Clarendon Press, 1967), Fifteenth Letter, and *passim.*
[70] See *Speech and Phenomena*, p. 159; "Structure, sign and play" in *The Structuralist Controversy*, p. 264.

own incarnated nature and in our intuitive apprehensions of powers and agencies which we encounter outside ourselves.[71] It is in this way that *nature* – which has been entirely banished by Saussurianism – must find its way back into our philosophical picture.

Saussurian theory has been valuable in so far as it has helped to undermine our theoretical interest in the individual writer's or reader's (or speaker's or hearer's) self-conscious *ego* and in questions about a literary artist's conscious or deliberate *intentions* (but such questions had for a long time been out of favor within Anglo-American literary discussions in any case). If the "thing-and-name" correspondence theory of language is wrong, then the notion of the individual author or ego as the sole originator of any literary "text" must be wrong also. But this does not take us very far towards understanding how we *should* think of the human subject or author, over and above his mere role as a passively "spoken" meeting-point of the public sign-systems which intersect in him. Any doctrine of the complete "deconstruction" of the human subject into the sign-systems which constitute him must be simply fallacious – a shift from a wrong (essentially Cartesian) concept of the self to (despite various post-structuralist protests to the contrary)[72] no concept of the self as such (in the sense in which Kant's system-transcending subject was an attempt to provide a concept of the self as such) at all. What we lack (and it is a lack which would be glaring, had we not, as in all such Emperor's clothes situations, been persuaded that there could not possibly *be* such a lack) is a notion of the subject which defines it in its relationship to apprehensible truth or reality: a partial resurrection (but a resurrection in all its corporeality and historicality – these being an ineliminable part of all human spirituality) of the old philosophical and religious notion of the soul.[73]

Saussurian theory has been valuable above all for its emphasis (1)

---

[71] These apprehensions may perhaps have their most primitive manifestations through dance and the mythic mode of consciousness. (See chapters 2 and 5 below.)

[72] For example Derrida's "The subject is absolutely indispensable. I don't destroy the subject; I situate it" (discussion following "Structure, sign and play" in *The Structuralist Controversy*, p. 271). Here again we are being offered a disingenuous concession to common sense, since there is no possible place for a concept of the self within the Derridean categories.

[73] We could perhaps sum up the demands of the re-spiritualization which is being called for here by saying that we need a notion of the soul which is both more corporeal than the one that Kant offers us but also more transcendent than the one that – for example – Aristotle offers us.

on the relational or structural dimension of signs and language, and (2) on the location of linguistic meaning within the institutions of language rather than within the conscious intentions or mental imagery of individual language-users. But as a complete account of the nature of language (rather than as an account merely of some of the principles according to which our actual languages should best be studied) Saussurian theory is philosophically bankrupt. The whole Saussurian tradition of linguistic and literary theory is philosophically adrift to the extent that it ignores, or has found no way to recognize (as well as perhaps having helped to suppress any awareness in us of a need to recognize), the necessities of human incarnation. The entire dimension of human *transcendence* is what constitutes the other term – the "presence" outside, or distinct from, the relational structures of language – which Saussurian theory has so briskly eliminated from its picture. If we were prepared to take the risk of merely replacing one kind of quaint jargon with another (and there seems to be little risk of losing anything very important, after all), we could say that this dimension is the dimension of what used to be called our *religious awareness*, and that the most fundamental objection to Saussurianism must in the end be understood to be a religious one. The objection which is being brought against Saussurianism here is not primarily an objection to the notion of the "deconstruction" of the subject (unless carried through to the point of an implicit *de*struction): Saussurianism is in many ways right as against the subject-centered or subjectist[74] notions of traditional humanism, and many of the arguments of "traditionalist" literary criticism against Saussurianism have for this reason been less effective than they might have been.[75] The most essential objection to Saussurianism is to its banishing of "presence" – to the Saussurian sleight-of-hand which makes us forget about "presence" by showing how it is a function of structure (which indeed it is), and therefore making us think of it as wholly "textual" and as having nothing to do with any dimension of extra-textual apprehension or intuition.

[74] See below, p. 65.

[75] For all the high unease-readings which have been registered by traditionalist criticism, no traditionalist has yet produced an argument which strikes at the main theoretical roots of Saussurianism: an argument which questions Saussurianism's fallacious banishment of ontology or transcendence. Until traditionalist criticism gets this part of its philosophical act together, therefore, this false Saussurian premise will remain built in to the ground floor of *all* our critical theorizing.

This dimension of apprehension or intuition, far from being effectively nothing ("there is nothing outside of the text") is in the end a great deal nearer to being the most important thing that we can ever hope to have or to have experiential access to. What Saussurian theory offers us, with its elimination from our lives of incarnation, transcendence, the self, intuition, creativity, apprehended extra-linguistic meaning, determinable textual meaning (if there is no "presence," then all readings are veridically equal), poetry (if there is no "naming," then all readings are poetically equal), historical context, and truth, is in effect the Abolition of Reality. But we are of course really left, as we always have been, with our (system-based but system-transcending) hunches or intuitions about what is real and what is not real: condemned – or free – as we always have been, to choose the one or to choose the other.

It might be asked what the implications of these arguments can be expected to be for the actual development of literary criticism – and even perhaps (at a further remove) for the actual present and future development of our imaginative literature itself. The answer is simple and can be easily enough stated. It is in the down-grading or elimination of the idea of *intuitive apprehension* or of *particular insight* that the problems of Saussurianism within literary theory irredeemably lie. The crucial weakness of Saussurian literary theory, which must go some way towards incapacitating it as any kind of value-establishing branch of literary *criticism*, is that it undermines our belief in – and must therefore indirectly help to bring about an actual withering of – our capacity for particular insights into the real meanings of particular life situations or of particular – and relatively stable, rather than indefinitely open or wholly self-referring – literary texts. This defect has sometimes been almost admitted by structuralist theorists – as for example by Jonathan Culler – but without any evident recognition of the magnitude of what is being conceded or of the philosophical importance of the issues which are involved:

> Structuralists have not succeeded in accounting for the distinction between acceptable and unacceptable symbolic readings ... It may well be that we stop [the process of interpretation] when we feel we have reached the truth or the place of maximum force and not, as Barthes suggests, that wherever we stop becomes the place of truth.[76]

[76] Culler, *Structuralist Poetics* (London: Routledge and Kegan Paul, 1975), pp. 225–29. Culler refers to Barbara Smith's argument in her *Poetic Closure: A Study of How*

Through a concatenation of false ideas (they are rarely arguments) the critic who works within an atmosphere of Saussurianism is likely to find himself progressively cut off from what must by definition[77] be his main strength as a critic or reader – which is his capacity to sense (and in a way which depends for its vitality on a continuing faith in the existence and value of that sensing) *what is really there*. Saussurian critics, like non-Saussurian critics, have done some valuable criticism, but their general theory can only have been a hindrance to them rather than a help in their having been able to do it, since the structuralist insistence that every element in a text is necessary to it by definition must inevitably get in the way of the intuitive apprehension of whether there are certain elements in a text which are aesthetically significant or effective and certain others which are not. The Saussurian critic is obliged to believe in the illusoriness or irrelevance to his enterprise of every kind of intuitively "felt" quality and of every kind of awareness of extra-linguistic "presence," and is therefore debarred from recognizing that the successful literary text is not merely a text along with all other texts but is also a capturing of some part of the essential nature of human life, and an insight into the nature of (humanly apprehended – but this is the only kind we can hope to know about) reality itself. ("Literature" differs from more "ordinary" language-using, here, only in the greater purity of its expressive or revelatory purposes.) It can hardly be a promising requirement for any critic or serious reader, and must be incapacitatingly more unpromising for any practicing literary artist, to have to believe in the unreality of *inspiration*. Both the critic and the artist who are condemned to such a disbelief are likely to become less and less able to discern, or to evoke, real human life wherever it breathes: to discover or to evoke the ghost, if there is ever to be allowed to be one, in the semiological structure which is the literary text.[78] (It has

---

Poems End (University of Chicago Press, 1968) to the effect that "allusions to any of the 'natural' stopping places of our lives and experiences – sleep, death, winter, and so forth – tend to give closural force when they appear as terminal features in a poem" (p. 102), but seems not to see how devastatingly such a dependence of literature on the "natural" must undermine the anti-naturalist premises of Saussurian theory.

[77] See also below, chapters 2 and 3.

[78] John Bayley, in *The Romantic Survival* (London: Constable, 1957), presciently remarked that "[t]he sad fact is that it is not difficult to write verse which will stand up to the methods of the analytic critic ... The old-fashioned romantic critic may have been overcome by an excess of respect for the poem's 'ghostliness,' but at least

fairly enough been remarked that Saussurian criticism's tendency to devote itself to comparatively inferior or marginal literary works, and its unwillingness entirely to disown the suggestion that any critic's reading may be as interesting as any other's *or as the literary text itself*, can very plausibly be "deconstructed" as the revenge of the categorizing intellectual upon the creative artist.)[79] In all of these ways criticism and imaginative literature within a Saussurian theoretical climate must find themselves distracted, or skewed away, from any recognition that literature is one of the main (because most intense) kinds of spiritual nourishment or sources of spiritual inspiration that we have, and that real criticism – which only means real reading carried on in more self-aware and more self-questioning ways – is itself a necessary part of that same existential and ontological enterprise. Since it is the essential function of literature to show us *how things are* – not by describing them in their actuality, but by revealing them in their essential forms and their essential rhythms[80] – it might also be valuable in this context to remind ourselves that the best of our actual literature, while readily enough allowing that there is such a thing in life as pleasure or *jouissance*,[81] also has ways of suggesting that there may still be circumstances in life where there is such a thing as *hubris* as well.

> this made him aware that ... it had a life of its own which was ultimately mysterious and irreducible ... A poem is both ghost and machine, and though a machine can be dismantled and demonstrated without reverence, a ghost is still entitled to be treated with something of the old romantic awe" (pp. 69–73).

[79] Denis Donoghue, in 'Deconstructing deconstruction" (*New York Review of Books*, 12 June 1980, pp. 37–41), has argued that post-structuralist literary theory "appeals mainly to the clerisy of graduate students" and "encourages them to feel superior ... to the authors they are reading." The poet Philip Larkin reputedly suggested that if a cow were to turn up at the headquarters of United Dairies she would be unlikely to find herself being made very welcome.

[80] No Saussurian theorist has yet had anything significant to say about rhythm; and yet rhythm, both within literature and outside of it, must – through its connection with temporality – lie close to the very essence of life itself.

[81] See Barthes, *The Pleasure of the Text*.

2

"ORIGINAL LANGUAGE"

To him who is compelled to pace to and fro within the
high walls and in the narrow courtyard of a prison, all
objects may appear clear and distinct. It is the traveller
journeying onward, full of heart and hope, with an ever-
varying horizon, on the boundless plain, who is liable to
mistake clouds for mountains, and the mirage of drouth
for an expanse of refreshing water.

COLERIDGE

1

The disembodied Kantian transcendental subjectivity of the *Critique
of Pure Reason*, if it is to be made philosophically coherent and
intelligible to ordinary thinking, needs to be re-interpreted – and
thereby provided with a "structure" – as the situated transcendental
subjectivity of real embodied life. As a necessary corollary of this, the
in-principle-humanly-inaccessible Kantian "thing in itself" needs to
be re-interpreted in terms of the embodied reality of the animate and
inanimate world which we pre-consciously inhabit. Kant himself in
fact leaves the various deeper questions about the nature of human
imagination, and therefore about the nature of human transcendence, almost entirely unexplored within the *Critique of Pure Reason*.
The function of "imagination" in the *Critique of Pure Reason* is
essentially to bridge the gap between "sense" and "understanding,"
by transforming whatever is given to us through our senses into
something which can be grasped by the thinking part of our minds.
There seems to be little that philosophy can say about this faculty,
and Kant even sounds rather dismissive of it when he calls it "a blind
but indispensable function of the soul, without which we should

have no knowledge whatever, but of which we are scarcely ever conscious."[1] In his later *Critique of Judgement*, on the other hand, where he devotes a great deal of his argument to the discussion of vital phenomena and of purposive behavior, he offers some formulations which (though they were never systematically developed by Kant himself) may help us to understand the relationship between an awareness or consciousness which is contingently situated in the world and a "thing in itself," or reality, which is not (as it was in the *Critique of Pure Reason*) wholly and by definition cut off from human experience. In an argument where he is directly concerned with art and artistic creation, Kant suggests that the "animating principle" (*Geist*) in the mind is "the faculty of presenting aesthetic ideas." He defines an aesthetic idea as "that representation of the imagination which induces much thought, yet without the possibility of any definite thought whatever, i.e. *concept*, being adequate to it, and which language, consequently, can never get quite on level terms with or render completely intelligible." He goes on to say that "such representations of the imagination may be termed ideas," and that "[t]his is partly because they at least strain after something lying out beyond the confines of experience." He proposes that in the creation of a work of art there takes place a process whereby the artist, "transgressing the limits of experience," attempts with the aid of imagination to "body forth" ideas to sense "with a completeness of which nature affords no parallel."[2] We seem here to be being offered a conception of the human imagination's power of "going beyond" experience which is very different from the "blind but indispensable" function that enabled us to build up the – mechanical and entirely lifeless – world of the *Critique of Pure Reason*.

Kant's suggestions about the function of imagination in art in fact provide us with the basis of a philosophically coherent account of the function of imagination – or we might prefer to say of creative insight or intuition – in every area of our experiential life. According to the account of imagination which this view points towards, it would be a necessity of *any* experiencing that it should comprise an element of "transgressing" or of "reaching beyond": of reaching beyond what is

---

[1] *Critique of Pure Reason*, B. 103.

[2] Kant, *Critique of Aesthetic Judgement*, trans. J. C. Meredith (Oxford University Press, 1952), sec. 49. This Kantian use of "idea" is of course quite different from – and almost opposite in meaning to – the use which was made of the term by the empiricists. Ideas, for Kant, belong to the faculty of reason and are the notions which are farthest removed from sense perception.

already clear to what is as yet obscure; of reaching beyond what we already are to what we have not yet become; of reaching into partly-grasped meanings beyond what language can "get on level terms with or render completely intelligible." In our experiencing at its most primal level, the subject, rather than being the (logic-based and disembodied) thinking subject of the *Critique of Pure Reason*, must discover himself *through* his worldly experience. The "blind but indispensable" process of what we might call human *meaning-creation* is the basis on which not only in art, but in experiential life generally, the "bodying forth" of rational ideas to sense takes place; and in so far as what is "bodied forth" is a meaning partly discerned "beyond the confines of experience," we may reasonably enough prefer to think of this meaning-creation process as (while wholly indispensable) no more than partly-blind, and as permanently partly-open to the disclosure or revelation of the nature of "things in themselves." The "noumenal" (to use Kant's term for what lies beyond or behind the realm of experienceable phenomena) must in some measure be present in every moment of our experiencing. Kant, in his *Critique of Pure Reason*, defines reality as it "really" is as lying beyond the reach both of our senses and of our understanding – and it was this aspect of his philosophy which most disturbed the post-Kantian philosophers and poetic theorists of the Romantic movement, who found themselves unable to accept the implication that we must be for ever cut off from "things in themselves" and that we can never really "know" anything but the objects of physical science or of common sense. The idea that we might somehow have contact, however incomplete, with things in themselves was an idea that earlier and more "mystical" ways of thinking had always supposed that we might attach a meaning to, and it seemed unlikely that we could be expected to abandon this idea altogether in the face of purely philosophical arguments. Between ourselves and ultimate reality there might be a veil, but it might also be possible for the veil to tremble or to be partly drawn aside: there might be special moments, or – in a later literary parlance – epiphanies, in which reality could be seen as revealing itself with special profundity in and through the appearances of ordinary life. Kant's rather unsystematic suggestions about the nature of imagination in his *Critique of Judgement*, by contrast with the role which he assigns to it in his fully-systematized account of experience in his *Critique of Pure Reason*, provide the basis for a view of human meaning-creation which will allow us to give a proper recognition to these non-conceptual and experience-transcending – but also immemorially well-attested – modes of awareness.

All consciousness, we could say, is oriented towards meaning in this fundamental sense, and can only come into existence through the meaning which reveals itself, or is revealed, in this primary process of meaning-creation. It is in fact the revelation of some meaning in reality which makes consciousness possible. This purposiveness, or orientation to meaning, is a pre-subjective and pre-objective intentionality which lies below the level of thought and of the conscious intentions of ordinary life (but at the same time is also something which must be present with, and surround, those conscious intentions, to the extent that none of our conscious thoughts or practical intentions can ever be wholly clear or explicit). This fundamental intentionality (we could perhaps borrow a phrase from Kant and speak of a "purposiveness without purpose")[3] is the matrix out of which all our thought and instrumental purposes must develop, and on which they must always continue to depend for their rationality and coherence. The world *arises* for us in response to our pre-subjective and pre-articulate desires, fears or aspirations; but the only way in which we can ultimately understand these primordial strivings must be not "objectively" but in terms of the imaginatively compelling patterns of meaning to which they have in practice given rise. This requires from us a sympathetic or "expressive" mode of comprehension, rather than a scientific search for causally-based laws or regularities. (It will in practice, perhaps, necessitate an exploration of the *myths*, or imaginative archetypes, which have become established in our own and other cultures, and within which the rest of non-human life and the inanimate order of things around us will have found some imaginatively comprehensible place.)[4] Since thought and knowledge belong to our conscious level of awareness, there is no way in which "behaviorism" or any causal-objective science can get a foothold from which to study the relationship between our pre-conscious needs or urges and the forms of expression to which they have given rise. We are in an area which is more fundamental than any science.

The process of falling into shape, or of taking on meaning or value,

---

[3] *"Zweckmässigkeit ohne Zweck"* (see for example *Critique of Aesthetic Judgement*, secs. 10, 15).

[4] See below, chapter 5.

is an intentionality below the level of conscious intention, and one which belongs neither to the subject nor to the world which that subject experiences, but which instead makes possible the coming into articulated existence of both. (The founder of phenomenological philosophy, Edmund Husserl, referred to a process of this kind in his later writings when he spoke of a "functional" [fungierende] intentionality which was the underlying foundation of all experience and the original source of unity of the experienceable world.)[5] This fundamental intentionality is the principle of the adaptive behavior of all life, and can properly be identified with the essence of life itself. Life, understood in this sense, is inherently creative, and the most exalted achievements of the human "creative imagination" are from this point of view merely a continuation of the humblest and most ordinary processes of biological adaptation. Language, and "the logical functions of judgement," are experientially subsequent to this primal creativity, even though language also establishes a special level of life which this fundamental intentionality governs in special (and for the philosopher specially central) ways. The fundamental process of meaning-creation is at work in our linguistic behavior as in all our other behavior, and – while being itself inaccessible to explanation – must be the principle which underlies all the explanation and intellectual comprehension which language makes possible: in this sense it must be recognized to be the most basic principle of "explanation" of anything. Construed as an ideal – to be pursued by us wherever we may, instead of our allowing ourselves to lapse into error and self-deception – this fundamental intentionality is at the human level perhaps the spirit behind the ἀρετή which was the moral basis of pre-Socratic Greek philosophy;[6] it may also perhaps be the spirit behind the *dharma* of Hinduism and of Zen Buddhism,[7] or the *tao*, or flowing with the stream of life, of the earliest tradition of Chinese mysticism.[8] The distinction between a "reaching beyond"

---

[5] See for example *Formal and Transcendental Logic*, trans. D. Cairns (The Hague: M. Nijhoff, 1969), p. 288. The notion also appears in *The Phenomenology of Internal Time-Consciousness*, ed. M. Heidegger, trans. J. C. Churchill (Bloomington: Indiana University Press, 1966).

[6] For an account of the thought of this period, see for example G. S. Kirk, J. E. Raven, and M. Schofield, *The Pre-Socratic Philosophers* (Cambridge University Press, 1983). On ἀρετή see also H. D. F. Kitto, *The Greeks* (London: Penguin, 1957), pp. 171–75.

[7] See for example D. T. Suzuki, *An Introduction to Zen Buddhism* (New York: Grove Press, 1964).

[8] See for example Richard Wilhelm, *The Secret of the Golden Flower*, trans. C. F. Baynes (London: Routledge and Kegan Paul, 1956).

into reality itself and mere instrumental purposes within a world which we have already understood is made explicitly – and in terms which Kant in his *Critique of Judgement* might have recognized – in the opening poem of the *Tao-Tê-Ching*:

> The secret waits for the insight
> Of eyes unclouded by longing;
> Those who are bound by desire
> See only the outward container.[9]

In the chapter of his *Biographia Literaria* where he prepares the way for his "deduction of the imagination, and with it the principles of production and of genial criticism in the fine arts" (which itself never materializes), Coleridge writes:

> We are to seek therefore for some absolute truth capable of communi-cating to other positions a certainty which it has not itself borrowed; a truth self-grounded, unconditional, and known by its own light. In short, we have to find a somewhat which *is* simply because it *is* ...
>
> Such a principle cannot be any thing or object ... [A]n object is inconceivable without a subject as its antithesis ...
>
> But neither can the principle be found in a subject as a subject, contra-distinguished from an object ... It is to be found therefore neither in an object nor subject taken separately, and consequently, as no other third is conceivable, it must be found in that which is neither subject nor object exclusively, but which is the identity of both.[10]

2

Language, we have traditionally been taught by those philosophers who have addressed themselves to the question, is in its primary function the means to our expression of our understanding of how things are. Since the time of Plato and Aristotle we have become accustomed to the idea of the human mind as making use of the concepts which we possess in order to understand, or to represent, the true nature of the world which we experience and within which we live. The judgements which we express through our thought or reason (the laws of thought are also the science of logic) are the means by which we grasp whatever it is about the world that we can

[9] *The Way of Life*, trans. R. B. Blakney (New York: Mentor Books, 1955), p. 53.
[10] Coleridge, *Biographia Literaria*, vol. 1, in *Collected Works* (Princeton University Press, 1983), pp. 268–71.

succeed in knowing; and truth (meaning the predicative truth of our propositions) consists in the conformity between the judgements which we make and the worldly states of affairs to which those judgements successfully relate. For some 2500 years, philosophy has worked with a model of – linguistically-based – human thought as "mirroring," or attempting to mirror, an external reality at which it is exploratorily directed by truth-seeking human thinkers.[11]

But language is also, as we have only recently come to be in a position to recognize, an expression of *how things are for us*, and must be an expression of the whole range of pre-conscious emotion, and of our sense of our own nature and powers, which we have found ourselves able to incorporate into our language-based behavior at the conceptual level. It is because it involves the expression of our entire range of pre- or extra-linguistically "experienced" emotion that the *gestural* aspect of language must be infinitely richer than anything which could be embraced by mere indicative (or exhortatory, or commendatory, or any other) *pointing* at items within a world of already-discriminated objects. Our vital or purposive involvement with the world must be metaphysically prior to our conscious or discursive involvement: we are animals before we are human beings, and primitive human beings before we are speakers or thinkers. The essential step into language[12] must occur – however gradual, inchoate or metaphysically complex the process may be – with the step beyond this merely vital involvement with the world to the first glimmering of an awareness of the world as a presence around us which is distinct or distinguishable from ourselves. (The philosophical question which is sometimes asked of "how language is possible" can in the end only intelligibly be construed as meaning, "How is it possible for us to have the mode of consciousness in which there are such things as *signs* for us?"[13] How is it that our mode of relating to reality can develop from the merely embedded or inhering relationship to life which is the mode of existence of the animals to

[11] The "mirroring" view of mind and reality has been well documented and criticized by Richard Rorty in *Philosophy and the Mirror of Nature* (Oxford: Basil Blackwell, 1980). Having disposed of the "mirroring" relationship, on the other hand, Rorty does not recognize any need to explore any *other* kinds of "relationship between language and reality."

[12] Here, as previously, we are in fact concerned with the necessary metaphysical *presuppositions* for the possibility of language, rather than with anthropological conjectures about its actual evolution.

[13] For this way of formulating the question I am partly indebted to Charles Taylor in his *Hegel* (Cambridge University Press, 1975), p. 474.

the kind of relationship to life in which we can achieve a detached or focused consciousness of things and can begin to have experience?) This crucial transition from a vital or purposive to a detached or conscious involvement with reality can only come about through our development of the capacity by some means to gesture, or to indicate, outside ourselves, in ways that will convey to others something about those aspects of our surroundings which we are making gestures towards or (in some spirit or other) indicating. It is some such process of gesture – whereby the "gap" between the "inward" and the "outward," between the "here" of "where we are" and the "there" of "what is outside us," is primally established – which we must recognize to be the process in which the particular mystery of "how language is possible" (as opposed to the more general mystery of how any meaning or life at all is possible) most essentially resides. The idea of gesture as a matter of simple *pointing* at already-discriminated worldly objects can only be a philosophical distraction in this context, since the "pointing" model of language-acquisition leaves quite untouched the question of how it is that we are able to *grasp* the notion of pointing in the first place. (Generally speaking, there is no way in which we can teach an *animal* anything by pointing, and yet certain animals are able to respond intelligently to some of our more complex gestural activities.)[14] What the "pointing" model leaves out – and in doing so it leaves out the very feature of language which makes it an institution as living and many-faceted as pre-linguistic life itself – is that the action of pointing can really be no more than an artificially narrowed aspect of the whole range of expressive bodily movements of which, as physically embodied beings, we must ordinarily be capable. For a person, or any imaginable organism, to be able to point, he must "first of all" be able to do innumerable other corporeally expressive things: pointing is necessarily an accompaniment to some kind of recognition of elements within a – to some extent – already conceptualized world, and other more primitive, but gesturally more complex, forms of bodily expression must go with other more primitive, but emotionally more complex, ways of expressing our relationship with the world on pre-

---

[14] Mary Midgley has pointed out that in a situation where the answer to the question "What on earth is that child doing?" is "He is play-growling and trying to pull the rug away to tease the dog," exactly the same answer is possible for the dog's play-growling and trying to pull the rug away to tease the boy. (See *Beast and Man* [Brighton: Harvester Press, 1979], p. 238.)

conscious and pre-conceptual levels. There is no way in which pointing can *itself* be a pre-condition for the establishing of such relationships. Just as our fully-conceptualized language depends for its meanings on our use of it within publicly-shared behavioral contexts, so, in order for such a language to come about, must we first suppose the existence of a process of sympathetic comprehension between individuals (who are nevertheless not yet conscious of themselves as individuals) within a publicly-shared realm of expressive bodily movement. Language can only be "attached" to the world that we experience if it has never in the first place been *de*tached from it.

The bodily-gestural aspect of language is in fact an entire *dimension* of language. It embraces the entire dimension of our possible modes of expression of our pre-linguistic "feelings" about ourselves and the world we live in, and in its broadest sense – taking into account all our possible modes of pre-linguistic awareness from the most immediate and concrete to the most remote and abstract – could properly be said to be an expression of the essential forms and rhythms of human life.[15] R. G. Collingwood, while insisting that he is concerned with the necessary nature of language as we possess it in the present and not with "that kind of *a priori* archaeology which attempts to reconstruct man's distant past without any archaeological data," has argued that

> [s]peech is ... only a system of gestures, having the peculiarity that each gesture produces a characteristic sound, so that it can be perceived through the ear as well as through the eye.

With an emphasis which runs in exactly the opposite direction to that of Saussurian (and in particular of Derridean) theory, he points out that

> [w]e get still farther away from the fundamental facts about speech when we think of it as something that can be written and read, forgetting that what writing, in our clumsy notations, can represent, is only a small part of the spoken sound, where pitch and stress, tempo and rhythm, are almost entirely ignored ... The written or printed

---

[15] The earliest formulations of the "how things are for us" view of language, and of reality, are to be found in the work of J. G. Herder and W. von Humboldt (they are also anticipated in the work of Vico). See for example F. M. Barnard (ed. and trans.), *Herder on Social and Political Culture* (Cambridge University Press, 1969); W. von Humboldt, *Linguistic Variability and Intellectual Development*, trans. G. C. Buck and F. A. Raven (Coral Gables, Fla.: Miami Linguistics Series 9, 1971).

book is only a series of hints, as elliptical as the neumes of Byzantine music, from which the reader thus works out for himself the speech-gestures which alone have the gift of expression.

Collingwood demonstrates some of the rich empirical implications of his argument when he goes on to suggest that

[e]very kind of language is in this way a specialized form of bodily gesture, and in this sense it may be said that the dance is the mother of all languages...

Different civilizations have developed for their own use different languages; not merely different forms of speech, distinguished as English from French and so on, but different in a much deeper way ... The habit of going heavily clothed cramps the expressiveness of all bodily parts except the face; if the clothing were heavy enough, only those gestures would retain their expressiveness which can be appreciated without being seen, such as those of the vocal organs; except so far as clothes themselves were expressive. The cosmopolitan civilization of modern Europe and America ... has limited our expressive activities almost entirely to the voice, and naturally tries to justify itself by asserting that the voice is the best medium for expression...

I said that "the dance is the mother of all languages"; this demands further explanation. I meant that every kind or order of language (speech, gesture, and so forth) was an offshoot from an original language of total bodily gesture ... I mean that each one of us, whenever he expresses himself, is doing so with his whole body, and is thus actually talking in this "original" language of total bodily gesture ... Rigidity is a gesture, no less than movement ... What we call speech and the other kinds of language are only parts of [this "original" language] which have undergone specialized development ... The language of total bodily gesture is ... the motor side of our total imaginative experience.[16]

When we see or hear another person speak, we see or hear an entire physical presence, and not merely a disembodied arrangement or assemblage of words: were this not so, there would be no way for us to have acquired any sense of a relationship between the words spoken – by ourselves and by others – and the world within which they are being used. For the infant language-learner, a particular

---

[16] *The Principles of Art*, pp. 243–47.

natural language arises for him as a gradual crystallization out of the gesturing and expressive noise-making which he has been engaged in since his birth, as he comes to learn which of his gestures and noises are of effective communicative use to him. (What the infant's gesturing and noise-making in fact expresses, on the other hand, will be at least partly determined by his condition of relative dependence and of biological immaturity.) Merleau-Ponty, on the basis of evidence from many studies of children's language-learning, has argued that

> [d]uring the first months of life, the child cries; he makes expressive movements; and then he begins to babble. One must consider this babbling as the ancestor of language ...
>
> Language is the indissoluble extension of all physical activity, and at the same time it is quite new in relation to that physical activity. Speech emerges from the "total language" as constituted by gestures, mimicries, etc. ... All the organs that contribute to language already have another function (Sapir).[17] Language introduces itself as a superstructure, that is, as a phenomenon that is already a witness to another order.[18]

Susanne K. Langer, in a bold speculation about the actual historical and pre-historical stages which lie behind the discursive and scientific modes of language which we now possess, throws a good deal of light on the hidden (and especially the mythic) presuppositions behind our ordinary language-using when she proposes that

> the gradual perfection of *discursive* form ... slowly begets a new mode of thought, the "scientific consciousness," which supersedes the mythic ...
>
> The primitive phases of social development are entirely dominated by the "mythic consciousness." From earliest times, through the late tribal stages, men live in a world of "Powers" – divine or semidivine Beings, whose wills determine the courses of cosmic and human events. Painting, sculpture, and literature, however archaic, show us these Powers already fixed in visible or describable form, anthropomorphic or zoomorphic – a sacred bison, a sacred cow, a scarab, a Tiki, a Hermes or a Korê, finally an Apollo, Athena, Osiris, Christ ... But in the first stages of imagination, no such definite forms embody the terrible and fecund Powers that surround humanity. The first

[17] See Edward Sapir, *Language* (New York: Harcourt, Brace, 1921).
[18] *Consciousness and the Acquisition of Language*, trans. Hugh J. Silverman (Evanston, Ill.: Northwestern University Press, 1973), pp. 11–12.

recognition of them is through the feeling of ... power and will in the human body and their first representation is through a bodily activity which abstracts the sense of power from the practical experiences in which that sense is usually an obscure factor. This activity is known as "dancing" ... Dance is, in fact, the most serious intellectual business of savage life: it is the envisagement of a world beyond the spot and moment of one's animal existence, the first conception of life as a whole – continuous superpersonal life, punctuated by birth and death, surrounded and fed by the rest of nature.[19]

Dance, we might say, already has a dimension of "aboutness," while not yet having progressed beyond being pure gesture. (That we have little empirical evidence about the actual evolutionary origins of language can hardly be an argument against philosophical speculation on the question, since our lack of evidence arises almost entirely from the accidental fact that there are no other cultures at a convenient stage of development for us to be able to watch these processes in action. The connection between biology and language is one of the most important metaphysical connections that we can be asked to explore, and it might well be argued that the whole official mainstream of Western philosophy – perhaps because of its dual over-dependence on the traditions of biblical theology and of natural science – has so far failed to register or to do any justice to this philosophical "missing link.")[20] In developing concepts out of pre-

---

[19] *Feeling and Form* (London: Routledge and Kegan Paul, 1953), pp. 189–90. Langer does in fact attempt to provide her argument with a measure of empirical support. Of the actual history of the development of the dance she notes that "Curt Sachs, in his compendious *World History of the Dance* [London: Allen and Unwin, 1937] remarks with some surprise: 'Strange as it may sound – since the Stone Age, the dance has taken on as little in the way of new forms as of new content. The history of the creative dance takes place in prehistory' [p. 62]." Criticisms of the idea that gestural language evolutionarily precedes auditory language almost invariably turn out to be concerned with gesture only in the sense of "pointing" or of other closely related forms of indication. (See for example G. Révész, *The Origins and Prehistory of Language*, trans. J. Butler [London: Longmans, 1956].) In fact an entirely silent gestural language would be quite possible, even if no such language has occurred naturally, while a language of sounds or other signifiers unrelated to bodily movement would be impossible altogether.

[20] Jane Lawick-Goodall, in *In the Shadow of Man* (London: Collins, 1971), has described, amongst other related activities, the dancing and rhythmically ritualistic behavior of a group of chimpanzees in response to the onset of a torrential rainstorm – seemingly a clear enough example of a primitive recognition of some kind of external presence or agency (pp. 58–59). Mary Midgley sums up a great deal of zoological and ethological evidence when she remarks that "[s]peech makes sense only for a species that is already constantly communicating by expressive movements" (*Beast and Man*, p. 243).

conceptual expressiveness, our language is in its own way pushing further the fundamental process of meaning-creation which is essential to all life. From this point of view, to be linguistically creative can be thought of as *inter alia* a new level of vital adaptive behavior: language, we might say, can from this point of view (there are many others which also need to be considered) be thought of as a continuation of biological evolution by other means.[21]

Any naturally used language must in its origins be expressive and gestural, and it is the development of bodily expressiveness as such, leading to the dawning of consciousness as we come to discriminate a reality distinct from ourselves, which must mark the most decisive experiential and ontological step. This step must perhaps remain mysterious; but we are at any rate nearer to understanding where its true mystery lies if we see it in terms of a general bodily expressiveness rather than in terms of something which is essentially hidden in the nature of verbal sounds or of written words on a page. The revealingness of language – its revelatoriness of how things "really" are – is therefore ultimately identical with our human expressiveness – which must mean our expressiveness, quite generally, of our sense of embodied life and of its over-all meanings and rhythms. It is in this comparatively profound, rather than merely "pragmatic," sense that *truth* (meaning here the capacity of our modes of articulation themselves to reveal reality, rather than the mere truth of "correspondence" as between "statement" and "fact") must necessarily depend on the bodily constitution of the organism of whose nature such a revelation is an expression. If a civilization came to be acquired by a race of giant crustaceans, it would necessarily possess a very different kind of language, as well as a very different kind of culture and art, from our own.[22]

3

When we once possess language, it must at the same time also become possible for us to raise questions about how far the particular conceptualizations of reality which we possess are adequate to the

---

[21] If this Clausewitzian formula sounds "reductive," we should perhaps remember that we are working here with a less reductive than usual notion of what biological existence itself is.

[22] For the same reasons we should have to agree with Wittgenstein when he remarks that "[i]f a lion could talk, we could not understand him" (*Philosophical Investigations*, p. 223).

pre-linguistic awareness which we use them to articulate. It is because there is necessarily an uncloseable gap between our sense of reality and the systems of concepts which we rely on to express this sense that there must always be room for such questions to be asked. The relationship between the linguistic and the pre-linguistic, or between the fully conscious and the as-yet-only-intuitively-sensed, must nevertheless be something which lies beyond the possibility of empirical investigation, since we can – by definition – never make a conscious (and therefore language-based) comparison between the words which we possess and the pre-linguistic intuitions which we call upon those words in order to give utterance to. Our speech relates to what we mean to express by it in the same kind of way that our expressive gestures relate to the emotions which we "use" them to convey (there are *also*, of course, practical or instrumental gestures – like pointing to a stone slab because we want someone to bring us a stone slab – where we can properly treat both the gesture and the "thought behind it" as separate items which are open to empirical investigation). The relationship between what we try to express linguistically and the language which we call upon to express it is in fact a radical instance of what (as Kant formulates the notion of his *Critique of Judgement*) our understanding, and conceptual language itself, must remain unable to "get quite on level terms with or render completely intelligible."

The feeling of approximating to truth – to the disclosure or revelation of how things really are – is a manifestation of the fundamental vital process of meaning-creation, and is a necessary component of every act of language-using where we feel that something has successfully been expressed. The "feeling" of getting nearer, or perhaps even of some particular break-through or discovery, is something which – though we may be deceived about it in particular cases – can in principle never be wholly irrelevant to the essential nature of language. The evolution of language which this "feeling" (or insight, or intuition) governs *is* the movement of our understanding or reason towards truth, since there is no way in which we could by-pass this history of individual language-using acts in order to arrive at truth by another method. These "feelings" which we have of *making* sense are not detachable psychological accompaniments of language-using, but are necessary components of the nature of language – and therefore necessary components also of the nature of truth or reality. Logic, we might say, deals with linguistic meanings which we have already acquired; meanwhile, in its actual use within the historical world, language deploys an "edge," or an intuitive "reaching beyond the confines of experience," which logic is by definition unable to "get quite on level terms with." This dual nature of language is what Nietzsche referred to when he said that "whatever we have words for, we have already got beyond."[23] Merleau-Ponty has pointed out that it is an aspect of the dependence of all linguistic meanings on contexts of *use* that these meanings should always lie beyond the reach of any final definition:

> It is the *value of use* that defines language ... [U]sage precedes signification *per se*. It does not occur otherwise, even at the level of the most elaborate language, for example, in the introduction of a new concept in philosophical language ... An entirely defined language ... would be sterile.[24]

There is the process of building up – or of laying down – the meanings which constitute our language-system as we at any time know it; but what enables this process to take place is individual creative speech-acts – or writing-acts – which take us a step beyond the various meanings which we have up to that moment possessed. There can be "rules" for applying our concepts only because the activity of applying a rule necessarily incorporates an intuitive (in a broad sense of the term, we might say "metaphorical") "reaching beyond" all the particular instances which have up to that time been comprised under that particular rule.

Feelings of rightness in this primitive linguistic area may nevertheless be subject to many kinds of error or self-deception. Since such feelings are less than fully conscious, they must necessarily take place on a level where we are less than fully ourselves, and they may therefore reveal to us things which – on a more conscious level – we are less than fully inclined to accept as being a real part of ourselves. The dynamics of human pre-consciousness (it might in fact be helpful if we could find a more corporeal-sounding word than either "soul" or "pre-consciousness" for this center of self which is already involved in the physical world) may very easily lead us into a kind of suppressive not-seeing which lies somewhere between genuine error on the one hand and wilful blindness on the other. These not-quite-blameworthy, but also not-quite-blameless, failings of human awareness are almost inevitably among the most important obstacles to the

---

[23] Nietzsche, *Twilight of the Idols*, sec. 26.
[24] *Consciousness and the Acquisition of Language*, p. 52.

evolution of language and to the revelation of truth. They are what Collingwood touches on with his notion of the "corruption of consciousness," when he argues that

> [c]oncealment of the truth is one thing, a bona fide mistake is another. But at the level of consciousness the distinction between these two things does not exist: what exists is the protoplasm of untruth out of which, when further developed, they are to grow.[25]

They are also a large part of what Heidegger (whose emphasis has been shared by other existentialist thinkers) comprises under the notion of "inauthenticity,"[26] as well as having a good deal in common with the Freudian and other psychoanalytic concepts of repression. They perhaps have one of their earliest formulations in Plato's allusion to "that deception in the soul about realities";[27] but even earlier than Plato they may perhaps be found at the basis of the pre-Socratic notions of ἀρετή[28] and of our ways of failing to achieve it. While it is a necessity that any measure of newly-articulated truth can only be arrived at through the activities involved in our ordinary language-using, we must also recognize that it is not at all a necessity that what we behaviorally classify as ordinary language-using will of itself ensure our access to any significant measure of truth. As well as mere verbal "behavior," there must also be a certain openness of disposition – in effect a concern for registering our not-yet-articulated intuitions authentically – which must manifest itself in the stance which we pre-consciously adopt towards our pre-linguistic experience.[29] This may seem hard to accept (not least if

---

[25] *The Principles of Art*, p. 219. In the present argument the term "pre-consciousness" is being used with some of the meanings which Collingwood here attaches to "consciousness."

[26] See *Being and Time*, sec. 9 and *passim*.

[27] Plato, *The Republic*, 382b.

[28] See above, p. 38.

[29] We are here of course dealing with the "internal" component of language-using which has made so many difficulties for post-Wittgensteinian philosophers. In *Philosophical Investigations* (pp. 213–26) Wittgenstein touches on the notion of what might be called "meaning-blindness." "For we want to ask, 'What would you be missing if you did not *experience* the meaning of a word?'" After acknowledging our inclination to *ask* such a question – the question, in effect, of whether our perception of meaning lies outside our mere "use" of language – he remarks that "[m]eaning is not a process which accompanies a word," and brings his argument to rest on the notion that "[w]hat has to be accepted, the given, is – so one could say – *forms of life*." We can accept these famous formulations, and even agree that "meaning it" is not a subjective "process which accompanies a word," without in the least agreeing that *all* aspects of experientially or pre-experientially discerned meaning can be allowed to drop out of consideration as irrelevant.

we think of "concern" as belonging only to the level of conscious purpose), in so far as the only criterion for the presence of this concern – since we cannot study it objectively – must in the end be nothing other than the success of the "concerned" individual or culture in achieving a deeper relationship with reality. In certain particular intellectual areas – as for example in the natural sciences – we may be able to call upon more definite-seeming decision-procedures or criteria of testability; but there remains a sense in which the ultimate validation of our concepts (as we may be readier to accept in the case of more "artistic"- or "imaginative"-seeming areas of language-using, such as poetry or literature) must be intuitive and based in the primal processes of gesture and of meaning-creation. The seeming circularity of this criterion is something which we have no alternative but to accept as a necessary part of the human condition itself.[30]

The element of pre-conscious openness, or of what might be called (since it must have its foundation in our vital purposiveness) *concern*, or *care*,[31] is something which we have no choice but to recognize as a condition for our possession of the kind of experience which we do have, since (this vital purposiveness being the only evident basis for our making of discriminations in the reality around us) the only alternative would be for every "presentation"[32] which comes to us to be meaningful – which would be impossible for a finite consciousness – or else for none of the "presentations" which come to us to be meaningful at all. Our pre-conscious openness to reality (which is nothing other than our human transcendence) must incorporate a

---

[30] Pragmatism, sensing the threat of this circularity, tries to avoid it by simply short-circuiting the whole process: truth is in the end only what "we" are inclined to accept. Any difficulties about who "we" may be in this context tend to be rather breezily bundled aside. (For example: "It would be foolish to keep conversation on the subject going once everyone, or the majority, or the wise, are satisfied, but of course we *can*" [Rorty, *Philosophy and the Mirror of Nature*, p. 159].)

[31] Compare Heidegger's concept of *Sorge*. (See *Being and Time*, sec. 39 *et seq*.) It might be a mistake, even so, to suppose that the notions of authenticity or of freedom which are being engaged with here must translate into anything quite so passive or docile as Heidegger himself makes of them. (See for example his Epilogue to *What is Metaphysics?*) Heidegger has little to say about the bodily-gestural or power-expressive (one might almost say Nietzschean) aspects of human transcendence – perhaps precisely because of what he seems to see as his central mission to save the meaning of reality from any capitulation to mere man-centered – or Nietzschean – will.

[32] See *Critique of Pure Reason*, for example B. 131.

freedom – and it must be a freedom on a level more primitive than any will-centered or instrumental freedom – to embrace or respond to the intuitions or intimations which come to us from the not-yet-articulated world around us. At the same time the "highest" truth which we can meaningfully speak of can be no "higher" than the truth which human language (or such other non-human or inter-galactic language as we have not yet come into contact with) has so far articulated through this pre-conscious experience of the "feeling" of approximating to truth. What lies beyond what has so far been articulated – which we might be tempted by a Kantian analogy to designate as Reality-in-itself – cannot yet be regarded as in any way a part of truth. The notion of "discoveries waiting to be made" is one which can be given meaning only within the context of some already sensed or formulated *problem*.[33]

Gesture, or pure non-referential bodily expression, must be the most fundamental form of language; but with the development of conceptual structures a mnemonic system comes into existence which enables us to make reference to things, and to express our "subjective" feelings or intentions towards them, whether or not we are immediately or physically in their "presence." The process of meaning-creation, as it occurs at the level of language itself, is the basis of what can be called the creative or *poetic* dimension of language, and it is this process which underlies the development of the structural or logical dimension which enables us to make comprehensible referential gestures towards items in a conceptual-ized world. The logical dimension of language arises out of, and must thereafter always continue to depend upon, its poetic dimension. However much the autonomy of our logic may be insisted upon by logicians, with an emphasis on its independence of all psychology (rather as the autonomy of our "understanding" was insisted on by Kant), our logic must retain, through its involvement with the

---

[33] The need for us to take an "existentialist" view of what lies – as yet – beyond human experience has been emphasized by Merleau-Ponty, when he defines Being, or reality itself beyond what has so far been articulated, as *"that which demands creation from us in order for us to have experience of it."* See *Le Visible et l'invisible* p. 251; author's italics in original. Rationalists or early-Sartreans, as well as Nietzscheans, may perhaps demur at the idea of freedom as a falling-in-with-reality (and at the idea that in some sense animals, in their attunement to life, might be free), but even they would presumably allow – even insist – that we must be less free if we see the world wrongly than if we see it rightly. The present argument is only suggesting that the same considerations must apply on the pre-conscious or pre-conceptual level of our awareness.

embodied nature of our existence, an unbreakable dependence on gesture and imagination and on the historical human situation out of which it contingently arises.[34]

4

There is the same mysteriousness at work in the ability of words to function as signs and to bring into existence a conceptually-articulated world for us as there is in the ability of a partial and "subjective" sensory experience (there being no pure "sense-data," and our imagination being involved in all our perception) to establish the presence of an independently-existing perceived object. Both processes involve what we may see as – in the most radical sense of the word – a *symbolic* transition from "sign" to "thing signified" which must be the basis of all our conscious experiencing and of its "transgressing" beyond contingent limitations. The notion of "symbolism" which we are concerned with here is one which is more fundamental than any notion of "agreed" symbolisms (such as the one-to-one correspondences of codes or technical systems), and is one which in fact necessarily underlies all such agreed symbolisms and makes them possible: it is the aspect of "symbolism" which is involved in any original *conferring* of significance, or in the very process of *naming* itself. The difference between the two senses of "symbolism" which is in question here in fact corresponds to the distinction which was made by Romantic writers such as Goethe and Coleridge between "symbol" and "allegory" in imaginative literature – whereby "allegory" is merely an intellectual encoding of something which has already been conceptually understood (what Coleridge called "a translation of abstract notions into a picture

---

[34] Hegel argues at length that the study of the logic of our conceptual understanding must be an artificial abstraction from the processes of actual thought (in a sense this might be seen as the whole project of his *Phenomenology*). Owen Barfield, coming to the argument from another direction, remarks that "Western philosophy, from Aristotle onwards, is itself a kind of offspring of Logic. To anyone attempting to construct a metaphysic in strict accordance with the canons and categories of formal Logic, the fact that the meanings of words change, not only from age to age, but from context to context, is certainly interesting; but it is interesting solely because it is a nuisance" (*Poetic Diction*, p. 61). Heidegger, protesting at the usurpations of reason and logic in the history of Western thought, is at one point goaded into calling reason "the most stubborn adversary of thought" (*Holzwege* [Frankfurt: Klostermann, 1950], p. 247).

language"),[35] while "symbol" is a genuinely original or heuristic disclosure of meaning (so that, according to Goethe, "whoever grasps this particular in a living way will simultaneously receive the universal too, without even becoming aware of it – or realize it only later").[36] But it is also a necessity, both in our perception and in our conceptual thinking, that the forms and directions which this fundamentally-symbolic meaning-creation process assumes should be in part governed by our physical nature as human beings. The most elementary forms of our gestures (to which all our verbally-articulated forms of language must ultimately be traceable) will necessarily be determined by our biological structure – the head thinks, the eyes see, the hands grasp, the feet tread – and only at comparatively sophisticated levels will the relationship between biological structure and expressive form begin to become more tenuous and hard to discern. With verbal language proper, the relationship may cease to be very evident at all.[37]

In its gestural or expressive dimension, which is also its poetic as opposed to its logical dimension, language is more usefully to be compared with such self-evidently expressive activities as dance or music than with the kind of cryptographic matching-up of "sign" and "thing signified" which has been taken as its paradigm throughout some 2500 years of Western thinking.[38] Like gesture, or like dance itself, the poetic dimension of language is an expression of our (or, because these processes occur on a pre-conscious level, we should perhaps say "our") sense of power, or of vital agency, in relation to the reality which surrounds us (and for which *we* are at the same time a means of coming-to-articulation, or of self-disclosure, into an experienceable world and a realm of propositional

[35] Coleridge, *The Statesman's Manual*, ed. R. J. White in *Collected Works*, vol. 6, p. 30.
[36] J. W. von Goethe, in *The Permanent Goethe*, ed. Thomas Mann (New York: Dial Press, 1948), p. 632; translation by Norbert Guterman.
[37] And yet it must continue on some level to be there – with destructive implications for the "structuralist" or "post-structuralist" linguisticians' key doctrine of "the arbitrary nature of the sign." See above, chapter 1.
[38] Anaximander (c. 610–547 BC), Heraclitus (c. 540–480 BC) and Parmenides (c. 540–460 BC) were perhaps the last philosophers to allow us to see reality in terms of a *creation* of meaning, or Λόγος as an original Word or revelation rather than as the principle of conceptual – i.e. logical – thinking. More recently (one might be reminded here of Mallarmé's remark in another context about "the original Homeric deviation"), it has become routine to oppose τὸ ποιεῖν and τὸ λογίςειν (or λογίςεσθαι) – the breaking-down of unitary meanings being opposed by the putting-together of poetry – as the Greeks themselves came to do, and as for example Shelley does in his *Defence of Poetry*.

truth). This may remind us in turn of those aspects of the "poetic" –
such as rhythm, symbolic structure, or emotional expressiveness –
which are the very aspects of the ordinary matrix of our used
language which the abstraction of "purely referential" (or of "purely
logical") discourse leaves behind.

Referentiality – the making of reference to things in an already
established world – can from one point of view be thought of as a
metaphysically derivative aspect of language, and as relying for its
significance on an institutionalized logic of meanings which has itself
been poetically elaborated out of the probings of human existence.
This creative development of language can of course itself be held to
depend on the antecedent existence of an elaborated language which
is in process of being further refined or extended – and it would be
true to say that both the referential and the poetic dimensions of
language must in some respects have been co-present in language
from its origins. But the most primitive language – as both dance and
the infant's gesturing and noise-making may remind us – does not
yet distinctly refer; and a pure form of linguistic expressiveness is also
possible, as in "poetry" or "imaginative literature," where the
making of reference to actually-existing – or to possible (or to impossible) – states of worldly affairs is in no way an essential part of what is
being done. In a scientifically- and technologically-dominated world,
our referential explorations – and in particular our factual or descriptive explorations – have become increasingly systematized and
abstract, and this has enabled them (construed not as empirical
science but as empiricist philosophy) to find their way back into our
common-sense thinking and to obscure the necessary creativity on
which they and all other conceptually-elaborated aspects of our
awareness must depend. But however systematized or abstract our
explorations may become (as for example in recent developments in
the natural sciences), they must ultimately rest on an unbroken
and – in principle – traceable relationship with the expressive matrix
of our used language. It is in this sense that poetry – meaning here
the poetic dimension of our ordinary everyday language – can
properly be said to be, in Shelley's words, "that which comprehends
all science, and that to which all science must be referred."[39]

[39] P. B. Shelley, *A Defence of Poetry*, in *Shelley's Works*, vol. 7, ed. H. B. Forman
(London: Reeves and Turner, 1880), p. 136.

3

POETRY

> [T]he poet makes the terms themselves. He does not make
> judgements, therefore; he only makes them possible –
> and only he makes them possible.
>
> OWEN BARFIELD

1

On one of the opening pages of his *Defence of Poetry*, and without
making excessively heavy transcendental weather of his argument
(he was "defending" poetry against his friend Peacock's account of it
as no more than a sentimental anachronism in the modern age of
reason and science),[1] Shelley tells us that "[i]n the youth of the
world, men dance and sing and imitate natural objects, observing in
these actions, as in all others, a certain rhythm or order." In the
same paragraph he suggests that

> [i]n the infancy of society every author is necessarily a poet, because
> language itself is poetry ... Every original language near to its source is
> in itself the chaos of a cyclic poem: the copiousness of lexicography
> and the distinctions of grammar are the works of a later age, and are
> merely the catalogue and the form of the creations of poetry.

The language of poetry, or of poets, he tells us,

> is vitally metaphorical; that is, it marks the before unapprehended
> relations of things and perpetuates their apprehension, until words,
> which represent them, become through time, signs for portions or

---

[1] See Thomas Love Peacock, "Four ages of poetry" in *The Works of Thomas Love
Peacock*, vol. 8, ed. H. F. B. Brett-Smith and C. E. Jones (London: Constable, 1934),
pp. 3–25.

classes of thought, instead of pictures of integral thoughts; and then, if no new poets should arise to create afresh the associations which have been thus disorganized, language will be dead to all the nobler purposes of human intercourse.

(Defence of Poetry, pp. 102–3)

Any philosophical exploration – or defence – of what we might unreflectively call "poetry," or "imaginative literature," might do well to start out from this recognition of the intrinsically expressive nature not only of poetry or literature itself but also of any kind of ordinarily or actually used language whatsoever. On the most fundamental level, this means the recognition of the essentially expressive, because not yet properly referential, nature of any "original language near to its source." "In the infancy of society," and also in the infancy of the individual human child, we must recognize the existence of a level of not-yet-fully-conceptualized language which is both gestural and emotionally expressive, but which has not yet been articulated into a referential structure which allows us to understand, or therefore even to experience, a world of objects around us; and it follows that we are obliged to see this pre-conceptual level of linguistic expressiveness as continuing to underlie the more sophisticated and fully-referential things that we are "later" able to do as a result of our possession of concepts.

As we apply or make use of it within our ordinary lives, our language will refer in various ways to the "things" which combine to make up our articulated world; but it will at the same time necessarily always continue to have an expressive dimension, even if not always an expressive dimension which is in any way an interesting or (in the most obvious sense of the word) a significantly imaginative one. A proposition or statement may tell us that "S is p," but it is only something "behind" or "beyond" the proposition itself which can give us our acquaintance with what S or p themselves really are. This "something beyond" is not reducible to any sum of possible states of affairs in which S or p may feature, even though it is only through our experience of such states of affairs (more generally through the "forms of life" in which S and p play a part) that the "something beyond" can come into presence for us and be intuitively or inwardly grasped. It is *naming* which provides us with the ultimate authentication of our language, and which constitutes the principle of its organization within this expressive or gestural dimension. (In terms rather different from those that Wittgenstein had in mind when he used the notion in his *Tractatus*, the proposition *shows* its sense.)[2]

But if our ordinary language is necessarily expressive, it is at the same time also necessarily bound up with the practical activities of our daily lives; and for this reason it must be equally essential to any philosophical exploration or defence of "poetry" that we should take into account the relationships which exist between the fundamentally expressive aspects of language and the whole pattern of practical and worldly activities which makes up the texture of our lives at the human level. Like the animals, we may be capable of eating, sleeping, fighting or running away without having to devote any conscious thought to the performance of such actions. On the other hand it can only be possible for us to plan, to cultivate, to bargain or to experiment when we are already in possession of a certain mode of conceptual language; and as thinking and experiencing human beings it must be more than an accidental fact about our lives that we should be capable of doing some at least of these conceptually-dependent things. It may perhaps be true that in the youth of the world men danced and sang and imitated natural objects, observing in these actions a certain rhythm or order;[3] but it is also philosophically certain (rather than merely humanly rather likely) that this cannot have been the whole way in which they spent their time. The dawning of expressiveness, we could say, comes with – is even from one viewpoint the same thing as – the dawning of language; but this first step in the emergence of subjectivity at the same time carries with it the – eventual – possibility of an instrumental relationship with the world whereby the things which have meaning for us in our surroundings are also capable of being made use of as means towards practical ends which (with the acquisition of subjectivity) we are for the first time able to formulate. What might be called a practically-oriented involvement with reality is a necessary part of life at the animal or pre-human level, and has at that stage not yet become separated from mere (but not yet conscious) awareness: both the practicality and the awareness are aspects of the fundamental process of meaning-creation which is the governing

[2] See Wittgenstein, *Tractatus Logico-Philosophicus*, trans. C. K. Ogden (London: Routledge and Kegan Paul, 1922), 4.022.
[3] See Shelley, *Defence of Poetry*, p. 102.

principle of life itself.[4] This practical orientation of pre-conceptual life, on the other hand, is not yet an *instrumental* orientation: it is only when life reaches the human level, and through the development of "concepts of objects," that there can arise both an objective world (of which we are subjectively aware) and also a practical mode of relating with that world which can properly be called instrumental (and which is determined in its shape or structure by our subjective intentions and our conscious will). But in addition to being made *possible* by the development of a subjective mode of awareness, this instrumental function of language must also be a *necessary* part of any culture or society in which subjectivity and objectivity have arisen. When once we have found ourselves in an articulated world, we cannot merely experience or contemplate that world passively: we must also *live* in it, with all that this entails of intending, trying, struggling, succeeding or failing in a range of practical projects. It may be true, as Shelley implies, that the development of conceptual comprehension may under some conditions deliver us over to rigidified ways of thinking (what Coleridge in a related context called "fixities and definites")[5] and that this may imperil our expressive abilities and leave us incapacitated for some of the "nobler purposes of human intercourse." But a degree of elaboration of words into "signs for portions or classes of thought" must be a necessary attribute of any culture whatever in which experience is possible, and not merely of a creatively-deadened one.

The possession of a fully experiential awareness depends on the possession of referentiality, and the possession of referentiality entails the possession of instrumentality or manipulativeness. It remains true, even so, that the referential systems which we possess are themselves won through to in a wide variety of expressive and pre-experientially exploratory ways.[6] We develop them, or they themselves come into articulation for us, in the course of our expressive probings within the obscurities in which we live, and in which, on the basis of our pre-conscious sensings or intuitions, we continually find new and previously undisclosed kinds of order. All language has its foundation in this process of pre- or extra-linguistic intuition, and even when we are already in possession of an objectively articulated language our particular kinds of linguistic expressiveness and our

---

[4] See above, chapter 2.
[5] See *Biographia Literaria*, vol. 1, p. 305.
[6] It is suggested below (chapter 5) that the mythic mode of consciousness may be a necessary stage in this process.

ability to "say new things" must rest on our pre-articulate sensing or intuition of the "thing which we need to express" and of the words in our available language which we can most effectively call upon to try to express it.[7] We are now in a position to recognize – as Kant, for example, was not yet in a position to recognize – that our true pre-subjectivity (in Kantian terminology, "transcendence") belongs to a level more primitive than the distinction between subject and object, and that our intuitive modes of awareness, given a certain necessary openness in our disposition, open up continually new *horizons* within the reality which we inhabit.[8] Since the primal appearances which "come to us" are primitively emotional as well as primitively perceptual, we must accept as a further corollary of our pre-subjective relationship to the world that – in a special but philosophically important sense – it is through our *moods*, which must underlie and surround all our conscious experience and conceptual formulations, that we have our most fundamental apprehensions of the nature of the reality around us.

"Mood," in this pre-conscious and pre-experiential sense, is something on a deeper level than – but must necessarily be something which can also accompany or surround – the kind of subjective emotional states in which we might be said to be in a mood "about" something. On this pre-experiential or ontological level, "mood" carries something of the poets' overtones of "intimation," or of "apprehension" ("What a piece of work is a man! ... in apprehension, how like a god),[9] and is what Wordsworth refers to, and begins to define, when he speaks of "that blessed mood, / In which the burthen of the mystery / ... / Is lightened" and "We see into the life of

---

[7] "Sense" and "intuition" are here of course being used to refer to our pre-conscious apprehension of significance or order, rather than to the wholly passive (empiricist or Kantian) reception of not-yet-mentally-structured data by an unembodied consciousness. Ordinary language (almost as though the notion of pre-conscious apprehension had to be kept alive *somewhere*) seems in fact to give an unusually good warrant for such a usage.

[8] In strict accuracy it should be said that "transcendence" is not itself Kant's term, but is used as a derivation from his term "transcendental." William J. Richardson, in his *Heidegger: Through Phenomenology to Thought* (The Hague: Nijhoff, 1974), argues from a Heideggerian perspective that "transcendence ... is ... that structure of the knower by reason of which knowledge is possible." He distinguishes "*transcendence*, which characterizes a knower as *self*, and the *consciousness* which characterizes him as a *subject*," and points out that "the genuine sense of self ... is not the stable identity of a subject but the unity of *concern* ..." (pp. 101, 113, 155–57); italics added. Some of the implications of this notion are discussed further in chapter 5 below.

[9] Shakespeare, *Hamlet*, II, ii, ll. 299–304.

things."[10] The special importance of lyric poetry among our various literary genres follows directly from this argument. Lyric poetry derives its revelatory power from the primitive unities of thought and feeling which lie at the very basis of language itself. The lyric genre has been identified by Northrop Frye with

> what we think of as typically the poetic creation, which is an associative rhetorical process, most of it below the threshold of consciousness, a chaos of paronomasia, sound-links, ambiguous sense-links, and memory-links very like that of the dream. Out of this the distinctively lyrical union of sound and sense emerges.

Frye proposes that "[t]he lyric is ... the genre which most clearly shows the hypothetical core of literature ..." (*Anatomy of Criticism*, pp. 271–72). Of this same pre-conscious verbal creativity, Susanne Langer has remarked that

> [t]his power of words is really astounding. Their very sound can influence one's feeling about what they are known to mean ... The vocal stresses that rhythmicize some languages, the length of vowels in others, or the tonal pitch at which words are spoken in Chinese and some less known tongues, may make one way of wording a proposition seem gayer and sadder than another. This rhythm of language is a mysterious trait that probably bespeaks biological unities of thought and feeling which are entirely unexplored as yet.
>
> The fullest exploitation of language sound and rhythm, assonance and sensuous associations, is made in lyric poetry.
>
> (*Feeling and Form*, p. 258)

To the extent that it is a discernment or disclosure of the most essential forms and rhythms of human life at the conceptual level of our awareness (the lyric genre is not so much subjective – an "I" talking to itself – as the core, or germ, of *all* our literary devices), lyric poetry might be thought of as the most essential of our linguistic modes of apprehension of reality.[11]

---

[10] "Tintern Abbey," ll. 37–49.
[11] It is to poetry, in the wider Shelleyan sense – and not, for example, to natural science – that we must look for a true comprehension of the nature of our ordinary naming. A. E. Housman was right when he remarked that "salt is a crystalline substance recognized by its taste; its name is as old as the English language and is the possession of the English people, who know what it means: it is not the private property of a science less than three hundred years old" (*The Name and Nature of Poetry* [Cambridge University Press, 1933], p. 15). Our living language mostly lies well clear of science, even though the whole of science has derived from it and bits of technical parlance are embedded in it.

2

All language, subject to the openness or authenticity of its users' dispositions (and here we must be speaking of a language-using collectivity, rather than of isolated *egos* or consciousnesses),[12] has an inherent tendency to try to attain a more truthful or expressive articulation of reality as we extra-linguistically sense it to be. In practice, on the other hand, and in the world in which we in fact live, a great deal of language-using occurs semi-automatically and largely unintuitively, with words being used inexpressively as "portions or classes of thought" and only the most minimal creativity being manifested in the application of those "classes of thought" to particular not-yet-articulated situations. This is linguistic creativity at its lowest level, and corresponds to a level of authenticity where language has almost lapsed from the condition of being language altogether and has begun to resemble a closed mechanical system. In this deteriorated condition language may already – *pro tanto* – have begun to be "dead to all the nobler purposes of human intercourse."

But it is also true, and may be true under the very same historical conditions, that certain other kinds of language-using can be found which are greatly more expressive, and that among these there are forms of language-using in which expressiveness, or creative insight, seems to be the main or even the exclusive purpose for which the form of language-using in question has come about. There are kinds of language-using (which belong not to the primitive level – like the events in Shelley's "infancy of society," or a real infant's cries – but to the level of fully-conceptual comprehension) where the immediate purpose of the linguistic activity seems not to be in any obvious sense a conscious or manipulative purpose or one which is determined by any preconceived or pre-describable intentions. Where language is expressive in this "pure" way, we are taken beyond any notion of "purpose" as understood in relation to preconceived ends within an already-comprehended world. As with expressive bodily gestures, we find that in such cases there is little that we can say about the extra-

---

[12] The notion of a "collective unconscious" may not be an altogether unuseable one. The main objection to it in its Jungian (we could perhaps also speak of a Lévi-Straussian) form is that it is made to seem unhistorical, timeless or universal, rather than being a dimension of the – differing but inter-related – awarenesses of particular historical contexts and cultures.

linguistic significance of the language-use in question except in terms of its expressiveness or inexpressiveness of some not-previously-articulated intuition. The kinds of language-using which seem most obviously to possess this quality – where it would be plausible to say that the expressive function is preponderant over all instrumental functions – is the range of language-uses which we ordinarily group together under the heading of poetry or imaginative literature.[13] Art, if we were to give this literary argument a wider application, could be seen from this point of view as a range of activities in which the expressive dimension is either the only one which is "present," or else is – in some sense – the only one which is immediately relevant or significant. In the case of poetry or literature, the art is made out of words; and because words make reference to, and have a descriptive dimension within, the world of human life, what a piece of literature (on this view) is "made out of" is in a certain sense the very stuff of human life, or of human history, itself. (What the other arts are made out of is, by analogy with literature, certain particular perceptual modes, or certain particular abstracted aspects, of human life or of human history.)

On this view of art, which might be called the *expressive-contemplative* view, poetry or literature is made out of the same "material" as ordinary everyday speech or writing; it is only created for different, and not (in any straightforward sense) for immediately instrumental, purposes. It is not meant to be attended to as though it were a part of our actual (or factual) understanding of the world. It is not documentary; nor, for the same reasons, is it moralistic or didactic (since moralism or didacticism are themselves ways of manipulatively handling a world which we already suppose ourselves to have understood). Literature is concerned with the *creation of terms* rather than with the manipulative handling of them: following Shelley we could say that this is because it marks or reveals the "before unapprehended relations of things and perpetuates their apprehen-

---

[13] It might be culturally wiser to say that – where our more formal or seriously-aspiring kinds of literature are concerned – it is language-uses of this kind which are *commonly held* to constitute literature in the estimation of a wide range of people who have taken a special interest in literature, including the writing of it. To talk in this way is no more question-begging than to say (as with T. S. Kuhn, Paul Feyerabend and others) that it is only physicists who can make statements within physics. The important questions are the questions about the place of these various activities within human life as a whole.

sion."[14] It requires us to attend to it contemplatively, and in "suspension of disbelief,"[15] because belief – of a world-representing kind – is not what is called for in the first place.[16] Meanwhile there are also mixed kinds of speech or writing, including instrumental kinds which are either more or less poetic in their manner (any piece of speech or writing must have a manner) and where the "poetry" appears only as the "style" with which the instrumental job in question is carried out. Since the expressive dimension of language can never be wholly suppressed or eliminated, every nuance, every suggestion of feeling, must be a part of the "real" meaning of any piece of language-using, and not merely of the user's intentions in using it. In "pure" art, or art properly so called, on the other hand, the style or form with which the language-using is carried out can properly be thought of as the very point or essence of the linguistic achievement itself. Coleridge remarked of poetry that "whatever lines can be translated into other words of the same language, without diminution of their significance, either in sense or association, or in any worthy feeling, are so far vicious in their diction" (*Biographia Literaria*, vol. 1, p. 23).

This expressive-contemplative view of art or literature has origins which can be traced a long way back in the history of Western thought; but it can also be seen as a conceptual aspect, or systematic formulation, of a distinctively modern phase of artistic theory. The notion of the "aesthetic" which was crystallized in the eighteenth century established a tradition within which the contrast between the "aesthetic" and the "practical" (i.e. instrumental) aspects of life

[14] *Defence of Poetry*, p. 103. Owen Barfield has remarked that "logical judgements [sc. judgements about the meanings of concepts], by their nature, can only *render more explicit* some one part of a truth already implicit in their terms. But the poet makes the terms themselves. He does not make judgements, therefore; he only makes them possible – and only he makes them possible" (*Poetic Diction*, p. 113; author's italics). Shelley, of course, is consistent, given the development of language into "signs for portions or classes of thought, instead of pictures of integral thoughts," when he implies that what the poet does is to counteract this process and to re-create (τὸ ποιεῖν) more primitive unities.

[15] Coleridge, *Biographia Literaria*, vol. 2, p. 6.

[16] The naturalistic manner of much literature may lead us to misunderstand its true nature. But a part of the reason for literature's naturalistic manner may be the history of its evolution along with other more descriptive or representational kinds of story-telling. A reason for literature's *continuing* use of the naturalistic manner, on the other hand, might be that such a manner can help to make literature more accessible to our practically-engaged minds; even perhaps that it can help literature to "feed back" into the practical world and to modify those minds as we make use of them in our ordinary lives. (See also chapter 6 below.)

came to be largely accepted as beyond question and as – therefore – possessing the status of something like a philosophical axiom. The notion first conceptualized by Heraclitus of the One in the many (῎Εν Πάντα) was from time to time, though only fragmentarily and intermittently, given hints of an aesthetic interpretation in various "mystical" Western writings between Plotinus and the eighteenth century.[17] At the basis of the fully-articulated modern notion of the aesthetic, on the other hand, we can perhaps see Schiller's concept of "appearance" or "semblance" (Schein), which provides the philosophical basis for a view of meaning quite different from either the practical-instrumental or the objective-theoretical. Schein – the semblance created in art, but also perceptible in nature when we view nature aesthetically – is something which calls for our disinterested contemplation for its own sake, and in abstraction from all our more practical worldly concerns. (Man, says Schiller, "is only fully human when he plays.")[18] There are less systematic expressions of this idea in Goethe, and it is given an explicit ontological or revelatory dimension by Fichte, Schelling and Hegel: for Hegel the aesthetic is a mode – though when set alongside religion and philosophy not the highest mode – of apprehension of reality. In more narrowly literary terms the "transcendental" outlook of German Romanticism finds its way into the English tradition through Coleridge, and there meets up with the more native (but still German-influenced) aesthetic philosophy of Blake and (at least in some of his moods) of Wordsworth. Both Keats and Shelley see art as visionary (Shelley says that poetry "lays bare ... the spirit" of the world's forms [Defence of Poetry, p. 109]). In the post-Romantic period the aesthetic view gains force with the "purism" of the modernist literary movement (Flaubert's novel "about nothing," Conrad's "the whole of the

---

[17] Plotinus tells us that the arts "go back to the Ideas from which Nature itself derives," and that the mind "gives a radiance out of its own store" to the objects which we perceive (Enneads, trans. Stephen McKenna and B. S. Page [University of Chicago Press, 1952], V, viii, 1, and vi, 1–3). Anticipations of the modern conception of the aesthetic can be found in Aquinas, Eckhart and Boehme. Hamann brings these ideas closer to the mainstream of philosophy – or the mainstream of philosophy closer to these ideas – when he sees language as the expression of the human soul rather than as a manipulative code: this is the point at which a revelatory notion of poetry becomes philosophically possible.

[18] Friedrich Schiller, On the Aesthetic Education of Man, trans. Elizabeth M. Wilkinson and L. A. Willoughby (Oxford: Clarendon Press, 1967), Fifteenth Letter, para. 9. Schiller's concept of Schein has affinities with Kant's notion of the artist's "transgressing" or "going beyond" the limits of experience.

truth lies in the presentation," Hopkins's "inscape" and the not-unrelated "emotional and intellectual complex" of Imagism, Joyce's "epiphany"). Modern philosophers of art (Croce, Collingwood, Santayana) have continued to explore the Romantic conception of art as expressive or visionary. More specialist writers about the other arts have adopted similar perspectives (for example Clive Bell's notion of "significant form," Roger Fry's identification of vision and design: behind much of this lies Walter Pater's notion that "all art ... aspires towards the condition of music" – an idea of direct visionary apprehension which also goes back to Herder and Novalis). The intellectual core of this movement is perhaps most centrally to be found in Hegel's formulations (importantly modified from those of Kant and Schiller) whereby art is indeed heuristic or world-comprehending – but in the sense of being ontological or revelatory of reality rather than of being descriptive or representative of it.

3

But why, it might be asked, even in the face of such a roll-call of distinguished opinion, should we be obliged to accept the view of literature, or of art in general, which is implied by all these – mutually supporting, and since Romanticism certainly very familiar – ideas? Can this expressive-contemplative theory really be anything more than a piece of verbal say-so, or at best merely a theory which must be seen as a theory in competition with many others – so that the whole issue (the point being perhaps purely verbal) may be one which still cannot be regarded as theoretically settled?

We could perhaps here introduce the term *subjectist* to denote all those philosophies – which begin to dominate Western thinking with Descartes (but which have their origins in Greek thinking as early as Socrates) which find their philosophical starting-point in, and base their view of the nature of truth or reality on, the notion of *the givenness of the conscious human subject*.[19] On the basis of this definition we could then say that subjectist theories of human life and of the human mind must of necessity only be able to leave room for subjectist theories of art and of artistic experience. When once we have interpreted human life and human experience as a whole in (for

[19] I have borrowed the term "subjectist" from William J. Richardson, who uses it in his exposition of Heidegger's relationship to the Western philosophical tradition. See *Heidegger: Through Phenomenology to Thought*, p. 326 *et seq.*

example) empiricist or scientistic terms, it is already too late to introduce a theory of art which would interpret art expressively or ontologically. The most that might be claimed about the "expressiveness" of art on the basis of a philosophy which takes the givenness of the conscious subject as its starting-point would be that art is "self-expressive" – meaning that it expresses the self, or the personality, or the emotions, of the artist who made it.[20] *Non*-subject-centered general philosophies of life, on the other hand, do at any rate make it *possible* for us to entertain non-subject-centered theories of art and of artistic experience: if human life as a whole requires to be understood in an expressive or intuitive rather than in an instrumental or subjectively-centered way, then we are at least not debarred *ex hypothesi* from understanding art – which is after all a part of human life – expressively or intuitively as well. If it can plausibly be maintained that artistic creation is an activity which is closely implicated in whatever is most fundamental in human life rather than something which is peripheral or secondary to it, then to take an expressive or intuitive view of what is most essential to human life will make it correspondingly more plausible that we should also take an expressive view of what is most essential to art.

An expressive view of what is most essential to human life is what we are in fact, by this stage in the history of philosophy, inescapably obliged to take. We now have no choice but to recognize – *pace* Kant in the *Critique of Pure Reason*, and all his predecessors in the mainstream of Western philosophy since Heraclitus and Parmenides – that the human mind is situated *in* reality, rather than being disembodied or detached from it, and that the world, or reality as we are able to apprehend it, is an expressive creation out of our embodied and distinctively human pre-consciousness. Life, at the *pre*-human level, is a creation of meaning in terms of biological purposiveness; and at the level of human existence proper, we must see our coming to a state of linguistic and experiential consciousness through our articulation of reality as being at the same time, but pre-consciously and pre-subjectively, an expression of *ourselves*. Reality is what we discern; but it is also what *we* discern. Given this background of philosophical necessities, the most important thing that

---

[20] This is a theory with a well-respected history (it goes back to Longinus, plays its part in "neo-classical" and "sentimentalist" thinking, and perhaps culminates in the Victorian notion of "sincerity"), but it is also one which rests on presuppositions which are entirely instrumental.

we should need to show in order to bring this mode of interpretation of human existence in general to bear on human art in particular – and thereby to provide a philosophically secure underpinning for the familiar Romantic, or transcendental, view of art – would be that art can be seen as closely associated with, or as having an essential affinity with, the processes which are involved in all our most fundamental and reality-discerning forms of ordinary experiencing.

This, with the help of philosophical arguments about the nature of perception which are now available to us, is something which is not in fact very difficult to do. We are now in a philosophical position to claim both that reality is ontologically revealed to us in our most ordinary experience – if it is not revealed to us there, it is not revealed to us anywhere – rather than (for example) by rationalistic argument which by-passes ordinary experience; and also that there is a kind of "imagination" at work in our most ordinary perception which is continuous with, and not self-declaringly distinguishable from, the kind of imagination which is at work in our more innovative or "creative" perceptions of form or significance. In the terms which were used by Kant, we could say that there is no possibility of perception without *con*ception. Kant himself makes it clear that it is only through the subjective organizing of our perceptual field or "manifold" that experience is possible, and that it is only our possession of concepts of objects which enables our subjectivity in the fully-developed experiential sense (i.e. where we can be conscious of ourselves and of the things which we experience around us as existing independently of each other) to come about. Our "seeing" of something must in effect – because of our necessary conceptual interpretation of the "given" sensory data – always be a seeing of something "as" something. This organizing or synthesizing of perceptual data is brought about within Kant's own system through the "concealed" activity of the imagination, which schematizes our empirical intuitions into something which can be grasped by the conscious part of our minds. Imagination – as Kant himself tells us – is "a necessary ingredient of perception itself" (*Critique of Pure Reason*, A. 120 n. a). In more analytical terms, we could say that the senses of the word "imagination" which have to do with the making of "images" or with mental "picturing" and the senses which have to do with "invention" or "creativity" are in fact closely connected, and that both are closely connected with the concept of "seeing" in the sense in which we apply that concept to our ordinary perception. Setting out from an ordinary group of usages of terms like "image," "imagine," and "imagination," P. F. Strawson has argued that the creativity or inventiveness of our imagination is inseparably involved in our most ordinary perception of the objects around us: that when we perceive something as a certain object (whether as a particular individual object or as an object of a particular type), our recognition of that object involves a relationship with certain other past or possible perceptions in such a way that – if we are to be true to the real nature of our experiencing – these perceptions must be said to enter directly (even though in what Kant might have called a "concealed" way) into our actual perception of the object before us. The linking or *combining* of different transient perceptions is one of the very things which it is the function of our "concepts of objects" to achieve: it is only because pastness and possibility are intrinsically involved in presentness that there can be any connection at all between "sense" and "understanding." Our immediate sensory experience of any object, Strawson suggests, is "*infused* with," or "*animated* by," or "becomes *soaked* with" the concept of the object in question. There also seems to be no simple distinction which imposes itself between cases of more or less "ordinary" (perhaps routine and "unimaginative") perception and cases which involve more sophisticated or "imaginative" kinds of seeing.[21] The same area of concepts to do with ordinary perception and imagination is touched upon by Wittgenstein, when he demonstrates that the process of "seeing" must depend on publicly established institutions or rules, and that an account of what we see must partly involve an account of how we publicly or outwardly behave. Purely "inner" sense data could never be publicly authenticated, and could therefore never form the basis of the experience – which we indisputably have – of a shared and publicly established world. Perceiving a similarity or difference – or therefore actually perceiving anything at all – depends for its sense on the "rule" we are following when we make a particular discrimination, and it is therefore "only if someone *can do*, has learnt, is master of, such-and-such, that it makes sense to say that he has had *this* experience." Our seeing of

---

[21] See "Imagination and perception" in *Freedom and Resentment* (London: Methuen, 1974), pp. 52–57; author's italics. Merleau-Ponty reaches a similar conclusion from another direction when he remarks of essential or conceptual meaning that "it is neither above nor beneath appearances, but at their interconnection; it is the link which secretly relates an experience to its possible variants" (*Le Visible et l'invisible*, p. 155).

something "as" something is like ' "[t]he echo of a thought in sight' –
one would like to say."[22] For all of these reasons, and setting aside
the "passively received data" prejudices of philosophical empiricism,
we have no alternative but to accept that there are in fact no neutral
"sensations" in the special philosophical sense of that word but only
a pre-objective experience which is already infused with (animated
by, soaked with) latent meanings, and which (though in a less than
conscious way) is already pre-objectively structured as a result of our
pre-experiential embodiedness in the world which we perceive; in
other words, which has the potentiality, given the application of
suitable concepts of "objects of experience," of being discriminated
into objects or occurrences which can be pointed to or talked about
by physically-embodied and located observers and agents.

No particular set of concepts or framework of understanding is
forced upon us, we might say – which is another way of saying that
no particular set of objects must inescapably be perceived by us:
there is no "given" reality "external" to the human mind which our
minds must "mirror" or conform to. When once we have accepted
this necessity of creative imagination, or of insight into an as-yet-
unarticulated reality, as a part of all our most ordinary experiencing,[23] it must begin to seem rather implausible to try to exclude *art* –
which is usually thought to involve creative imagination, whatever
else it may also involve or not involve – from the same kind of
participation in reality. To do so would mean *denying* the access of art
to truth (which we may perhaps be tempted to do on social-
propagandist, law-and-order, or other not *per se* philosophical

---

[22] *Philosophical Investigations*, pp. 209, 212. Wittgenstein may nevertheless be thought
to have confused the issue when he suggests that our "seeing" of something "as"
something is subject to our will. A great deal is comprised in this question, since
"the will," in Wittgenstein's sense, is necessarily the will of a conscious and
individuated subject – and yet the way in which we articulate reality is in fact the
very means to our individuation as subjects. On the pre-experiential level, the way
in which we articulate our awareness may be governed by qualities in our
disposition – such as spiritual authenticity or the lack of it – which cannot themselves be explained *in terms of* such categories as "passive experience" or "will." (A
multitude of spiritual paths lead off from here in all directions.) Both Strawson and
Wittgenstein remain within a subjectist framework, and therefore leave their
discussions cut off from what may be very important transcendental implications.
One of the aims of the present essay is to show that there must be such implications
and to give a sense of where they might lead.

[23] An early formulation of this idea is to be seen in Schiller's notion of the aesthetic as
the basis underlying *all* our comprehension, including morality and reason as well
as art itself. See *Aesthetic Education*, especially Twenty-Third Letter.

grounds) and saying that art involves imagination only in the pejorative sense of that word which connects it with things which are "imaginary," "fanciful," or "unreal."[24] (Coleridge made a well-known distinction between the "primary" and the "secondary" imagination – between the imagination inherent in "all human perception" and the imagination of the artist which "dissolves, diffuses, dissipates, in order to re-create"[25] – but the distinction is in fact philosophically groundless. Coleridge had his own reasons for wanting to hold on to his doctrinally-underwritten notions of virtue and true religion – in his case Christianity – and for not wanting to allow the human imagination to become our *only* arbiter of what can count as real.)

4

It is arguments of this kind about the necessary expressiveness, or probingness-into-obscurity, of human life as a whole which we are now in a position to bring to bear on all our more specialized discussions of art and of artistic experience. Recent theories of art and of artistic experience themselves, meanwhile – sometimes, but not always, deriving from Romantic philosophy – have intensified the older and more mysterious assumptions about the inspiration-dependent and obscurity-probing qualities of art and artists (from ancient times the poet or artist has often been seen as a divinely-inspired madman or priest). What was once only an aspect of our ideas about art, perhaps with a good deal of self-mystifying support from among artists themselves, has now become the mainstream of our aesthetic thinking and has prevailed over almost every other kind of artistic theory. (Where literary art itself is concerned, the world-rejecting dreaminess of the "Symbolist" movement – Rimbaud's "systematic derangement of the senses," Villiers de l'Isle Adam's character Axel's "as for living, our servants can do that for us," Rilke's "Earth has no refuge but to become invisible" – might

---

[24] We must recognize that such a sense of "imagination" exists. What is less clear is the notion of "reality" with which such "imagination" is being contrasted. It seems mainly to be an empirical or empiricist one – so that the reality with which such "imaginings" fail to engage is the reality of the actual or factual world of science or of common sense.

[25] *Biographia Literaria*, vol. 1, p. 304. Coleridge's distinction in fact parallels the distinction between Kant's concept of imagination in the *Critique of Pure Reason* and his concept in the *Critique of Aesthetic Judgement*.

best be seen as a late heresy, rather than as the original formulation of this hieratic conception of poetry or literature.)[26] Given the convergence of modern lines of thinking about ordinary life and modern lines of thinking about art, it must begin to seem a persuasive philosophical option to *fall in* with the notion of art as a "pure" non-instrumental creation of art-objects or art-work for contemplation which is also *eo ipso* a pure revelation or expression of ontological truth. How far we are willing to do so may perhaps depend on the view which we take of other, at one time more unquestioningly honored, candidates – such as religion or philosophy – for this privileged ontological status.

We have reliable enough philosophical grounds for claiming that art has a dimension which is transcendental, since these are the same grounds that we have for claiming that our ordinary experience has a dimension which is transcendental. Can we, nevertheless, go further than this, and claim that art is by definition *truth-revealing* – or are we only justified in saying that art takes place within the dimension of transcendence but that it may just as easily lead us to untruth or illusion as to truth or reality? One thing which seems certain is that it must always be open to us to *misread* the nature of such truth as any work of art (and the same must be true of any experience in ordinary life) authentically can reveal to us. What we grasp as being revealed, both in art and in life, may in itself be genuine enough, but it may at the same time be susceptible to misinterpretation in various ways with regard to the relationship in which it stands to the rest of reality. A naturalistic story or novel in which some of the more essential realities of life are not allowed to intervene may properly be considered to be artistically false, but it may still contain valuable elements of truth if only we are able to discern these for what they are. Dr. Johnson was perhaps right to say of "metaphysical" poetry that its writers "fail to give delight, by their desire of exciting admiration,"[27] or Coleridge to see Pope's poetic matter and diction as "characterized not so much by poetic thoughts as by thoughts *translated* into the language of poetry" (*Biographia Literaria*, vol. I, p. 19), or T. S. Eliot to complain that "even in his most mature work, Milton does not infuse new life into the word, as

---

[26] This heresy perhaps has its real origin with the German poets known as the *Frühromantiker*.

[27] Samuel Johnson, *Lives of the English Poets* vol. I (London: Oxford University Press, 1968), p. 28.

Shakespeare does,"[28] or F. R. Leavis to object to Shelley's "notable
inability to *grasp* anything – to present any situation, any observed
or imagined actuality, or any experience, as an object existing ... in
its own right";[29] but this does not mean that there is no way in
which the writings which gave rise to these famous adverse judgements can authentically extend our apprehension of reality. One of
our most ordinary, and seemingly most necessary, literary-critical
responses is our habit of singling out for admiration particular lines
or passages or qualities in what we otherwise feel to be bad or
unsuccessful pieces of writing. (Consider, for example, Wordsworth's
"It will easily be perceived, that the only part of this Sonnet which is
of any value is the lines printed in Italics" [Preface to *Lyrical Ballads*,
1802]). Does this mean, in that case, that we are in danger of having
to say that *any* artistic muddle can reveal truth to us if only we can
manage to discern the truth that it reveals? The realistic answer can
only be that it must depend on whether and how far such a detailed
process of critical discerning turns out to be worth the effort. Art –
and in the present context, particularly literature – we may have to
say, is what we in the end *find it worth our while to attend to* for its
expressive qualities alone.[30] In our response to individual art-works,
or to our artistic tradition in its entirety, we may sometimes be
tempted to see the order of art as revealing a greater degree of order
in the world than is really "there" to be revealed. We may therefore
be tempted to turn our traditional art into a false consolation about
the nature of reality or – which is the same thing – about the kinds of
meaning which are to be found in ordinary human life as a whole. In
the same spirit, we may be tempted in our own times to *create* the
kind of art which lends itself to being used in this falsely reassuring
way. It must always be an obligation on us to *read* the reality-which-
is-to-be-found in a particular art-work or life-situation and to test
these revelations intuitively against the comprehension of reality

[28] *Selected Prose of T. S. Eliot*, ed. Frank Kermode (London: Faber and Faber, 1975),
p. 260.

[29] F. R. Leavis, *The Living Principle* (London: Chatto and Windus, 1975), p. 80.

[30] This will of course be true *mutatis mutandis* of our contemplation of natural beauty
also; and it may in fact sometimes be less essential to art that it should be a human
product than that it should be revelatory of truth or reality (there is also "found"
art). How do we know that we are creating or attending to something "for its
expressive qualities alone"? There is no simple answer: A. E. Housman believed that
"most readers, when they think that they are admiring poetry ... are really
admiring, not the poetry of the passage before them, but something else in it, which
they like better than poetry" (*The Name and Nature of Poetry*, p. 34).

which we already possess. There will often be art-works, just as there will often be life-situations, which in our experiencing of them greatly outreach the range of comprehension which we have up to that time achieved: these works or situations *read us*, we might say, more significantly than we are yet in a position to read them. (Owen Barfield, elaborating on Wilde's dictum that men are made by books rather than books by men, remarks that "there is a very real sense, humiliating as it may seem, in which what we generally venture to call *our* feelings are really Shakespeare's 'meaning'.")[31] Our coming to terms with art or with life must nevertheless always be a two-way process: no works of art – and no sequences of natural or historical events – can ever entirely transcend the various readings or interpretations which particular historically- and culturally-situated human beings are cumulatively and collectively able to make of them. (The history of Western art might from one point of view be seen as the history of our gradual coming to terms with the degree of chaos which – within the total meaningfulness of life as a whole[32] – reality "really" comprises.[33] Shall we – if we pursue this line of argument to its conclusion – have to say that *The Divine Comedy*, or the art of Michelangelo, or the music of Mozart, are inauthentic *for us*? The real questions here must concern what we are *doing* when we allow ourselves to read or to experience these older works. Mozart expresses – perfectly – a more ordered, but less all-embracing, vision than we now feel life to demand of us – as the music of Beethoven very soon came along to make clear. Older, or "classical," art may be valuable for the enduring insights which – with all its over-formality – it can still give us: Shakespeare may seem to embrace us still, even though his view of women, or of man's insignificance, or of the meaning of death, may not. But such art can also be "used" as a substitute for religious devotion, or as a tranquilizing drug, or in various other not particularly ontological ways. Vivaldi gives us a certain outlook on, or aspect of, things – but he can also – for that reason – be especially useful for helping to clear a hang-over. Art which was authentic in its own time cannot be authentic *in the same way* for us now, or it would still be possible for us to create the same

---

[31] *Poetic Diction*, p. 136. It seems to have been the Danish story-writer Hans Andersen who first spoke of literature as "reading us."

[32] The Camusian notion of *life itself* as meaningless is in fact quite incoherent.

[33] Nietzsche argues in *The Birth of Tragedy* that the pre-Christian art of Greek tragedy measured up to this demand, and that our vision only deteriorated into self-delusion with the post-Socratic and Christian ages.

kind of art today. To appreciate older art without bad faith, we must approach it either in a spirit of genuine naiveté, or else with a measure of historical detachment.)

5

By any ordinary linguistic criteria we are perhaps in a position where we can settle the question of whether or not to tie art definitionally to the revelation of truth in whichever direction we choose. It may be worthwhile, even so, to recognize that the modern tendency towards an increasingly "aesthetic" view of art is tied to genuine discoveries in philosophy as well as to various less systematic insights which have been generated by the artistic process (as well as by modern life) itself. Insights of an essentially Romantic-transcendental kind are expressed in the increasingly truth- or authenticity-related critical language which we have come to rely on[34] in most of our ordinary talk about art and about life – as when we say of art-works, as of people's behavior or utterances, that they are "authentic" or "genuine" or "coherent," or that they are "spurious" or "pretentious" or "false."[35] These truth- or authenticity-related idioms do not seem to be ones which we can dismiss as merely transiently fashionable, and it seems almost certain that to insist on the transcendental nature of art and on the connection between art and truth would be to consolidate a re-settling of values, or a re-ordering of conceptualizations, which has been under way in Western culture for many centuries – but which has also been accelerated and brought to greater consciousness by the philosophical insights of Romanticism. There may be good reasons, not all of them yet obvious or explicit, why it may be metaphysically demanded of us, and a great gain in the re-structuring of our problems, to regard the connection between art and ontological truth as a necessary and definitional one. (The historically-established key terms which we possess in fact let us down in this area, not least because of their traditional and philosophically-sanctified emphasis on the distinction between art and natural beauty. It may be that we do not in fact *need*

---

[34] At least until the supervention of "post-structuralist" discourse.

[35] In actual linguistic practice, authenticity-related usages of this kind rest on a substructure of slang or colloquialism which – as in modern English and American-English – is continually being recreated: the spirit of the concern for authenticity persists, even where the idiomatic letter of it is constantly changing.

to make any very clear distinction between art and natural beauty, and that the man-madeness of art should not be thought of as among its most essential characteristics.[36] The distinction between art and beauty seems to be largely a product of Western monotheistic religion, and is certainly not very prominent in early-Greek or oriental thinking. There is in fact no very compelling reason why we cannot learn to attend to anything, whether man-made or natural, in a contemplative and reality-revealing way.)[37]

To accept the option of connecting art with truth or reality (the two concepts are as yet undifferentiated in the early-Greek notion of ἀλήθεια) does in fact correspond to some of our most central and familiar modes of critical thinking, since the category of "failed" art already exists, and is heavily relied on, in our modern critical language.[38] Since the time of Romanticism we have been inclined to mark off a category of artistic failure – which may be where the art falls back into accident or contingency, or into autobiography, or into the inessential in whatever fashion – which seems on the face of it to be defined by criteria of merely *formal* failure. (It was with the "holistic" notions of Coleridge that such habits first gained their foothold within English criticism.) The formal failure is a failure, and furthermore *matters*, we tend to argue, because it fails to secure any coherent creation of meaning or comprehension of truth within what purports to be the order of a single artistic work.[39] Such notions as "poetic truth," or "the truth of the imagination,"[40] have long been familiar to literary critics as ways of talking about literature – but they have also been assumed to be merely "poetic" or meta-phorical in themselves, and not to be concerned with truth or reality in any sense which would be of interest to philosophers or to ordinary worldly-minded people. (This is the practical-rationalistic spirit which underlies Peacock's "rattle and plaything" criticism of

---

[36] The "aesthetic" – still a very new concept – is so far the only notion we have for marking out this particular experiential or pre-experiential region. What we really need is a concept of something which is insightful, revelatory, or a disclosure; but we in fact have no adequate word for this. "Beauty" sounds too uplifting; "art" too man-made.

[37] Zen Buddhism, in particular, has tried to teach us how to.

[38] Or at least has been until the supervention of "post-structuralist" discourse.

[39] We must take care not to construe "failure" too narrowly here, since there may be many different things which a single art-work is doing. "Holistic" theories and the search for unitary meanings can become over-simple weapons in the face of the deliberate complexities of many modern, or modernist, art-works.

[40] See for example Keats, letter to Benjamin Bailey of 22 November 1817.

poetry.)[41] These notions of artistic truth, despite the efforts of Romantic philosophers such as Schelling and Hegel, have so far made little impression on philosophers as affecting their – or what they take to be our – notions of truth in general and outside of any artistic or literary contexts.[42] But there is really no way in which we can go on making art subservient to, or else irrelevant to, such supposedly more fundamental ideas as we may have about truth if we are unable to give any convincing account of what those more fundamental routes to truth can authentically be believed to be. The claims of rationalist metaphysics or of empirical science to be our "real" access to truth – our true "mirroring" of reality – can now be rejected; and it may be that the claims of doctrinaire religion will need to be rejected also unless they can be given a more convincing basis in intuitive life – which will also mean in art – than they were given during the centuries when their doctrines were accepted unquestioningly and art was obliged to maintain a subsidiary existence in their shadow. Art, which has spent so many centuries being outshone by more solemn or ceremonious apparelings of truth (which have themselves gradually taken on an Emperor's clothes-like quality of incredibility) and has been pressed into various philosophical molds which it could not fit, has itself meanwhile pressed steadily, both in the seriousness of its practice and in the theories which have grown up about it among artists and critics, its claims to the highest ontological status. The time may have come for these claims to be recognized and properly allowed.

If we decide to fall in with such a metaphysical claim, we shall of course immediately place a correspondingly greater ontological burden on the practicing or self-proclaimed artist (or on the practicing or self-proclaimed critic or artistic experiencer) himself.[43] One of

[41] See Peacock, "Four ages of poetry."

[42] The notion of ontological truth, which has for the most part been banished from official Western philosophy, has in fact maintained a largely underground existence within the tradition of artistic theory and criticism for almost two centuries.

[43] We lack any satisfactory word for the "experiencers" of art in general, as well as for the "experiencers" of some of the individual arts in particular. "Observer" seems too detached, "audience" too collective and auditory, "client" (though one can see its point) too suggestive of improper soliciting on the part of the artist. "Experiencer" is hardly an improvement (experience being subjective, while our apprehension of art is ontological), but it may serve in its awkwardness to remind us that the word which we really need does not yet exist.

the results of doing so – of insisting, above all else, on the duties or obligations of art to truth or reality – would almost certainly be to bring the tradition of art itself nearer to such a truth-revealing ideal than it had already come to be during the Romantic and post-Romantic (and more unknowingly during the pre-Romantic) periods. If both artists and critics were to take up this burden – building the pursuit of truth into the very depths of their creative pre-consciousness (not pursuing beauty *out of* life, as the "Symbolist" artists did, but seeking the luminous or the numinous within life itself) – it might be possible for art to break through into a tradition of truth-achievement more self-awarely and effectively than had previously been possible. (Only a small proportion of the art of the past has broken through the ideas of its age into a substantial measure of revelation. *Classical art*, we may very well find ourselves having to say, *is really only the pre-history of art*.) Under these conditions, the problems for critics and experiencers of art – as well as for artists themselves – of discriminating the true from the false, the genuinely insightful from the illusorily idealized, the achievement of revelation from the "applied art" achievements of serving more immediately worldly purposes, would remain to be faced in every particularity of our aesthetic responsiveness: the distinction between reality and unreality would increasingly come to be subsumed within the finer texture of our spiritual awareness. Some of our problems might in this way seem only to have been shifted on to a new basis (we may seem only to have further "internalized" some of our familiar anxieties about evil, authenticity, the "deception in the soul about realities," and much else); but with the removal of false theories about art (the Romantic-transcendental doctrines about art being seen as metaphysical truths for us, rather than as mere stepping-stones in the "history of ideas") and the taking on of these new responsibilities, we shall at any rate be providing ourselves with something genuinely demanding on which to exercise those aspects of our spiritual faculties which have been left in abeyance by the decline of our belief in various (no longer easily believable) systems of doctrinaire religion. Art, instead of being rejected by, or ignored by, or a mere handmaid to, religion, may in future – if there is to be anything in the future which can be distinctively identified as religion at all – need to be seen as, and effectively to become, the reality-inscribing heart and soul of it.[44] Poets in particular (and we are all, potentially, poets: "every [authentic person] is necessarily a poet, because [authentic] language itself is poetry")[45] would in this metaphysically-transformed situation necessarily be – and even perhaps eventually be recognized to be – "the hierophants of an unapprehended inspiration," or – through their obscure, continuous and unacknowledged activity of re-creating the very terms by which we live our ordinary lives – "the unacknowledged legislators of the world."[46]

6

One of the philosophical conceptions which came most to dominate discussions of art and of artistic theory during the early-Romantic period was the notion that the artistic process might best be understood in terms of the organic concepts of biology (as they were at that time) or through various more or less detailed analogies with the processes of animal and vegetable life. Herder declares that

> [e]very noble species sleeps, like any good seed, in silent germination: is there, and remains unaware of itself ... How does the poor shoot know, and how should it know, what impulses, powers, vapors of life streamed into him at the instant of his coming into being?[47]

Coleridge claims of poetry that

> its spirit takes up and incorporates surrounding materials, as a plant clothes itself with soil and climate, whilst it exhibits the working of a vital principle within independent of all accidental circumstances.

The true poet's work, he tells us, "is distinguished from all other works that assume to belong to the class of poetry, as a natural from an artificial flower ..."[48] To the historically-distanced modern reader it might seem that these ways of thinking about human creativity

---

[44] The artistic "purity" which is in question here is of course relative, and is mainly to be contrasted with immediately practical or instrumental intentions. All texts will necessarily be "deconstructible" from some standpoint sooner or later, but the texts of poetry or literature will – by definition – be those which most resist the deconstructive process.

[45] Compare Shelley, *Defence of Poetry*, p. 103.

[46] *Defence of Poetry*, p. 144.

[47] J. G. Herder, "On the knowing and feeling of the human soul" quoted in translation by M. H. Abrams in *The Mirror and the Lamp* (Oxford University Press, 1953), p. 205.

[48] Coleridge, Lectures of 1818, sec. 1, in *Collected Works*, vol. 8.

are really no more than new kinds of literary or philosophical metaphors – arrived at partly as a reaction against the Cartesian or Newtonian (and no longer very illuminating) metaphors of the early Enlightenment. In his study of the literary theories of the Romantic and pre-Romantic periods, M. H. Abrams has described the Romantic poets' substitution of "the conceptual model of organic growth" for the various mechanical models which had previously been in fashion, and has spoken of the general embracing of these new metaphors within criticism as "the age of biologism." Coleridge's central problem, he goes on to suggest,

> was to use analogy with organic growth to account for the spon-
> taneous, the inspired, and the self-evolving in the psychology of
> invention, yet not to commit himself so far to the elected figure as to
> minimize the supervention of the antithetic qualities of foresight and
> choice ... The solution is that genius, however free from prior precept,
> is never free from law; knowledge, diligence, and the reflective
> judgement, as a preliminary and accompaniment to creation, are
> necessary but not sufficient conditions to the highest aesthetic
> achievement; eventually, the work of imagination must start sponta-
> neously into independent life and by its own energy evolve its final
> form in the same way that a tree grows ...[49]

What may be misleading in this account is the emphasis which it places on the idea of an "analogy," or of an "elected figure," with the implication that these are really no more than expository (in effect rather superficially literary) devices which may serve some temporary explanatory purpose but which must sooner or later become dispensable when that purpose has been served. The truth is rather that what we are faced with in the Romantic "age of biologism" is not merely the substitution of a new metaphorical fashion for an older and no longer stimulating one, but the breaking through into critical theory of a deeply-sensed philosophical recognition of the necessary relationship between art and life and of the necessarily embodied or incarnated place of art itself *within* life. Herder, at the very beginning of the Romantic movement, concerned himself with

---

[49] M. H. Abrams, *The Mirror and the Lamp*, pp. 224–25. The idea of one fashion or "model" replacing another within literary thought is not an uncommon one: Fredric Jameson, for example, in *The Prison-House of Language*, has said that he would like to see the "organic model" of Romanticism replaced by the "linguistic model" of structuralism (p. vi).

the basis of human language in organic life, and with the question of how it is that a transition can occur from the kind of awareness which is characteristic of non-language-using creatures to the kind of awareness which is characteristic of human beings. For Goethe, the dominant conception which links all his artistic and scientific preoccupations is the idea of nature, or of life, as a universal current or force of which man is only a part, even if he is also at the same time its highest expression. Schelling provided Schiller's notions of "play" and of aesthetic "semblance" with an ontological basis when he argued that in art and aesthetic experience the conscious and free activity of the human spirit becomes unified with the unconscious life of nature which is at work in the depths of the human mind. Although not developed into a distinctive philosophical outlook until the post-Romantic period (there is a line from Hegel to Bergson and A. N. Whitehead which emphasizes organicism as a metaphysical principle *per se*), the almost universal use of the organic "metaphor" during the early-Romantic period is really the intuitive recognition of the structure of a metaphysical argument. To invoke *life*, in this context, is not merely to invoke a disposable analogy (the artist is more like a plant, less like a machine or a logician); it is to see that art essentially *is* life at the human level – and not merely comparable with life – and that the forward-striving of life, or of meaning-creation, which is present in all human existence is present most purely and quintessentially in our creation and appreciation of art. It is to *situate* the creativity of art, or of poetry, within the process of all life – which is itself creative. This is a philosophical result of very great importance. It obliges us to see that many of the objections which have been brought against the Romantic theorists' biological "metaphor" cannot in fact be sustained: the metaphor is indeed a metaphor, but it is also one which effectively embodies a philosophical truth, given the present state of our concepts in these areas.[50] It has been claimed, for example, that the Romantics' use of the organic growth "model" to explain art is in effect a way of eliminating the artist's own creativity, and that "to substitute the concept of growth for the operation of mechanism in the psychology of invention seems merely to exchange one kind of determinism for

---

[50] The comparison of life as a whole to a plant or flower ought perhaps properly to be called a philosophical metonymy or synecdoche, rather than a philosophical metaphor.

another."[51] The reason why this is not so, and why there is no
problem about a new "kind of determinism," is that the concept of
life with which we are working in this context (and which such
writers as Herder or Coleridge had in mind in their own discussions)
is not a concept of a mere "natural" or blind (in effect mechanistic)
process (a *natura naturata*) but is equally essentially a form-giving or
spiritual process (a *natura naturans*),[52] so that the idea of life or nature
at the human level already incorporates, or accommodates, human
spiritual autonomy or self-direction. Life, in this sense, is not a
process in which human transcendence is merely swallowed up.[53]
The creation of meaning at the human level (which is not a
subjectist, or individual, or *ego*-based process, but a pre-conscious
and communal process) is a special form of the meaning-creation
process which is definitional to all life. Art is a special and "pure"
form of this creation at the human level; but in the sense of "nature"
or "life" with which we are here concerned, we can also say that
nature or life at the same time "gives the form" to art. Polixenes, in
Shakespeare's *The Winter's Tale*, observes:

> Yet Nature is made better by no mean
> But Nature makes that mean; so over that art,
> Which you say adds to Nature, is an art,
> That Nature makes.[54]

There is no reason why such a process should be regarded as an
undermining of human freedom or spiritual autonomy when it is in
fact – in our free choosing of truth or authenticity where we are by
definition equally free to choose otherwise – its highest expression or

---

[51] Abrams, *The Mirror and the Lamp*, p. 173.
[52] On the Renaissance distinction between *natura naturans* and *natura naturata* see
for example R. G. Collingwood, *The Idea of Nature* (Oxford: Clarendon Press, 1945),
p. 94 *et seq.*
[53] In terms of the earlier stages of the present argument, we might say that it follows
from the necessity of human *embodiedness* that we at all times apply to our
experience the understanding, or logic, that is available to us up to that time, and
that in each individual act of experiencing we at the same time necessarily reach
beyond and modify that understanding or logic. The argument from embodiment is
in fact the missing philosophical piece that we need in order to justify in more
general philosophical terms what the Romantic writers have asserted on the basis of
their own intuitive experience as artists and critics.
[54] *The Winter's Tale*, IV, iv, ll. 89–92.

manifestation.[55] This does not mean that there is nothing left to be said about the freedom or authenticity – or ontological or religious awareness – which are comprised within this extended (and at the human level, spiritualized) notion of life; only that whatever is to be said still needs to be said *within* such a philosophical understanding of the life process rather than against it.[56] The Kantian insistence (in the *Critique of Practical Judgement* and the *Fundamental Principles of the Metaphysic of Morals*) on the priority of our moral or spiritual autonomy over every kind of natural inclination has left us with a heritage of moral "disembodiment," and of a false setting of moral or spiritual autonomy *against* nature, which we are only slowly beginning to overcome.

7

Poetry does not have any particular or distinctive subject matter of its own – as poets have known in practice for a very long time, and as poets of the Romantic period such as Blake or Coleridge or Keats have found their own very individual ways of telling us. No subjects are more proper to poetry than any others, and the revelations, or luminous details, or epiphanies, of poetry must be thought of as capable of occurring, or as liable to occur, almost anywhere in our experiencing. These are lessons which Romanticism has given us overwhelmingly convincing reasons for accepting. (The truths of Romantic literary theory are *also* truths about our linguistic life as a whole. "Inspiration" is integral to any experiential life, and not merely to art or poetry. "Genius" is only a more intense form of ordinary human transcendence. The natural is *also* the supernatural.) Nor, on the other hand, is poetry a particular kind or quality of language, distinguished by the presence of particular linguistic properties such as "irony," or "tension," or – except in an unfamiliarly general sense[57] – "ambiguity." Any kind of language-

---

[55] The emphasis placed by a critic such as F. R. Leavis on the concept of *life* is often misunderstood as a merely puritanical assertion of a moral preference. The truth is rather that Leavis has seen (and in his late books has begun to explore) the necessary metaphysical connection between life and art and the metaphysical necessity for art to be seriously life-affirming – rather than, for example, moralistic or sentimental.

[56] Mary Midgley, in *Beast and Man*, remarks that "[o]ur dignity arises *within* nature, not against it" (p. 196).

[57] See below, chapter 4.

using – any spoken sentence, any snatch of journalism, any passage from a scientific textbook, any entry in a diary, any note to a local delivery man – may be poetry if they have the right (which is to say an ontological or expressive) kind of interest for us. The majority of people's notes to their delivery men may not be worth preserving as poetry, but a few of them just conceivably might be.[58] Earlier and more traditional kinds of poetry or literature have usually been comparatively restricted in their subject matter, as well as – for historical reasons – being tied to a rather narrow range of literary modes or devices. In our earlier tradition poetry often occurs in the course of narratives which are themselves mainly history or legend, and which therefore have *inter alia* – but perhaps also primarily – a moral or some other practical function. There exists, historically, a whole complex network of *devices* of literature – the continually-changing conventions of verse, of the play, of the novel – which between them make up the whole complex network of ways in which we are able to *attend* to a text as literature. These devices may in some cases have their origins in the remote past, or they may have been brought into existence for artistic reasons which are no longer valid or applicable. Our writing and reading practices will always change, and the ones which make up our present understanding of the nature of literature may even now, for all that we can be sure of to the contrary, be dissolving away before our artistic or critical eyes. Poetry is not a particular area of concern, nor is it a particular way or set of ways of using language. It is all the kinds of language-using which we find worth attending to[59] for their expressive – meaning their ontological, rather than their egoistically *self*-expressive – qualities alone.

[58] There are kinds of imaginative writing which have exactly this "found" quality, whether or not the experiences which are conveyed in them have had a "real" or an "imaginary" origin. The "found," or seemingly-"found," poem has become a significant genre in modern poetry, and there are other comparable devices at work in the non-fiction, or seemingly non-fiction, novel or short story. Whether the events or situations depicted in the poem or story are in fact "real" or "imaginary" is not in itself a very important question. See also chapter 4 below.

[59] The question of *who* finds art worth attending to and in what ways is of course an important one, but it is also one which does not undermine the argument which is being developed here. It is an aspect of the traditional "problem of ideology," and is a problem which needs to be re-structured in cultural or socio-historical terms. It is also a problem which relates not just to art, but to science, philosophy, and the whole structure of human reason in general.

8

Something should perhaps be said in the present context about the kinds of "self-expressive" notions of art which have in fact widely been supposed to have been characteristic of Romanticism. The historian A. O. Lovejoy, in a well-known essay "On the discrimination of Romanticisms,"[60] pleased many academic commentators when he appeared to demonstrate that Romanticism could mean almost anything; but the things which it could mean appeared particularly to involve this kind of emphasis on the expression of the self. A number of twentieth-century poets and poetic theorists, usually regarding themselves as "classical," have either rejected or distanced themselves from Romanticism on the grounds that it appears to be based on this kind of egoistic assertion of the individual personality. T. E. Hulme, T. S. Eliot, and at times W. B. Yeats, have apparently felt themselves to be driven towards such a view by a fear of what might now be called the "confessional" element in poetry. They have claimed, in deliberate contrast, that poetry is an "escape from the self," is "hard and clear," that the poet "is not the bundle of accident and incoherence who sits down to breakfast," and that he needs a "mask" to protect him from "the hot-faced bargainers and the money-changers." Hulme in fact came close to a profound insight when he spoke of Romanticism as "spilt religion."[61] The false assumptions of this kind of neo-classical theorizing in fact tend to support or depend on one another. Classical art – although these writers were not likely to acknowledge the fact – did not attain to a total impersonality, for the inescapable reason that no kind of art, or of human expression, could ever do so. This modern neo-classical view of literature tries to by-pass the essentially Romantic, but philosophically profound, recognition of the necessarily embodied and located nature of all human experiencing. Equally, and on the other hand, Romanticism was not, as these writers supposed, centered on an assertion of the subjective *ego* or personality; and we could now say that this was because no art, or human expression – because of the necessarily transcendent nature of art or of human expression – could ever be so. To the extent that these "personality-

---

[60] See A. O. Lovejoy, *Essays in the History of Ideas* (Baltimore: Johns Hopkins University Press, 1948), pp. 228–53.
[61] See also below, chapter 5.

expressive" doctrines are a feature of Romantic theory, they are really, along with the concept of "authorship" according to which the author is supposed to be in sole command of a text's true meaning, more of an inheritance from the Longinian tradition of the ancient world and from the "sentimentalism" of the eighteenth century. Taken together, they amount to a distortion – almost an inversion – of the ideas which in fact constitute the main intellectual and artistic tradition of the Romantic movement.

4

PRESENCE

Art is neither the impression of natural objectivity nor
the expression of spiritual subjectivity, but it is the work
and witness of the relation between the *substantia humana*
and the *substantia rerum*, it is the realm of "between"
which has become a form.

MARTIN BUBER

1

We have sometimes been reminded by structuralist or post-structuralist literary theorists that reading is not an entirely naive or
innocent activity. "To read a text as literature is not to make one's
mind a *tabula rasa* and approach it without preconception," writes
Jonathan Culler in his *Structuralist Poetics*:

> [O]ne must bring to it an implicit understanding of the operations of
> literary discourse which tells one what to look for.
>
> Anyone lacking this knowledge, anyone wholly unacquainted with
> literature and unfamiliar with the conventions by which fictions are
> read, would, for example, be quite baffled if presented with a poem. His
> knowledge of the language would enable him to understand phrases
> and sentences, but he would not know, quite literally, what to *make* of
> this strange concatenation of phrases ... He has not internalized the
> "grammar" of literature which would permit him to convert linguistic
> sequences into literary structures and meanings.
>
> (pp. 113–14)

It must follow – since this claim is obviously quite justified – that
however much we might want to argue (and here we should be
agreeing with the semiologists) that our "ordinary" ways of seeing

or talking about the world are not sharply discontinuous from our more "imaginative" or "artistic" ways,[1] there will still remain genuine questions to be answered about the nature of the literary conventions or devices – the "literary structures or meanings" – which we rely on whenever we create or experience any text as literature. Even the most unassuming or naturalistic of our conventions are still conventions, and (to complicate things further) there is the philosophically challenging fact that almost any text whatever *can* be read as literature if we choose to read it in that way. The news item which can also be read as a poem is only one of the many favorites among such literary theorists' examples, and there is in fact no necessary limit to the amount of found, or as-it-might-be-found, "textuality" which may turn out to have a significant literary value for us.[2]

We could grant this, even so, without thereby having to grant the need for the reader to have any explicit knowledge or awareness of the older-fashioned categories of literary "rhetoric" or of the newer-fashioned categories of post-Saussurian literary theory. What really *is* it, we perhaps need to ask, for the reader to be aware of "literary structures and meanings," or to be familiar "with the conventions by which fictions are read"? Reading may not be an entirely naive or innocent activity, but neither are horse-riding or singing or speaking foreign languages entirely naive or innocent activities; yet all of these are things which we *can* learn to do simply by learning to do them. In practice, we learn to read literature in the same kind of way that we learn to do most other things, and children learn to understand stories (or poems, or plays, or television programs) without needing first – or therefore perhaps ever – to familiarize themselves with rhetorical categories or with post-Saussurian literary arguments.

---

[1] See above, chapter 3, Sec. 3.

[2] See for instance Gérard Genette, *Figures of Literary Discourse*, trans. Alan Sheridan (Oxford: Basil Blackwell, 1982), pp. 96, 100–1. Literary structuralists are generally agreed that it is the quality of our attention to a text which determines whether it is a piece of literature or not. A related point is made by the present writer's daughter (aged 11) when she claims that "poetry means: you read it in a silly voice, with lots of pauses in between." Marxist critics such as Fredric Jameson, Raymond Williams or Terry Eagleton are surely right when they claim that there is no such thing as literature as defined by a type of writing or a type of subject matter. "Literature" in this sense may indeed be a bourgeois concept. But they must be wrong when they imply that there is no such thing as literature at all. Literature is any text which we (any of us) find worth attending to for its revelatory qualities. The reason why Marxist critics have no need or room for any notion of literature in this sense is simply that they have no need or room for any notion of the revelatory.

(The painter we call "primitive" is, after all, the painter who has never studied traditional painting, not the painter who has never studied the theory of how to paint.) Since the time of Aristotle we have acquired a great deal of knowledge about the kinds of things that literature can do, and the "innocent" reader will not find his way around in his reading without some kind of awareness of the conventions and devices which have traditionally been used. But is the kind of "implicit understanding of the operations of literary discourse" which a perceptive and competent reader needs to have really anything more than the kind of awareness which he can acquire simply by reading a great deal of literature?

To some extent, very possibly, it is. There will always be times when the reader, or the literary artist himself, will be able to strengthen his grasp of what he is experiencing through a certain kind of making-conscious of the intuitive processes in which he is involved; having done so, he will then, with a deepened understanding, be able to revert once again to the intuitive levels of apprehension on which we necessarily depend in all of our moment-by-moment dealings with the world. The question which arises here is how far these processes of making-conscious are likely to be helped or illuminated by the official categorizings of literary theory: they may be more a matter of registering what Shelley called "before unapprehended relations of things" (*Defence of Poetry*, p. 103) – connections or transitions about whose presence or absence in any particular work a general theory of literature can have almost nothing of interest to say. Whatever concessions the literary theorist may make to the individuality of the particular work, the fact remains that his systematizing can have little to show us about how that work is to be understood – in the sense of how it succeeds where it does succeed, or therefore of why it deserves to be counted as a piece of literature at all. The literary work will always lie to one side of, or beyond, anything that we can systematically say about it, and the essence of the most valuable literary criticism must always lie in a kind of indirection – an indirect gesturing (which will be both systematic and unsystematic, just as the work itself is both systematic and unsystematic) at the various ways in which we sense the work to "go beyond" whatever we and the rest of our literature have otherwise comprehended;[3] comparison with other literary texts will

---

[3] Iain McGilchrist has argued the case for indirection in criticism with much subtlety in his *Against Criticism* (London: Faber and Faber, 1982).

only be one of our many possible means to this end. (A classifying theorist such as Northrop Frye, while being intimately familiar with the history of literature, has no way of making sense of that familiarity within his classificatory scheme. Much of the argument of Frye's *Anatomy of Criticism* rests on generalizations which beg the main questions at issue,[4] and he has only the most improvisational things to say about why our literary conventions have changed as they have.[5] The flaw in Frye's approach is that it is standpointless and unhistorical rather than based in a present-day creative sensibility, and that it can therefore offer us little more than an academic exercise in literary taxonomy. Nothing is changed, from this point of view, if we decide to regard Frye's categorizing as a categorizing of reading-procedures rather than as a categorizing of modes or genres. Frye is both right, and also disastrously wrong, when he tells us that "[p]oems can only be made out of other poems" [p. 97].) Like any other kind of reading process, the critic's activity is a probing of the mysteriousness, or the incomplete articulation – sometimes misleadingly spoken of by semiologists as the "empty meaning" – of the text itself, and the critic's special role is to read in such a way as to help us to bridge the gap between what we consciously and rationally know and what we only intuitively sense through our participation in the text's "going beyond"; in doing so he of course helps to *create* the text for readers who share some of the cultural ground on which he stands (when the text is read by different readers in different situations, it will have correspondingly different meanings).[6] The critical process, like the process of writing itself, is in part necessarily irrational and beyond explanation, and we ought perhaps to remind ourselves that the attempt to explain how a poem "works" can have a good deal in common with the attempt to explain how a joke works: in the case of the joke, we are usually ready to allow that

---

[4] For example: "During the last hundred years, most serious fiction has tended increasingly to be ironic in mode" (pp. 34–35).

[5] For example: "Then a new kind of middle-class culture introduces the low-mimetic" (p. 34).

[6] Is the critic's own text itself a poem? Almost certainly not, since it will rarely have the particular kind of rhythmic or gestural quality which poems have, but will instead have the rhythmic or gestural quality of practical discourse about things (in this case words or meanings). Since any "found" text may be capable of being experienced for its expressive qualities alone, a critical text can be a poem in so far as it can be *attended* to as a poem – just as a newspaper article can be a poem in so far as it can be attended to as a poem. Most critical texts simply do not have this degree of expressive or revelatory interest, and are therefore not a part of literature.

there is either something there or there is not – that it either works for us or it does not – and that there may otherwise be very little that we can usefully say about what is taking place. (To adapt Wittgenstein's early phrase about linguistic meaning in general: "what *can* be shown *cannot* be said" [*Tractatus Logico-Philosophicus*, 4.1212].)

Whether in terms of the older categories of rhetoric (or modern versions of these such as Northrop Frye's) or of the newer categories of semiological theory, there exist indefinitely many kinds of "literary structures and meanings" and an indefinite variety of ways in which we might set about trying to "recover" or to "naturalize"[7] our literary (as well as our non-literary) texts for our ordinary understanding of the world. Whatever value there may be in trying to reduce such structures or strategies to a limited number of types, it will continue to be the case that the essential function of the literary text is one of revelation or disclosure, and that the essential requirement for a piece of writing if it is to have any significance for us as a piece of literature is that there should be a sufficient degree of reality or truth in it to be revealed or disclosed. To the semiological theorist who argues that "our notion of the range of possible speech-acts which a literary text might perform is the very basis of literary naturalization," and who goes on to give examples of such speech acts from the history of literature (the praise of a mistress, the meditation on death, etc.) and to claim that "our notions of literature do not permit just any speech act to serve as the determinant of a poem,"[8] the only sensible reply is that in fact *anything will do*, and that there is no way of knowing where our models for "possible speech acts which a literary text might perform" will come from next. Effective modern verse has been based on speech acts as varied and un-traditionally-literary as the inventory or list, the biology textbook, the newspaper profile, the overheard conversation, the exchange of love letters, the travel brochure, or the nuclear-attack warning; and the speech acts underlying effective modern prose fiction have been almost as heterogeneous. The notion that there must be a distinctive "grammar" of literary discourse is in effect little more than a piece of defensive professional obscurantism: the neo-

---

[7] See for example Culler, *Structuralist Poetics*, pp. 134–60. Other words used in semiological writings for this process include "recuperation," or the establishing of "*vraisemblance*."

[8] *Structuralist Poetics*, p. 147.

rhetorician or semiologist has simply replaced the old notion of literature as a special kind of language or subject matter with the new notion of literariness as a variety of special ways of reading or of special "structures and meanings." In fact, there are no such special structures or meanings. The literary theorist really has no choice but to recognize that the question of revelation or disclosure *cuts across* all questions of modes or genres – the only qualification to this being that there may be modes or genres which by their nature, as well as by their historical provenance, simply happen to be better suited to revelation or disclosure and others which are better suited to more instrumental or manipulative purposes. (There are also conventions which are meta-poetic rather than poetic, and which show us more about the institutions of literature, or about the work in which they appear, or about language in general, than about the world itself – of which language and literature are of course only a very small corner. But these meta-poetic conventions must necessarily depend on other conventions, including much ordinary language-using, which are simpler and more directly world-revealing.) The semiological theorist's practice of aggregating together, and taking as his field, the entire possible range of "literary structures and meanings" (the over-all study of these constituting "poetics") obscures the fact that while many of these "operations of literary discourse" involve a direct revelation of aspects of the world, others, though no less "literary," and with perhaps just as impressive a literary ancestry, may belong to kinds of activity which are not primarily expressive or revelatory at all. The revelatory content of a medieval morality play was not very significant, but it was a useful way of re-acquainting its audience with the moral verities and of holding contemporary vices up to scorn. The instrumental usefulness of a lyric poem may be minimal, but it may have a pivotal importance for our ontological comprehension of the world.

Anything that we might do by way of classifying or categorizing our literary conventions or reading-procedures can tell us almost nothing of real value about what is living or dead for us either in our literary past or in our literary present or immediate future. More useful than any trans-historical systematizing of devices must be the notion of a literary *tradition*, or of a specifically literary culture, to which everything which (as it now seems) has been significant in our literary history has necessarily belonged, and within which all our historically-used conventions and devices have had their actual

place and life. The idea of a literary tradition comprehends everything which is of importance in the ideas of literary devices or
reading-procedures; but it at the same time comprehends the idea of
life, and of what may now be literarily vital for us and what may be
literarily dead. (The idea of tradition is one which writers themselves
have usually had a place for, while being conspicuously uninterested
in rhetorical theorizing for its own sake.) T. S. Eliot's famous
formulation gives us a view of tradition as something which has both
weight and permanence, but which can also – and must also – be
open to modification through every contribution from a creative
newcomer:

> Tradition is a matter of much wider significance ... It involves, in the
> first place, the historical sense ... No poet, no artist of any art, has his
> complete meaning alone ... You cannot value him alone; you must set
> him, for contrast and comparison, among the dead. I mean this as a
> principle of aesthetic, not merely historical, criticism. The necessity
> that he shall conform, that he shall cohere, is not one-sided; what
> happens when a new work of art is created is something that happens
> simultaneously to all the works of art which preceded it. The existing
> monuments form an ideal order among themselves, which is modified
> by the introduction of the new (the really new) work of art among
> them ... [9]

This conception of tradition is a genuinely temporal and historical
one, and corresponds closely to the notion of the development of our
ordinary language through its continuous exposure to contingency
within new historical contexts.[10] A sometimes overlooked corollary
of this view of literary tradition is that we can only know what our
tradition actually *is* from a standpoint which is more or less that of
the present-day creative artist: we are in effect obliged to be (in some
sense) creative artists ourselves if we are to have anything significant
to contribute to literary criticism at all. Genre-theorists and reading-
procedure-theorists have usually tended to have very little that is
interesting or persuasive to say about *new* literature; and yet the
ability to respond to new literature is probably the most important
critical requirement of all, since if the critic does not know where he
is with the literature of his own time he can have no standpoint from
which to appraise the literature of the past. Coleridge suggested that

[9] T. S. Eliot, "Tradition and the individual talent" in *Selected Essays* (London: Faber
and Faber, 1951), pp. 14–15.
[10] See above, chapter 2.

"[t]he question should fairly be stated, how far a man can be an adequate ... critic of poetry who is not a poet, at least *in posse?*" (He did also go on darkly to reflect that "there is yet another distinction. Supposing he is not only a poet, but is a bad poet? What then?")[11]

The process of literary evolution must involve a continuous modification of our literary conventions (which is not to say that the modification of literary conventions is usually the point, or the real achievement, of significant works of literature);[12] and it must always be possible, and may at any time turn out to be necessary, for us to re-draw our entire scheme of literary-critical categories from the standpoint which we currently occupy. "No work of true genius dare want its appropriate form," said Coleridge, trying to escape from the timeless and Aristotelian notions of literary form which had prevailed in the age before him, "neither indeed is there any danger of this. As it must not, so genius cannot, be lawless: for it is even this that constitutes it genius – the power of acting creatively under laws of its own origination."[13] "Tell Arnold Bennett that all rules of construction hold good only for novels which are copies of other novels," said D. H. Lawrence; "[a] book which is not a copy of other books has its own construction, and what he calls faults, he being an old imitator, I call characteristics ..."[14] "Whether we call it life or spirit, truth or reality, this, the essential thing, has moved off, or on, and refuses to be contained any longer in such ill-fitting vestments as we provide," said Virginia Woolf in one of her denunciations of the formal hide-boundness of her Edwardian predecessors.[15] Our understanding of tradition, unlike our understanding of rhetoric, can – by incorporating history into the very bloodstream of literature – provide us with a living physiology of literature rather than merely

---

[11] Entry in *Anima Poetae* (London: Heinemann, 1895) dated March 1805 by E. H. Coleridge.

[12] It *is* of course the point of some; but they occupy only a small place in the whole of literature – and should perhaps be encouraged to go on doing so. The tendency of semiologically-minded criticism has been to read the whole of traditional literature as proto-modernist (see for example Gabriel Josipovici, *The World and the Book* [London: Macmillan, 1979]); but what we see revealed in this anti-naturalist program may be not so much something about the true nature of literature as something about the modern literary intellectual's troubled relationship with nature.

[13] "Shakespeare's judgement equal to his genius" in *Shakespearian Criticism*, vol. 1 (London: Dent, 1960), p. 197.

[14] D. H. Lawrence, letter to J. B. Pinker of 16 December 1915.

[15] Virginia Woolf, "Modern fiction" in *Collected Essays*, vol. 2 (London: Hogarth Press, 1966), p. 105.

with a dead anatomy of it. Instead of studying our reading-procedures for their own sake, the literary theorist could perhaps more valuably concern himself with such questions as why we cannot write novels with a prose style like Dickens's today, or to what extent or in what ways the psychological assumptions of the Balzacian novel have been legitimately overthrown by the theorists of the *nouveau roman*, or why modern poetry has increasingly moved away from metricality and towards one form or another of free verse.[16]

If we are willing to take the notion of literary tradition or of a literary culture seriously,[17] we shall in fact be correspondingly better able to respond authentically to the literature of our own time. Only an intuitive knowledge of where we are at the moment enables us to understand our literary past; but an historically educated awareness of our literary past is also a necessary prerequisite for our understanding of where we are at the moment. (The interplay of literary "structure" and "event" which is here in question parallels the interplay of structure and event which is essential to the nature of any ordinarily used conceptual language.) Against the longer sweep of the past, much of our new literature could come to seem little more than a product of our literary practitioners' inability to escape from the spiritual limitations of their own culture: much of what is now called "post-modernist" writing may come to strike us as inturned and divorced from existential obligation – where a true post-modernism would need to be more directly revelatory or expressive of reality than any of the literature of our past has succeeded in being. (In a culture where our ontological needs have often seemed both to have been monopolized and also at the same time betrayed by the claims of organized religion, we might expect to find a poetic form such as the romantic lyric occupying a central place in our literature; yet living in a culture where this apparent ontological betrayal has scarcely yet begun to be philosophically explored, we have allowed the romantic lyric to become eclipsed and have turned to more easily

[16] The theorist who wants to help us to understand the modern history of English and American verse, for example, might usefully focus on such things as the irregular odes of some of the Romantic poets, the *avant-la-lettre* confessional manner of Browning's dramatic poems, the way in which a poem like Hardy's "The Voice" breaks meter in its fourth stanza, the internal rhyme- and sound-pattern of Yeats's "The Wild Swans at Coole," or the autobiographical prose basis of Lowell's *Life Studies*.

[17] The notion of "culture" which is involved here is not meant to prejudge any social or political questions about one form of culture being superior or inferior to any other.

rewarding and less existentially ambitious kinds of verse.[18] In our prose fiction, a reflexive literary irony and various kinds of meta-writing may indeed have become the dominant forms of the modern period;[19] but at their best – as for example when they operate satirically – they ought perhaps to be seen mainly as defensive responses to the world's evils rather than as any adequate literary recognition of what it would most deeply satisfy us to be able to read.)

2

Yet we can be helped to see. An intuitive critic such as William Empson can be explicit and straightforward about his rationalistic urges ("unexplained beauty arouses an irritation in me, a sense that this would be a good place to scratch") while still giving us insights which help us to see some of the revealing things that may be going on in particular pieces of writing; his classifications, as he himself seems to be very ready to admit, are of only secondary importance. In *Seven Types of Ambiguity* he writes of the famous lines on winter-bound trees in the first quatrain of Shakespeare's 73rd Sonnet that

there is no pun, double syntax, or dubiety of feeling, in

Bare ruined choirs, where late the sweet birds sang

but the comparison holds for many reasons; because ruined monastery choirs are places in which to sing; because they involve sitting in a row, because they are made of wood, are carved into knots and so forth ... because the cold and Narcissistic charm suggested by choir-boys suits well with Shakespeare's feeling for the object of the Sonnets, and for various sociological and historical reasons (the protestant destruction of the monasteries; fear of puritanism), which it would be hard now to trace out in their proportions; these reasons, and many more relating the simile to its place in the Sonnet, must all combine to give the line its beauty, and there is a sort of ambiguity in not knowing which of them to hold most clearly in mind ...

Such a definition of the first type of ambiguity covers almost

---

[18] Gabriel Pearson has demonstrated the modern importance of the romantic lyric ("Romanticism and contemporary poetry," *New Left Review*, 16, July–August 1962: 47–69), and has shown that it can be revelatory while at the same time being complex, self-referring, and many of the other things that post-Saussurian critics like their literature to be.

[19] Compare Frye, *Anatomy of Criticism*, p. 34.

everything of literary importance ... [T]here is a sort of meaning, the
sort that people are thinking of when they say "this poet will mean
more to you when you have had more experience of life," which is
hardly in reach of the analyst at all.[20]

The process of critical suggestion which is at work here is as intuitive
and mysterious as the process of the poem itself, and its acknowledged lack of system (its recognition of the "ambiguity" of not
knowing which reasons or connections to hold most clearly in mind,
and that this kind of "ambiguity" covers "almost everything of
literary importance") is essential to its nature and to its critical value.
Elsewhere, and by way of a partial explanation, Empson remarks
that "[w]hat I would suppose is that, whenever a receiver of poetry is
seriously moved by an apparently simple line, what are moving in
him are the traces of a great part of his past experience and of the
structure of his past judgements" (p. xv).

When the critic is not helping us to see, the other traditionally
familiar critical activity that he is likely to be engaged in is showing
us where, and how, things have gone artistically wrong. The later
phase of the Saussurian movement has given us more sophisticated
and intellectual ways of interpreting this traditional critical concern
or undertaking: such things as lapses into the author's own personality, or into his fantasies, or into the ideology of his own time and
situation – all of them falling within the accepted domain of the
exploratory critic – have come to be treated in newly systematic and
philosophically-oriented ways by the "deconstructive" analyst. But
literary texts do not merely declare their weaknesses in an unlocated
vacuum and without the need for particular capacities of insight or
qualities of spirit on the part of the deconstructing critic, and the
anti-spiritual language of much post-Saussurian theory has gone to
incoherent lengths[21] to avoid acknowledging the necessary role of
insight – of insight into a reality which is revealed or disclosed, *by*
someone in a cultural and historical situation – in the literary-critical
process. The arguments of post-structuralists against the systematic
theory of, for example, Saussure himself[22] – *inter alia* that (in effect)
its classifications presuppose a contextless and Olympian classifier –
are in fact valid against the entire apparatus of rhetorical theory in

---

[20] William Empson, *Seven Types of Ambiguity* (London: Chatto and Windus, 1953),
    pp. 2–3, 9.
[21] See above, chapter 1.
[22] See for example Derrida, *Of Grammatology*, pp. 27–65; *Positions*, pp. 17–36.

general; but the post-structuralist can go no further than this, because his conceptual framework prevents him from giving any account at all of what it is for us to recognize literary (or any other artistic) *success* or *failure*. For post-structuralism, all texts, whether they be popular television drama series or celebrated masterpieces of literature, can seem of equal interest, and there is no way within the premises of post-structuralism (quite apart from what post-structuralist critics themselves, as intuitive individuals, may be able to do) for us to identify any work as being a partial success, or as being incompletely realized, or as having dead patches within it – all of which are critical judgements which we ordinarily and untheo-retically make as a part of the process of coming to terms with the meaning of literary texts. The semiologically-inclined theorist tends to argue that "every work is clear, provided we locate the angle from which the blur becomes so natural as to pass unnoticed,"[23] or that "we can always make the meaningless meaningful by the production of an appropriate context";[24] and yet these notions can come very close to being abdications of critical responsibility, since they lead us to suppose that every text is a satisfactory totality as it is (and yet in that case how do any texts come to be singled out as particularly worthy of our attention in the first place?) – which is a supposition that academic commentators in the analytical tradition have often been more than ready to fall in with. (Frank Kermode has brought this post-structuralist tendency to a lucid *reductio ad absurdum* by suggesting that the literary canon is simply what we give our readerly or critical attention to.[25] This particular notion of what we "find worth attending to" seems likely to need some drastic qualification before it can give us the kind of definition we really need. In a more spiritual climate than the one we in fact live in we might find things worth attending to mainly for their expressive or spiritual qualities. In a post-graduate English seminar, we will be rather more likely to find things worth attending to for their complexity, their cleverness, or their discussability. Much of our best literature is poor material for post-graduate English seminars, precisely because of its ability – by very simple means – to set moving in us what Empson calls "the traces of a great part of [our] past experience and of the

[23] See Fredric Jameson, "Metacommentary," *PMLA*, 86 (1971), p. 9.
[24] Culler, *Structuralist Poetics*, p. 138. As an epigraph to his opening chapter, Culler ominously quotes Victor Hugo's "Tout dit, dans l'infini, quelquechose à quelqu'un."
[25] See Frank Kermode, *Forms of Attention* (University of Chicago Press, 1985).

structure of [our] past judgements." We might even go so far as to feel that work of this kind, which "is hardly in reach of the analyst at all," "covers almost everything of literary importance." How many seminar-hours have been spent on, say, the "ambiguities" of Hardy's poems as compared with, say, the "ambiguities" of *Finnegans Wake*?)

The "deconstructive" critic who exposes hidden private assumptions or ideological presuppositions will be doing valuable criticism if he does so in the name of truth or reality; but not if he only resembles the psychoanalyst who can think up countless ingenious interpretations of his patient's behavior but who has no idea which of them are likely to be more true than any of the others or than the patient's own account of his situation. Likewise the notion (Barthes)[26] of "absorption" in the text and of release from the demands of the "real world" can be persuasive (we could perhaps see it as a rather French way of talking about contemplation) as against the metaphysically unsustainable idea of the "one correct reading"; but it will be unpersuasive if it can tell us nothing about the *return* of the text to the "real" world and about the spiritual obligations which lie on us to distinguish more whimsical, or merely cleverer, readings from more profound ones, to come up sooner or later with our own readings rather than with just any readings, and thereby to attempt to make what we can for the purposes of our own lives of the text we have been dealing with. Since we live in a practical world, we will inevitably naturalize the text back into that practical world, and we will therefore perhaps do best to be as aware and as explicit as possible about what is involved in this necessary eventual commitment. (The Barthesian notion of "*jouissance*" takes us – in a joyful and Nietzschean manner – beyond any mere docility before given meanings; but there must still remain an obligation on us to hold on to the notion of truth or reality, or ἀλήθεια, rather than simply allowing it to be anthropocentrically eliminated.) When poststructuralism comes to acknowledge that the demands of human spirituality must either be recognized and faced up to, or else must be expected to find their own uncomprehended way back into our experience from some unanticipated direction, the theoretical wheel will have come full circle and we shall be likely to find ourselves back once again with some version of the time-honored notion of critical intuition.

[26] See *The Pleasure of the Text*.

These arguments may help to make more comprehensible the familiar fact – sometimes troubling to practical critics – that it nearly always seems to be easier to say what is wrong with a particular poem or piece of imaginative writing than it is to say what is right with it. What is right with a piece of writing is what cannot quite be said at all – but which can only be gestured at – because it is what the poem or piece of writing itself *shows*, and what language itself "cannot get quite on level terms with or render completely intelligible."[27] It may be useful, even so, for the critic to keep in mind some of the essential qualities which a text needs to possess if it is to be able to impress us as deserving to be treated as a piece of literature at all. It is this that a critic such as F. R. Leavis is doing when he speaks repeatedly of "maturity," or of "life," or of the absence of such qualities, in particular pieces of writing: to emphasize these qualities is to give us a philosophical reminder, and not merely to assert a moral prejudice. Literature must express life, because literature is language at its most expressive, and because expressive language is our centrally human way of grasping life, or of acceding to the process of meaning-creation (or of *tao*, or ἀρετή) at the human level.[28] Any vocabulary of praise in a critic is now likely to seem cloying or supererogatory; and it was the lack of the necessary philosophical background for understanding this, and the consequent confusion of critical responsiveness with moral gentility, which made a great deal of traditional literary criticism fall into what is now likely to strike us as decorativeness or floridity. What survives from the best criticism of the past is its particular illuminations; otherwise it is its scalings-down – one might almost say deconstructions – of fashionably exaggerated reputations. The critic's proper function is not to give praise (it should be taken for granted that, as Matthew Arnold insisted, he "welcomes" everything that is good): it is to illuminate or to interpret; or else it is to find fault, and to suggest, perhaps as systematically as possible, some of the reasons for the faults that have been found.

It is the connection with life or with the process of meaning-creation which justifies us in relating literature to truth or reality, and therefore (which is only to say the same thing in different terms)

---

[27] Kant, *Critique of Aesthetic Judgement*, sec. 49.

[28] See above, chapter 2. Leavis, in his later writings, makes many references to the "*Ahnung*," or intuition, embodied in literary works, and is obviously much nearer to seeing literature in transcendent, or religious, than in moral terms.

with the dimension of our religious awareness. Language, through its basis in gesture, is life and meaning-creation at its most distinctively human and spiritual level; literature is only the most concentrated or intense form of this spiritual meaning-creative process. The perception of literary meanings therefore cannot be the special province of the academic commentator (whether semiological or non-semiological) or of any other specialist or expert – unless we are in fact prepared to accord to him (there might be marginally more of an argument for doing so in the case of the poet or imaginative writer himself) the status of a priest. Since reading is not a "naive or innocent activity," the reader or critic needs to have more than "a certain experience of the world"[29] in order to be a reader or a critic in a literarily effective way; but he does, nevertheless, need to have a certain experience of the world. With the dangers of narrowly literary-critical specialization in mind D. H. Lawrence once remarked that "[a] critic must be a man of force or complexity himself, which few critics are."[30] What the reader of literature – like anyone who lives or experiences life at all – needs to have is a sense of reality; and to have such a sense he must have an entire education and knowledge of human life *built in* to his intuitive faculties. The reader or critic needs to have his knowledge and his intellectual capacities (including whatever he may need to know of literary theory) in his bloodstream rather than in his head; he then needs to respond intuitively to what he is reading, in order to establish with as much authenticity and certainty as he can what is really there. The artist, likewise, needs to have his knowledge in his bloodstream also; and he needs to have the same realistic kind of knowledge as the reader or critic. To be a creative reader or a creative writer means to possess a sense of reality. To possess a sense of reality means – because it is only another name for the very same thing – to possess a religious sense.

3

In its dispute with "the metaphysics of presence," and with any notion of an experiencing subject which lies outside the structures of human language and sign-systems altogether, post-structuralist theory has been astutely ready to endorse the claim which was once

[29] Compare Culler, *Structuralist Poetics*, p. 121.
[30] Lawrence, *Selected Literary Criticism* (London: Mercury Books, 1961), p. 118.

made by Heidegger that "it is language that speaks" and not man himself.[31] For Jacques Derrida, there is no conceptual room for any experiencing awareness within the open-ended linguistic process which he labels *"différance."* Michel Foucault has claimed on related grounds that "man is a recent invention and will soon disappear."[32] Elaborating on the Saussurian premise that words cannot have their meanings through their correspondences with already-discriminated things or items in the world, post-structuralism insists that the basis of linguistic meaning must be relational and only relational: the meaning of a word, or of any other sign, is a matter of the relationships or differences which obtain between the word or sign itself and the other words or signs which make up the system to which it belongs. If we were to describe this state of affairs in more material and less formal terms, we could say that every thing or item which forms a part of the world we live in must therefore in the end be understood to be a part of everything else.

With its emphasis on the interconnectedness of all things, and its pressure towards a dissolution of the self or *ego* such as we experience it in ordinary life and our ordinary linguistic usages, post-structuralist theory bears important resemblances to certain traditional modes of religious thinking. Post-structuralism is in fact at one with any mode of religious thinking whatever to the extent that it sees itself as in conflict with the *ego*-centered humanism, and the idea of the individual self as the sole arbiter of what can count as reality, which has dominated Western philosophy since the time of Descartes. The most important contrast or difference between post-structuralism and religious thought is that where religious thought, in its preoccupation with the state of the individual human soul or spirit, has always found it necessary to give a place to experienced meaning and experienced apprehension of reality (while not allowing such apprehensions to be wholly *constitutive* of reality), post-structuralism has eliminated any conceptual means for giving expression to such notions altogether. For post-structuralism, language simply evolves as it does, and no questions can usefully be asked about the spiritual – or even the physical – situation of the experiencing human beings who are the means by which such

[31] See Heidegger, *Der Satz vom Grund* (Pfullingen: Neske, 1957), p. 161. "Die Sprache spricht, nicht der Mensch. Der Mensch spricht nur, indem er geschicklich der Sprache entspricht."
[32] Michel Foucault, *Les Mots et les choses* (Paris: Gallimard, 1966), p. 15.

evolution occurs. It is at this point that post-structuralism falls into incoherence, since the pre-experiential human awareness, or Man as a source of experienceable meaning, cannot in fact disappear unless he reverts entirely to nature and loses altogether the conceptual and world-referential mode of comprehension which comes to him through his possession of language.[33] In the post-structuralist eschatology of Michel Foucault, Man will shortly disappear before the ever-more-brightly-shining structures of language; but the truth is rather that for Man – or any other imaginable transcendent center of awareness – to disappear must at the same time be for language to disappear also. Post-structuralism eliminates the very process of perceptual and embodied articulation-out-of-obscurity which makes language itself possible, and which must therefore be an ineliminable aspect of our nature as conscious and language-using beings. (If we were to suppose, as some post-structuralists suppose, that the evolution of human language or sign-systems can only be understood as governed by blind forces, then our very ability to be aware of this fact – were it indeed a fact – would *eo ipso* give us a measure of freedom to escape from the fact as well.) It may be true that language speaks; but it is also true that language only speaks through, and by means of, man's embodied vision.

When once we have abandoned the idea that the concepts of vision or of perceived meaning are philosophically dispensable, we shall find ourselves in a position where we are able to look more closely at what such concepts really involve, and in particular at such affinities as they may have with certain religious notions to which they bear obvious resemblances. That it is a part of the human condition that we should be faced with the possibility, or the task, of striving for a relatively authentic, rather than a relatively inauthentic apprehension of the world around us follows directly from our nature as embodied and striving beings. As conscious and language-using organisms, it is a part of our nature that our language should both give structure to, and be dependent for its evolution upon, our transient perceptions, and that the capacity of our language to reach beyond, or to transcend, the forms of experience and understanding which we at any time possess should be shaped by a pre-conscious purposiveness which is partly governed by our physical and biologi-

---

[33] To adapt Kant's formulation in the *Critique of Pure Reason* (B. 197), we might say that "the conditions for the possibility of human transcendence are likewise conditions for the possibility of the objects of experience."

cal organization. Our pursuit of such authenticity, or our embracing of such transcendence, is a care, or a concern, to relate authentically to reality, and is a continuation at the human level of the adaptiveness which is the essence of all life.[34]

This quality of care or concern,[35] or of the pursuit of authenticity, is in fact more or less identical with what has come to be spoken of in modern theological discussions as "the religious requirement."[36] When the demands of particular religious creeds or dogmas have been isolated for what they are, it is precisely this care or concern for the achieving of authenticity which has in more "liberal" theological quarters come to be seen as definitional of the essence of religion. Historically existing religions have always emphasized the difficulty of this process; and many religions, perhaps partly for accidental historical reasons, have come near to identifying it with joylessness, or with the renunciation of the commonly sought-after things of this world. It may be for this reason that theological discussions have tended to favor the notion of concern, with its overtones of unremitting watchfulness and scrutiny, rather than the more relaxed-seeming notion of care which a philosophical argument based in ordinary usage might seem to point towards. Care – with its implications of caring, rather than primarily of worry or of anxiety – has no difficulty in accommodating the notion of play, which (though it has been taken up by post-structuralism in something of a Nietzschean spirit) has been noticeably absent from almost all traditional religions. "Man is only truly human when he plays," claimed Schiller – thereby also suggesting a foundation for a new, non-instrumental and non-theoretical understanding not only of art but of human life as a whole.[37] (A dance movement, a piece of music, a sexual embrace, an arrow shot at a target, may all be manifestationsof care – and may certainly also be manifestations of play – where concern, in such contexts, would almost certainly carry with it an excess of anxiety which would interfere with the activities in question.) But whether we speak of care or of concern, the root concept seems in any case to be inseparable from the more purely philosophically derived concept of accepted transcendence or of

[34] See above, chapter 2.
[35] These are the terms which have often been used to translate Heidegger's version of this concept (Sorge). See Being and Time, sec. 39 et seq.
[36] See for example Don Cupitt, Taking Leave of God (London: SCM Press, 1980), passim.
[37] Aesthetic Education, Fifteenth Letter.

authentic human living. Where (for example) on empiricist or idealist views of human life there may be no room for religious awareness as an irreducible mode of apprehension of reality – either because there is no such thing as transcendence, or because all transcendence can ultimately be taken up into conceptual knowledge[38] – on an embodied or incarnational view of human life, which is the only view which is now philosophically sustainable, we may find that there can be no way of keeping religious considerations out of any area of our experiencing at all.

4

A literary text or fiction, although it makes use of the various referential or descriptive resources of our ordinary language, nevertheless does not make use of them in a referential or a descriptive manner. Its function is, or we are to attend to it as if it were, entirely expressive or creative – or, in the sense in which the term has been used at an earlier stage of the present argument, gestural. Reference may indeed seem to be made to persons or circumstances or events, in the sense that such things are mentioned within the literary text and may even be linked together by it into some kind of story; but reference is not made to them, in the sense that these persons or circumstances or events have no existence in the actual world in which the text is written or read, or else that it is irrelevant to the nature of the text as a piece of literature if they do have such an existence.

Attempts have sometimes been made to analyse the conditions governing the truth of fictional writings in terms of certain facts or circumstances which obtain within what we commonly speak or think of as the "real" world. An early attempt of this kind forms a part of Bertrand Russell's "theory of descriptions," while more recent analyses have introduced such notions as "make-believe" or "pretending" in order to account for the ways in which the assertions made in fictions differ from the assertions which are made in the descriptive or information-conveying situations of "real life."[39] A

---

[38] As for example in the philosophy of Hegel.

[39] See for example Kendall L. Walton, (1) "Pictures and make-believe," *The Philosophical Review*, 82 (1973), 283–319, and (2) "Fearing fictions," *The Journal of Philosophy*, 75 (1978), 5–27; David Lewis, "Truth in fiction," *American Philosophical Quarterly*, 15 (1978), 37–46; Gareth Evans, *The Varieties of Reference* (New York: Oxford University Press, 1982), ch. 10.

necessary defect of these approaches is that – precisely because of their commitment to analyzing fictions in terms of their relationships to the information-conveying statements of the "real" world – they must by definition only be able to engage with literature from an actuality-dependent or instrumental viewpoint, and must therefore be incapable of coming to terms with – or even of recognizing the existence of – its aesthetic dimension. The truth-conditional analyst may suggest, for example, that "fictionally true" means true "in the game of make-believe" which we enter when we write or read any fiction. Or he may propose that "representational works of art generate make-believe truths."[40] Or he may tell us that "story-telling is pretence."[41] Or he may define literary fictions in terms of "cases in which empty singular terms are knowingly used, not in the first instance to state how things stand in the world, but to convey the content of some *representation* of the world."[42] What these approaches most significantly share is that they are by definition dependent or parasitic upon actual or possible "literal truths" or descriptions of "how things stand" in the "real" world.

Among the advantages which have been claimed for analyses of this kind is that they enable us to see why we might want to *re*-experience a story whose outcome we are already familiar with. The reason suggested is that *in make-believe* we do not know the outcome until the story – once again – reveals it to us. For example:

> But how can there be suspense if we already know how things will turn out? ... *Some* works, to be sure, fade quickly from exposure, and familiarity does alter our experience in certain ways. But the power of many works is remarkably permanent, and the nature of their effectiveness remarkably consistent ... Children, far from being bored by familiar stories, often beg to hear the same ones over and over again.
>
> None of this is surprising on my theory. The child hearing *Jack and the Beanstalk* knows that make-believedly Jack will escape, but make-believedly she does *not* know that he will – until the reading of the passage describing his escape.[43]

But advantages of this kind are in fact illusory, in so far as they are only solutions to the illusory problems which are generated by the

[40] Walton (1), p. 287 *et seq.*, and (2), p. 12.
[41] Lewis, p. 40.
[42] Evans, p. 343; author's italics.
[43] Walton (2), p. 26 – who acknowledges Lewis's concurrence on this point.

supposed, and therefore supposedly puzzling, resemblances between the statements of fiction and the information-conveying or description-based statements of "real life." If we were to cease to treat fictional statements as dependent in this way upon "real life" statements, we should no longer be liable to find ourselves subject to this kind of puzzlement – and the far greater disadvantages of the would-be truth-conditional, or representation-dependent, analysis of literary fictions would be likely to crowd in upon us.

These disadvantages would include, first of all, that there are fictions which do not make any statements at all – for example certain kinds of poetry. This is true not only of nonsense poetry, which may be literally quite meaningful,[44] but also of such poems as William Blake's "Ah! Sun-flower," which (lacking a main verb) makes no statement whatever and cannot very sensibly be paraphrased as one (we might do better to treat it as an emotional elaboration of the word "Ah ... " from which it sets out):

> Ah, Sun-flower, weary of time,
> Who countest the steps of the Sun,
> Seeking after that sweet golden clime
> Where the traveller's journey is done:
>
> Where the Youth pined away with desire,
> And the pale Virgin shrouded in snow
> Arise from their graves, and aspire
> Where my Sun-flower wishes to go.

Secondly, that not all literature is even seemingly representational in its form or style: not all fictions create worlds, and there is no way in which the "make-believe" or "pretending" analysis can gain a foothold on those which do not; and yet any theory which would sever representational from less representational or altogether unrepresentational literary modes seems *prima facie* unlikely to get close to the most essential qualities of literature or therefore to be able to provide a very convincing philosophical analysis of it. Thirdly, that the notion that "story-telling is pretence," and that "[t]he story-teller purports to be telling the truth about matters whereof he has knowledge,"[45] in fact fits only certain very restricted genres of

---

[44] See for example Frye, *Anatomy of Criticism*, p. 270 *et seq.*

[45] Lewis, p. 40. It must surely be significant that Lewis's examples are drawn from a genre such as the Sherlock Holmes stories – and more generally, perhaps, that many of the philosophical analyses of literature which try to reduce it to something

traditional literature (in particular, literature of the "omniscient narrator" variety), against which a significant amount of modern fiction (as well as a not entirely insignificant amount of traditional fiction) has been a critical reaction. Fourthly, that the truth-conditional or representation-dependent approach can have nothing very helpful to say about the *identity* of a work of literature: the truth-conditional theorist may suggest, for example, that "the proper background [for filling in the fictional "world" of any work] ... consists of the beliefs that generally prevailed in the community where the fiction originated: the beliefs of the author and his intended audience" – an idea which anyone who has reflected seriously on the problems of literary meaning would be likely to regard as too naive to be worth taking seriously.[46] This notion would entail, for example, that the identity or meaning of a literary fiction must be entirely hostage to its creator or to the ideas of his time. An entire realm of critical inquiry – known as hermeneutics, and originating in biblical studies – has in fact been devoted to questions about the cross-cultural significances, and therefore the nature of the identity, of literary texts. The idea that the meaning or identity of the stories in the Bible are dependent solely on "the beliefs of the author and his intended audience" (and are quite *in*dependent of the beliefs of the unintended audiences who might read the stories centuries later) is obviously absurd – and the same must be true for all other literature.

The list of such disadvantages might be extended considerably, but it would in the end perhaps have to come to rest on the insistence that what these would-be truth-conditional analyses really offer us is not properly speaking an account of literary art *qua* art at all. What they offer us is in many respects closer to being an analysis of certain kinds of literary *fantasy*. It will be likely to occur to anyone who has tried to make a realistic assessment of the part which is played (or which might be played) by literary fictions within the institutions of human life as a whole that "make-believe," or "pretence," are (when once we have entered the realm of literary fictions at all) rather closer to being definitions of certain kinds of literary *failure* than of

else are based on genres which are only marginally art at all. It is hard to resist the suspicion that on some unconscious level analysts of this kind may be trying to de-nature art, or to de-mystify it, in order to turn it into something which they find less threateningly ambiguous or less spiritually demanding than art – like, for example, logic.

[46] Lewis, p. 44.

the essential nature of literary success.[47] From a literary point of view, analyses of the truth-conditional kind must be almost entirely devoid of explanatory value: there may be certain kinds of truth within them, but in terms of getting at what literary art really consists of they are no more useful than would be (for example) analyses of a dance program in terms of geometrical theory or of the kinetic energy which might be expended in it: they do not help us to see what the art in question *is*.[48]

A literary fiction may take the form of a story, but it need not do so (the truth-conditional approach has no way of making sense of literature which does not tell stories). The fictional story, if there is indeed a story, may seem to link events together within something which resembles our actual (or what the truth-conditional analyst uncritically calls the "real") world. But what makes a story – or any literature which is not in the form of a story – significant is that it gives us insights into, or that it reveals or discloses, something of importance about what human life, or therefore reality as it is humanly experienced, is essentially like. This is not something which it makes statements about or tells us. What a poem or story says or tells us (if it says or tells us anything) is only the means by which it *shows* us something. What it shows us is something which we can recognize only through the sense of a certain rightness (the sense of a certain fidelity to the essential nature of human life or reality) which it gives us as we experience it. Robert Frost's poem "The Cow in Apple Time" tells us something about the behavior of a certain cow in rather unusual circumstances, but what it shows us is something about duty, temptation, security, exposure, and the life of the artist:

---

[47] Coleridge, for example, taking many of his ideas from Kant's *Critique of Judgement* and from Schelling, insisted on the metaphysical primacy of the distinction between "imagination" and "fancy" in literature as a way of discriminating between true and false art, and the main tradition of modern literary criticism has tended to follow him on this point.

[48] It would be possible to see in the "make-believe" analysis of literature a survival of something of the positivistic spirit of certain literary discussions of the 1920s. See for example I. A. Richards's distinction between "the scientific use of language" and "the emotive use of language" in *Principles of Literary Criticism* (London: Routledge and Kegan Paul, 1924). The "make-believe" theory of art was in fact tellingly dismissed by Collingwood in his section entitled "Imagination and make-believe" in *The Principles of Art* (pp. 135–38). Collingwood points out that "[m]ake-believe involves a distinction between that which is called by this name and that which is real," but that imagination as we use it in art "is indifferent to the distinction between the real and the unreal."

Something inspires the only cow of late
To make no more of a wall than an open gate,
And think no more of wall-builders than fools.
Her face is flecked with pomace, and she drools
A cider syrup. Having tasted fruit,
She scorns a pasture withering to the root.
She runs from tree to tree where lie and sweeten
The windfalls spiked with stubble and worm-eaten.
She leaves them bitten when she has to fly.
She bellows on a knoll against the sky.
Her udder shrivels and the milk goes dry.

The reason why (for example) we may want to re-experience a story whose "outcome" we already know is that it is not usually the story's outcome that we are primarily interested in[49] (it is hard to imagine a poetry reader pretending – yet once more – that he does not *really* know what is going to happen to Robert Frost's cow). We are more likely to be interested in it, and may therefore want to re-experience it, because it helps us to make sense of the disparateness or randomness of our ordinary experiencing by finding a certain kind of meaning or order within it. In so far as it is a story with an outcome, it symbolizes, through its own crises and resolutions, other kinds of crises and resolutions which we may have experienced in our lives, but without yet having properly comprehended. Such comprehension, when we have achieved it, will be likely to be less like the intellectual acquisition of a piece of knowledge and more like the emotional acquisition of a certain kind of disposition or habit. We can make no sense of the idea of literary art without the idea of the poetic symbol which both belongs to the actual world – which may either be, or (as in a fiction) appear to be, a part of the actual world we live in – and which also, through its inter-relations with other things which are simultaneously presented for our contemplation or attention, shows us something more universal about how that world coheres or has meaning in terms of our human aspirations or purposes. (When, for example, at the end of Joseph Conrad's novel *Under Western Eyes* the central character Razumov is harshly punished for his betrayals of his fellow human beings, we are likely to feel his punishment to be just and that it strengthens our sense of a certain moral order in human life. When the ancient mariner in Coleridge's "Rime of the Ancient Mariner" shoots an albatross but

[49] In the case of the Sherlock Holmes stories, of course, it may be.

subsequently recognizes the power of love to help him to expiate his crime, we are likely to be persuaded of the possibility of an at least partial escape from the kinds of affliction which such violations may bring upon us.)

An inescapable difficulty for the "make-believe" or "pretending" analysis of literature is that the stories of literary fiction and the stories of "real life" can in fact *alike* be revealing or aesthetically significant, and that this similarity between them is far more important than any difference in terms of whether or not the events or circumstances depicted in the story actually "happened to happen." The "make-believe" or "pretending" approach starts out from a relatively superficial problem or puzzlement – how do these fictional events which did not "really" happen relate to certain other events which did or do "really" happen? – and can therefore only end up with relatively superficial conclusions. *Referring* (or pretending to refer, or making-believe about referring) to the actual world is simply not one of the things which enters into the definition of any literary fiction or of any aesthetically revealing "real life" anecdote. Charles Taylor, in the course of an interpretation of Hegel's aesthetic theory, has written:

> But it can be that the descriptive dimension does not apply ... The work of art renders something, is faithful to something ... If this initial inspiration can be thought of as a sense of reality ... then the work of art is a vehicle of a higher awareness of reality ... It is non-arbitrary, it results from a striving to render something faithfully and in its entire depth. But it is not description. It is not to be judged by correspondence, since the initial dim, implicit sense is quite incommensurable with the articulate expression of insight.[50]

Roger Scruton makes a related point when he argues that an "abrogation of reference" is a necessary aspect of the aesthetic dimension of fictional writings.[51] Rather than being unreal or less real, the "world" (in so far as such a term may be appropriate) of the aesthetically significant fiction is a discerning of a deeper reality within the actual ("real") world in which we live – and in this respect is no different from any aesthetically significant story drawn from actual ("real") life. It is a common enough experience, in

[50] *Hegel*, pp. 474–75.
[51] See Roger Scruton, "Public text and common reader," *Comparative Criticism: A Yearbook*, 4 (1982), 85–105.

critical discussions of poetry or of prose fiction, to come upon events
or circumstances which are present in a fictional text because they
were present in a "real life" situation on which that text was based –
but to know nevertheless that from an aesthetic point of view these
things ought *not* to have been there: the events or circumstances
were actual, but from the point of view of the deeper truth to life
which the aesthetic standpoint is concerned to disclose, they were
not significant.

This does not mean that there can be no point in asking such
questions as "How many children had Lady Macbeth?",[52] on the
grounds that *Macbeth* is a fiction and that the fiction does not contain
within itself any mention of the number of the lady's children. A part
of the problem here is precisely to determine what *is* contained
"within the fiction itself," since the notion that such a question can
be settled by any simple appeal to "the words on the page" must
obviously be unsustainable. The question would make perfect sense
if it could be shown to be relevant to the play's drama (a new
psychological theory might find unexpected relationships between
the murderous propensities of parents and the numbers and ages of
their children). Likewise we can quite sensibly talk about the kind of
person that such a character as the J. Alfred Prufrock of T. S. Eliot's
(otherwise misleadingly-titled) poem "is," even though the words on
the page tell us little about him: it would be a pointless piece of
critical abstinence to avoid constructing a context of life around such
a character where the poem "itself" seems more or less to invite us to
do so. In the limiting case of a short lyric, the tone or diction alone
may entitle us to read many things into the poem which it neither
states nor mentions:

> For a moment she rested against me
> Like a swallow half blown to the wall,
> And they talk of Swinburne's women,
> And the shepherdess meeting with Guido.
> And the harlots of Baudelaire.[53]

Much, but not all, literature tells a story: it conveys a piece of history,
or of human life, and if the background of the story is filled out in

---

[52] See L. C. Knights, "How many children had Lady Macbeth?" in *Explorations*
(London: Chatto and Windus, 1958).
[53] Ezra Pound, "Shop Girl" (quoted entire).

sufficient detail we may be prepared to say that the text creates its own world. But if it does these things, it also does them, *qua* literature or art, without referring (or pretending to refer, or making-believe about referring) to any actual situations: when we are told, "One may as well begin with Helen's letters to her sister,"[54] or of "the great wings beating still / Above the staggering girl,"[55] or even how "There was an Englishman, a Scotsman and an Irishman," we know that we are in a fictional world or life and we have no inclination to ask whether, or where, any of these things happened (even though it is perfectly possible that they may have done so) – and we may have no inclination, either, to think of ourselves as pretending or making-believe that they happened, even though there might be cases where we would accept this as a description of one of the things we were doing in the process of reading a text. "Pretending" or "making believe" may in fact be one of the possible *means* – and for children, perhaps, may even be the commonest means – whereby we gain *access* to the meanings which stories offer us; it cannot be an essential part of the analysis of those literary meanings themselves. On the formal or linguistic level, what we are mainly entitled to say is that the literary fiction reveals something about the linguistic *terms* which are involved in its composition: on this level, poetic creation alters (and in its widest sense, is the only means of altering)[56] the logic of our language. On the material level, we can say that the poem reveals "before unapprehended relations"[57] between the various things which are mentioned in it, whether or not these things are in fact articulated into a distinct fictional "world" of their own. Like music (which has no logical dimension to distract us from a proper understanding of its function), it gives us an immediate presence of meaning; it shows us something about how the actualities of our "real" world really hang together.

It seems to be commonly enough accepted in modern literary-critical parlance that the fictions of imaginative literature may offer us alternative "worlds" in something like this sense. Schiller, in a discussion of the common underlying nature of the arts in general, gave the name *Schein* ("semblance") to the kinds of appearance

[54] E. M. Forster, *Howards End*, opening line.
[55] W. B. Yeats, "Leda and the Swan," ll. 1–2.
[56] See also above, chapter 3. We should remind ourselves, perhaps, that we are all of us, some of the time, poets.
[57] Shelley, *Defence of Poetry*, p. 103.

which what we should now think of as more realistic or descriptive-seeming kinds of art-work (as well as the ordinary things of the world when we view them under an aesthetic aspect) are by virtue of their aesthetic organization able to exhibit.[58] Art of this realistic kind has also been spoken of as creating an "illusion,"[59] or – in the particular case of literature – as conveying or evoking "virtual life."[60] A necessary requirement, if such a literary semblance or illusion or virtual life is to be worth contemplating or taking a reflective interest in, will be its ability to reveal something significant about how language, or therefore reality itself, coheres or is organized: a great many literary illusions or imagined worlds may be illusions only in the pejorative sense that – like certain other kinds of pretending or make-believe – they express (for example) only our egoistic fantasies or our urges to escape from the real problems of our lives. (Schiller distinguished clearly between the "semblance" [*Schein*] of true art and the counter-factuality or fantasy of mere "deception" [*Betrug*] – a distinction which the later critical distinction between "imagination" and "fancy" partly rests upon.[61] Recent philosophical analyses of literature from the "make-believe" standpoint have helped to re-confound these essential distinctions.) To the extent that literature may be world-evoking or life-evoking, and because it must by definition be genuinely revelatory, it is perhaps easy enough to understand the inclination of many poets and of certain philosophers to speak of it in terms of its power to transcend the world within which we do our practical daily living. The poet Rilke claimed that poetry offers us "the sensuous possibility" of new worlds and new times, and that "[t]he artist is eternity projected into time."[62] More philosophically, it has been suggested that "[t]he truth of art lies in its power to break the monopoly of established reality ... to *define* what is *real*. In this rupture, which is the achievement of the aesthetic form, the fictitious world of art appears as true reality."[63] The poem or fiction (and this will be a part of its definition whether it evokes a world of its own or

[58] Schiller, *Aesthetic Education*, Twenty-Sixth Letter and *passim*.
[59] See for example Ernst Gombrich, *Art and Illusion* (London: Phaidon Press, 1977), *passim*.
[60] See Susanne K. Langer, *Feeling and Form*, ch. 13 *et seq.*
[61] *Aesthetic Education*, Twenty-Sixth Letter, para. 5.
[62] See Rainer Maria Rilke, *Tagebücher aus der Frühzeit* (Leipzig: Insel-Verlag, 1942), pp. 38–39. See also his letter to Witold von Hulewicz of 13 November 1925.
[63] See Herbert Marcuse, *The Aesthetic Dimension* (Boston: Beacon Press, 1978), p. 9.

not) gives us the truth of, or the truth behind, the world which we ordinarily inhabit. It takes us to where the real life of that world lies; or as D. H. Lawrence said of the novel, "[i]t can inform and lead into new places the flow of our sympathetic consciousness, and it can lead our sympathy away in recoil from things gone dead."[64]

[64] D. H. Lawrence, *Lady Chatterley's Lover* (London: Penguin, 1960), p. 104.

5

SPILT RELIGION

Poetry raised to its highest power is then identical with
religion grasped in its inmost truth ...

SANTAYANA

1

In the opening sections of the *Critique of Pure Reason* Kant attempted
to lay bare the necessary conditions for our possession of self-
conscious experience – for our awareness of being surrounded by a
world of things or objects which endure quite apart from our perceptions of them – but did not in fact succeed in laying bare these
necessary conditions in their entirety. In leaving out from his philosophical picture any consideration of our necessary embodiedness,
he not only failed to give an adequate account of the full conditions
for the possibility of self-conscious experience, but he also deprived us
of any means of understanding how language itself – on which the
possibility of our self-conscious experience partly depends – should
have come into existence in the first place. How is it, we may find
ourselves wanting to ask, that we can ever *arrive at* the kind of
concept-using subjectivity which Kant simply took to be definitional
to the experiencing subject's nature – in other words, at the Kantian
"I think" which must be able "to accompany all my presentations"?[1]
A part of the answer must lie in the biological development, or from
another point of view the metaphysical transition, which takes place
from mere animal movement to a form of bodily gesturing which
gives us our most fundamental, or most primitive, basis for the

[1] *Critique of Pure Reason*, B. 131.

distinction between ourselves and that which is not ourselves.[2] It is on some such basis as this that all of the more specialized forms of gesturing which make up our various kinds of word-using and sign-using must depend. But how is it that this kind of bodily-gestural involvement with reality allows us to make the transition to a fully conceptually-articulated *language*, and to the relatively sophisticated forms of conceptuality which we in fact eventually come to possess?

Myth, and the mythic mode of apprehension of reality, seems in actual historical and prehistorical fact to be a universal stage through which the developing human linguistic consciousness passes, and the mythic mode of awareness can perhaps best be understood as another aspect or dimension of the corporeally-based awareness of our own powers and agency (and of their relationship to other powers and agencies in the world around us) of which gesture or dance is the most primitive manifestation. The seeming universality of myth and of mythic consciousness in primitive cultures[3] must on its own be a *prima facie* justification for supposing that these corporeally-based and pre- or incompletely-conceptual modes of awareness may be not merely a universal, but also a necessary, aspect of human existence on which our fully-articulated and discursive conceptual language has its experiential foundation. The mythic mode of consciousness is a vision of reality, and therefore also of men's place in reality, in which the perceived presence and activity of certain gods, super-human creatures, or cosmic forces, is accepted by a community as an adequate and satisfying perception of all the main events of the world as it is ordinarily experienced. Since all language must be based in gesture, and must arise out of a dawning consciousness of bodily power and its limitations,[4] the gods and cosmic forces which populate myths can perhaps best be seen as satisfying a pre-objective need to give form and comprehensibility to powers or agencies which lie outside our human power or agency and which it must be among the first functions of a developing language to try to come to terms with. It seems beyond question that it must be a necessary rather than an accidental fact that the personification or embodiment of these extra-human forces should take forms which bear resemblances or relationships to the forms of

---

[2] See above, chapter 2.

[3] The anthropological evidence is overwhelming.

[4] See above, chapter 2. Here, as previously, we are concerned with a metaphysical, rather than an evolutionary-temporal, kind of priority. See chapter 1, n. 25.

human embodiment itself. (If a mythic presence takes the form of an animal or other non-human being, it will be because of the relationship in which that animal or being's form and natural behavior stands to our own human form and natural behavior.)[5]

One of the most common misunderstandings of myth is to see it as a primitive form of *theory*, the purpose of which is to account for facts of nature which – with the development of more systematic and objective knowledge – we have subsequently learned to explain in more satisfyingly theoretical ways. On this interpretation, myth would need to be seen simply as a more primitive and more superstition-ridden form of natural science. The objection to this view is that in the world in which myth and mythic consciousness predominate there do not yet exist any objective "facts," or therefore any need for theories to account for such facts: there is nothing as yet which needs explaining, or (if we prefer to express it in that way), the world is already quite satisfactorily explained in the very way in which it is *seen* – through the myth itself. Myth is a form of integrated perceptual awareness which unites "fact" and "explanation," because it is a form of awareness in which fact and explanation have not yet become *dis*united. It is a mode of perception or of vision, rather than a mode of explanation, and myths which involve (for example) the heavenly bodies are not usefully to be thought of as failures to do the same kind of thing that the natural-scientific theories of Newton or Einstein successfully did later; nor, likewise, is the myth of Demeter and Persephone usefully to be thought of as a primitive way of explaining the earthly facts of seasonal change. Natural science itself, by contrast, is a mode of comprehension which must for its own purposes be as far as possible purged of the emotional or spiritual peculiarities of human perception: when nature has for these special purposes been dissociated into "facts" and theoretical "explanations" of facts, it will only be poetry (in the sense of the creative use of language in general – which in Shelley's words "comprehends all science" [*Defence of Poetry*, p. 136]) – which

---

[5] In the religion of ancient Egypt, for example, the earliest gods were locally-based animal gods such as the cats of Bubastis, the bulls of Memphis or the crocodiles of the Fayum basin. Gods with animal heads included the jackal-headed Anubis, the ibis-headed Thoth, and the hawk-headed Horus. In a progression from a religion merely of animal forces towards a religion of human ideals, there came the gods in human form such as Isis and Osiris, the gods of the cosmos such as Ra (the sun) or Hapi (the Nile), as well as such abstract gods as the gods of creation, truth or writing.

will allow us to reconstitute the unities that have been lost and to reinstate our human vision. But poetry, in this Shelleyan sense, must also lie at the very basis of all our language and consciousness, since it is the very principle by which language itself evolves and develops. It is hard to see any alternative to the view that myth is the form of not-yet-dissociated world-articulation that poetry – "[i]n the infancy of society," and when "language itself is poetry" (*Defence of Poetry*, p. 103) – must most primitively take.

Since there is little reason to suppose that human biological nature has significantly changed during the period in which our more rational and intellectual modes of comprehension have come about, it seems likely not only that myth and mythic consciousness must lie at the origin of our subsequently more fully-articulated linguistic awareness, but also that the most important structures of our fully-articulated linguistic awareness will continue to fall within the outlines of myth and will be most satisfyingly open to "explanation" through an assimilation to mythic patterns – some at least of which we share with the mythic consciousness of the ancient world. Such widely different orders of human comprehension as literary criticism, religious doctrine, psychoanalytic theory and anthropological research have all converged towards such a conclusion, and if it seems possible that we can be entirely (at least on a conscious level) unaware of mythic patterns when we view the world through our ordinary modes of awareness, the most likely reason may be that mythic patterns continue to lie at the basis of our over-all vision of the world, but that in our more ordinary modes of awareness we have been taught to look for other more rational kinds of explanation and to find them satisfying. If it should be claimed, as against this supposition, that children who are in the process of learning language do not in fact seem to pass through any stage which could be identified as mythic, a part of the answer may be that in a technologically-structured world – in which water comes out of taps, in which food is gathered from shelves, and in which warmth, light and darkness are controlled by switches on walls – it is hardly reasonable that they should be expected to; yet because we do not speak in overtly mythic ways where more objective or scientific modes of description might be appropriate, this does not mean that the over-all sense which we have of the world may not continue to be deeply mythic. Another and perhaps more important part of the answer may be that there is a sense in which the child's over-all comprehension of the world may indeed be mediated through myth, in so far as it may be on the basis of the myths, fables or fairy stories which we read or otherwise encounter in early childhood that our deeper (and perhaps subsequently rarely questioned) sense of the world's meanings may come to rest.[6] The child will be likely to interpret or make sense of his or her own situation in terms of *Beauty and the Beast* or *Cinderella* or *Jack and the Beanstalk* before he or she can begin to interpret or make sense of it in terms of psychology or sociology or economics. If we were to recognize this as a possibility, then it might be easier for us to recognize the possibility also that more objective or theoretical modes of explanation – such as natural-scientific ones, which in effect determine much of what we experience, as well as of what we do, in a technological world – may remain dependent on quite different, and ultimately more primitive, modes of comprehension which are essentially mythic.

Since all knowledge must be based in bodily awareness,[7] there is necessarily a sense in which "explanations" which embrace the peculiarities of human emotion and of the human spirit must be more profound than explanations – such as natural-scientific ones – which do not. Beneath our objective or scientific awareness, a mythic awareness may need to persist if we are to have any sense of meaning in the world at all: the configurations within which human life can most fundamentally be understood as falling – the patterns in terms of which it can most satisfyingly be *seen* – may in the end need to be understood as a matter not of scientific order but of a poetic order which is inherently mythic. Coleridge, taking such a view for granted, saw any possible "science of realities" as being necessarily and by definition founded in myth, and argued that "children [should] be permitted to read romances, and relations of giants and magicians and genii" because "I know no other way of giving the mind a love of the Great and the Whole";[8] but, being Christian, he

---

[6] This will include, of course, the whole of what is conventionally called "religious upbringing," as well as mythic or myth-based stories of other kinds. (There also need be no essential distinction – if the present argument is sound – between stories which are impersonally mythic and those which are the product of more conscious literary creation.)

[7] Only beings who are capable of intention, for example, could have the notion of cause, and our intentions must ultimately be informed by an awareness of ends in themselves – a way of seeing the world – rather than merely of practical means to such ends.

[8] Letter to Thomas Poole of 16 October 1797.

also insisted that "[t]he Bible alone contains a science of realities."[9] Emerson, more pagan in his inclinations, said of the primitive orders of perception which underlie our more rational kinds of language-using that

> [t]hese are not the dreams of a few poets here and there, but man is an analogist, and studies relations in all objects ... [N]either can man be understood without these objects, nor these objects without man ...
>   Because of this radical correspondence between visible things and human thoughts, savages, who have only what is necessary, converse in figures.[10]

This last contention echoes, and amplifies, Shelley's claim that "[i]n the infancy of society ... language itself is poetry" (*Defence of Poetry*, p. 102).

2

The possibility of our distinguishing ourselves from the "external" world around us depends on our possession of concepts of objects which endure quite apart from our perceiving of them, and it follows that in cultures in which mythic awareness predominates, and to the extent that their awareness is therefore pre-objective and pre-logical, there can be no state of fully-developed self-consciousness or of fully-developed awareness of an "external" world. The conditions for fully self-conscious or objective experience in the Kantian sense[11] will not have been satisfied. Within actual primitive cultures which are historically and anthropologically accessible to us, on the other hand, we shall necessarily (this being a pre-condition of such accessibility) find ourselves faced with a stage of development in which subjective and objective modes of awareness have already begun to detach themselves from mythic consciousness – but in which they have not yet made any significant progress towards an understanding of the world in terms of systematized knowledge or of abstract science. (The history of Greek culture from the quasi-mythic apprehensions of Homer to the survivals of primitive animism in the natural science of Aristotle might be understood as the history of an

[9] *The Statesman's Manual*, p. 49.
[10] R. W. Emerson, *Nature* in *Essays and Lectures* (New York: The Library of America, 1983), p. 21. This passage is also quoted by Barfield in *Poetic Diction*, p. 92.
[11] See *Critique of Pure Reason*, especially B. 131. See also Strawson, *The Bounds of Sense*, pp. 26–29.

emergence from such a phase.)[12] A cultural stage may later be
reached in which there exists a mode of objective consciousness,
together with a fully-developed sense of the self and of its relationship
to an "external" world – but in which there also continues to exist a
deeper mode of awareness beneath this self-consciousness which
remains mythic in its over-all patterns. The dualism of subjectivity
and objectivity is not, *pace* Kant, given with the human condition,
but can only be acquired as a result of a certain evolution of human
thought. (We might choose to say that it is acquired only with the
evolution of human thought as such.) What *is* given with the human
condition, by contrast, may be an integrated mode of vision which
comprises both the perceptual and the subjective or spiritual, and
which we can recapture from the viewpoint of a later cultural stage
only through a unifying and metaphorical effort of poetic imagination.[13] To understand more primitive – and perhaps more profound –
ways of experiencing the world, we are in effect obliged to make our
way back from what has come to be regarded in Western philosophy
as the axiomatic distinction between the experiencing self and the
experienced world. (To do this has of course always been seen as an
indispensable first step in all kinds of religious thought, as well as in
most kinds of non-Western philosophy.)

If we were to accept such a view of mythic consciousness, and in
particular if we were to accept that myth cannot usefully be regarded
as a primitive (and as it happens untrue) variety of theoretical
explanation, a question which we would then be obliged to consider
would be that of how far, and in what sense, the notion of "truth" is
properly to be predicated of the mythic mode of consciousness at all.
On what basis, if any, can a particular mythic interpretation of the
underlying realities of our modern spiritual life be offered or accepted
as more "truthful" or more "explanatory" than any other? If we
should be asked by an interpreter of human behavior to understand
some particular aspect of our conduct in terms of the lives or stories
of Oedipus, or of Buddha, or of Jesus of Nazareth, on what basis are
we to decide whether or not such an explanation is to be seen as true
or illuminating? Attempts to engage with such questions in a

---

[12] For Aristotle there are forty-nine gods which manifest themselves in appropriate
ways through the phenomena of nature.

[13] This is the imaginative activity which Coleridge called "esemplastic," meaning
"making-into-one" (*Biographia Literaria*, vol. I, p. 168), or which Shelley called τὸ
ποιεῖν (*Defence of Poetry*, pp. 100–1).

seriously critical way have in practice largely been confined to the realm of art – especially poetry or literature – and of art criticism, rather than having been recognized as constituting an identifiable dimension of thought or province of inquiry in their own right. Other modes of study or comprehension which have worked in this area have very largely disqualified themselves from a critical standpoint, precisely because of their lack of any real openness to questions about the nature and criteria of mythic truth. Traditional religion has been one such approach, but has always dogmatically privileged certain myths – such for example as the myth of Christ crucified and reborn – and has thereby prejudged questions of truth in a way that largely precludes critical discussion. Psychoanalytical theory has explored some of the modes of untruth or of deception, but has often leaned uncritically on a very few (as with Freud) or very many (as with Jung) myths or imaginative archetypes without showing any real sensitivity as to whether these are in fact – or as to which of them are in fact – the most revealing patterns which are to be found in the human psyche. (Where psychoanalysis has been more "existential," it has in effect led inquiry back towards the relatively unsystematized mythic patterns of ordinary life and of imaginative literature.) The approach of social or cultural anthropology has been very similar in many respects.[14]

In the history of the West, and only comparatively recently, it has been in the area of literature and literary criticism that questions of the truth or satisfyingness of myth have come the nearest to being pursued in an unprejudiced and critical spirit. They have been pursued in a critical spirit simply because they constitute an inherent aspect of questions about the truth or satisfyingness of literature itself. A literary fiction or poem (in this respect it can be seen as comparable with a piece of music, or any other art-work) gives us an immediate presence or presentation of ontological meaning. It reveals in a more concentrated or intense way what ordinary life reveals in its expressive aspects. In giving conceptual form to such

---

[14] Claude Lévi-Strauss, for example, can seem both empirical in his method and at the same time – as he himself comes near to acknowledging – notably subjective in his classifying of what empirical research discovers. See for example his Overture to his four-volume *Mythologiques* (in *The Raw and the Cooked: Introduction to a Science of Mythology*, trans. John and Doreen Weightman [New York: Harper and Row, 1969], p. 6), where he speaks of his own categorizing of myths as "itself a kind of myth." Derrida criticizes this aspect of Lévi-Strauss in *Of Grammatology*, part II, ch. 1.

disclosures, literature *inscribes* reality, and is a concentrated or intensified expression of life as it occurs at the distinctively human level.[15] Where perceptual and emotional meaning were once unified primitively, the literary fiction or poem is the form which this unified perceptual and emotional inscription of reality takes within the rational framework of the modern understanding. The literary critic's activity rests on the premise that certain literary texts participate in reality more fully than others do – that as "symbols" in the Coleridgean sense[16] they inscribe more of the "felt life"[17] of the world in which they were created than certain other texts do, or that to a greater extent than other texts they present "[an] original plenitude [where] form and meaning [are] simultaneously present to consciousness and not to be distinguished."[18] The critic's function is to find ways of recognizing and judging the epiphanies of literature which, like those of life itself (Joyce borrowed his use of the term "epiphany" directly from theology), are partial disclosures or revelations, or spiritual "matches struck unexpectedly in the dark."[19] At times, literature will be seen to be inscribing reality within mythic forms which are easily recognizable – and it will be a part of the critic's function to decide how far such an assimilation is a true disclosure or imaginative "explanation" or how far it may be merely falsely "literary." (Many writers have questioned whether the explicit or deliberate use of myth, or of certain particular myths, is any longer authentically possible. Keats wondered in his preface to *Endymion* whether he had not "in too late a day touched the beautiful mythology of Greece." Hopkins believed that "[t]he Greek gods are a totally unworkable material; the merest frigidity, which must chill and kill every living work of art they are brought into."[20] Philip Larkin more than once referred to certain poets' reliance on "the myth-kitty.") At other times, it may not be so easy to assimilate the "before unapprehended relations" which are revealed in a work

---

[15] Certain other arts or media, including drama, film and television, must of course in their own ways be capable of doing this also.

[16] See *The Statesman's Manual*, p. 30.

[17] See for example Henry James, "The art of fiction" in *The House of Fiction*, ed. Leon Edel (London: Rupert Hart-Davis, 1957).

[18] See Culler, *Structuralist Poetics*, p. 19. For Culler and all structuralists or post-structuralists, the belief in the possibility of such a "plenitude" can only be a pre-Saussurian illusion.

[19] See Virginia Woolf, *To the Lighthouse* (London: Dent, 1938), p. 186.

[20] Gerard Manley Hopkins, letter to Robert Bridges of 17 May 1885. We may of course suspect Hopkins of special pleading for his own preferred mythology.

to any identifiable mythic pattern; yet they will perhaps necessarily have some place in a mythic order – even if it is not the critic's main function to determine that place[21] – simply because the same may be necessarily true of any aspect of our spiritual life whatever. Since myths must always be open to the assimilation of new contingent experience, our mythic patterns themselves, like our concepts themselves, must always be indefinitely open to historical change.

3

Modern theology, for the most part basing its arguments on Kantian premises, has increasingly come to abandon the notion of God as a necessary entity who has His being above or outside the natural world and whose existence can be in some way established by human reasoning. For Kant, there are no valid arguments which could demonstrate the existence of such a being,[22] and even if there were any such arguments there would be no consequences which could be drawn from them with regard to our proper behavior or obligations. That such a supernatural being commanded or enjoined us to behave in certain ways could not provide a basis for morality, since to follow such commandments or injunctions would involve what Kant calls the "heteronomy" of our will and would not be truly moral. In morality it is only our autonomous free choice in the pursuit of duty which is valid.[23] (It should be noted, perhaps, that the Kantian transcendental self, of which in the *Critique of Pure Reason* nothing could be known,[24] has here taken on sufficient substance to possess a moral identity and to be able to have dealings with the world of behavior.) The basis for any belief in God must rather be that if we are to be rational in our pursuit of duty, then we must believe such a pursuit to be realistically possible and that we are not in fact living in a world which renders such a pursuit senseless.

---

[21] A recently common way of not doing literary criticism was underwritten by Northrop Frye when he implied that the mythographic locating of a literary text within the context of the rest of literature was the extent and limit of the critic's interest in myth. (See *Anatomy of Criticism*, Third Essay.) There is in fact no room for questions about literary truth within Frye's classifications.

[22] See *Critique of Pure Reason*, B. 612–70.

[23] See for example *Fundamental Principles of the Metaphysic of Morals*, trans. T. K. Abbott (London: Longman's 1909), pp. 51–59; *Critique of Practical Reason*, trans. T. K. Abbott (London: Longman's, 1879), p. 169.

[24] See for example B. 157.

"Therefore it is morally necessary to assume the existence of God,"
Kant concludes – attaining to monotheism with a single fictional
bound[25] in which modern theologians have usually been more than
ready to follow him.[26] It is our autonomous moral conscience alone
which reveals to us God's will.

Accepting these arguments, an influential part of modern theology
(ignoring the alternative and more "aesthetic" road which was long
ago opened by Schleiermacher) has proposed that we should re-
interpret religion not as an account of reality but as a pattern of
"religious values,"[27] where this means a freely chosen embracing of,
and commitment to, certain aspirations or ideals of behavior. In
identifying religion with choice or commitment rather than with a
picturing of reality, the modern theologian has usually been very
willing to associate himself with the conclusion of a writer such as
Kierkegaard when he tells us: "[f]or God is that all things are
possible, and that all things are possible is God."[28] (Such theologians
as Nicolas Berdyaev, Martin Buber, Reinhold Niebuhr or Paul Tillich
might all, with certain reservations, be comprehended within this
post-Kierkegaardian tradition.) Where traditional religion, and certain theistically-based philosophies (for example Spinoza's), have
tended to subordinate the individual to a reality which embraces and
transcends him, the modern theologian, like the existentialist philosopher, places his main emphasis on the point of discontinuity
between the experiencing individual and the world within which he
makes his choices or commitments. Don Cupitt, one of the more
prominent among current exponents of this "internalized" view of
religion, has written that

> we are and have been for many generations in a position where not
> one single religious doctrine (of the sort that mentions supernatural
> beings, events and causes) can be established by a reputable intellec-
> tual method ... Yet it is also the case that there are many obviously

---

[25] Kant's more philosophical-looking word for our legitimate use of such ideas as God,
freedom and immortality – which cannot be rationally grounded but to which we
must accord an "as if" status – is "regulative." See *Critique of Pure Reason*, especially
B. 647, 672 *et seq.*

[26] See *Critique of Practical Reason*, p. 222; *Religion Within the Limits of Reason*, trans.
T. M. Greene (New York: Harper, 1960), p. 142; *Critique of Pure Reason*, B. 836,
843–44; *Critique of Teleological Judgement*, trans. J. C. Meredith (Oxford: Clarendon
Press, 1938), pp. 113, 119.

[27] See for example Don Cupitt, *Taking Leave of God*, p. 82.

[28] Søren Kierkegaard, *The Sickness Unto Death*, trans. W. Lowrie (Princeton University
Press, 1941), Part First, III, A, (b), (2).

admirable and beautiful religious attitudes, values, practices and so forth which ought not to pass away altogether. Here are some of them:

> It is good that one should appraise oneself and one's life with an unconditional religious seriousness that tolerates no concealment or self-deception...

> It is good that one should come to transcend the mean defensive ego and learn absolute disinterestedness and purity of heart.

> It is good that one should commit oneself to existence in religious hope and receptivity to grace.

> (*Taking Leave of God*, p. 82)

Cupitt has argued – for example – that "*the doctrine of God is an encoded set of spiritual directives*," that these directives (which may also be called "the religious requirement") entail "a ceaseless struggle after self-transcendence,"[29] and that "the resurrection is a religious reality – that is, a state of the self and a form of salvation" and that "compared with this tremendous religious reality, 'historical' claims about walking corpses and empty tombs are foolish and irrelevant" (p. 45). What were once wrongly taken as descriptive stories about the creation of the world, the fall from innocence, the resurrection, or the after-life, are instead properly to be taken as moral allegories about the religious possibilities which are available to us here and in the present.

An approach to religion along these lines might be defensible if we could rest securely in Kant's moral arguments and in the Kierkegaardian intensification of them in terms of choice or commitment; but this is in fact something that we are not in a philosophical position to be able to do. The post-Kierkegaardian theologian's "internalized," or "de-mythologized" (meaning that the scriptural myths are not to be taken literally) version of religion must certainly be defensible in so far as it transforms what were sometimes understood as descriptive accounts of the origins of the world, along with certain other mythic stories related to those accounts, into some kind of disguised expression of behavioral ideals or aspirations.[30] "Religious" stories or

---

[29] *Taking Leave of God*, pp. 100–1; author's italics.

[30] The term "de-mythologization" (*Entmythologisierung*) has mainly come to be associated with the writings of Rudolf Bultmann, and is used by him primarily in the sense of the purifying of a religious tradition of its extraneous mythological elements. See for example his *Theology of the New Testament*, trans. K. Grobel (New

fictions, like any other aesthetically significant stories or fictions, cannot sensibly be interpreted as descriptions or representations of the world, and if there is to be a valid meaning for them it must be an "internalized" meaning in just the same way that the meaning of any kind of aesthetically significant fictions whatever must be an internalized meaning. But this religious meaning must also, from another point of view, be *just as little* an internalized meaning as the meaning of any other aesthetically significant fictions is an internalized one. Fictions reveal reality – and in this sense are not usefully to be thought of (as the post-Kierkegaardian theologian might wish to think of them) as being "internal" *rather than* "external." They merely reveal reality in a way which does not involve their being literal descriptions or representations of reality. When Blake proposed that "[a]ll deities reside in the human breast,"[31] he was not thereby denying the sense in which they might also be disclosures or revelations of the true nature of the world in which we live.

The "internalized" conception of religion which modern theology has widely accepted has given us an "internalization" which is cut off not only from literal description but also from any kind of evocation or presentation of the "external" world at all. It offers us instead – and interprets religious meanings as being little other than – a spiritual pressure towards commitment, self-scrutiny and the pursuit of moral ideals, but in a stripped and bare landscape which has been almost entirely shorn of any natural context or content. As a corrective to worldly possessiveness or manipulativeness this may have a religious value, but to construe it as the very essence of religious awareness itself can only be to confuse spiritual means with spiritual meanings. It is in the meanings of aesthetically significant fictions that the essence of religion lies – as well as of course in the ways in which such meanings may be "applied" to practical life. These meanings are meanings of, or within, the world itself, and the value of the de-mythologizing insistence that these are not literal or representational meanings is mainly that it allows us room in which to recognize that they must be treated as existential or ontological meanings instead. The practical results of religious "internalization" may very easily be to leave us with an imagistically

York: Charles Scribner's Sons, 1951). Some version of de-mythologization must nevertheless always have been at work whenever religious scriptures have been read in a non-literal way.
[31] See *The Marriage of Heaven and Hell*, in *Complete Writings*, p. 153.

denuded or deserted landscape, along with a generalized commitment towards the transcending of all the baser or more instrumental
aspects of our natures; yet this commitment seems in practice to
amount to a renunciation not merely of worldly desires or pos-
sessions but also of the greater part of worldly experience itself – in a
way which might precisely help to equip us for living in an actual (as
opposed to merely a metaphorical) desert landscape. The underlying
motivations which have led theologians towards this kind of world-
repudiating austerity – over and above a perhaps worthy enough
measure of anti-instrumentality – have rarely been explored,[32] and
their almost wholly contingent or accidental nature with respect to
the true essence of religion has never yet been properly recognized.
There is in fact no way in which a taste for austerity or for desert
landscapes follows from the abolition of the metaphysical "God of the
philosophers."[33] Nor does the Kantian-"autonomous" notion of
religion itself entail any particular commitment to monotheism,
Christianity, or the privileging of the teachings of the historical Jesus.
If there is to be an argumentative basis for such beliefs, other
arguments than those of religious internalization or religious de-
mythologization will need to be found for them. (Of course not all
modern theologians are Kantians. But almost all modern theologians
in the post-Kierkegaardian tradition have tended to transpose the
language of revelation into the language of morality and to give new
and moralistic interpretations to such words as "God." Bultmann, by
contrast, does not himself see de-mythologization as a process of
moral de-coding: following Heidegger, he regards such a view as
based on a false – we might say "subjectist" – conception of human
awareness, and insists instead that myths must be interpreted
"existentially." Bultmann's view of myth as a mode of vision of
reality, which is only with difficulty to be metaphorically interpreted
or paraphrased, is philosophically sound. Objections might nevertheless be made to his actual critical practice, and in particular to his
extreme selectiveness – he gives us a New Testament from which
Hell is absent – as well as to his misanthropic fervor. More importantly, we might question the religious privileging which he is
prepared to accord to these particular texts. Bultmann has in fact
opened the way for all and any myths whatever to take on an

[32] Some of the most significant explorations are perhaps to be found in Nietzsche's *The
Genealogy of Morals*.
[33] See Anthony Kenny, *The God of the Philosophers* (Oxford: Clarendon Press, 1979).

existential force for us – but has chosen not to follow that way himself. Any text, read selectively enough, can be made to yield almost any meaning – as literary critics have long known, but as they have also recognized as imposing a heavy demand on their own tact and openness to the truth. The problem for the theologian is that he has usually staked a good deal on the results that his texts will produce in terms of their relationship to the way we live our lives. The unavoidable problem with the *via negativa*, for the theologian, is that there can be no knowing where it might lead – except, as John Keats saw, towards the fullness of our development as human beings. If we were to take a more Nietzschean – not to say "deconstructive" – view than is usually adopted in theology, we might find ourselves wondering why so much austerity, humility, self-scrutiny and self-rejection have found their way into modern religious thought, and why so little dance, play, animal vitality or creative power.)[34]

The radical problem which faces the post-Kantian and post-Kierkegaardian theologian is that myths seem in practice to be quite ineliminable from human perception or vision, and that their function in human life appears to be a primal, and an irreplaceable, expressive one. Myths occur universally throughout human experience – not merely as a primitive residue which has not yet been superseded by rationality[35] or true belief, but seemingly as a continuing substratum of the basic structures of our experiencing. The well-intentioned but rather impoverished handful of precepts which the religious de-mythologizer finds himself left with is the result of the fact that to de-mythologize has by him usually been interpreted as meaning to *de-allegorize* – in other words to seek for the extractable, and separately expressible, moral content of the texts he studies. To do this is to misunderstand or to violate the true nature of myth – which is that it is originally, and must subsequently most valuably continue to be regarded as, a form of *poetic symbol* rather than a form of allegory. (Bultmann is in fact making this point about religious scriptures when he insists that they must be interpreted "existentially." That the distinction between "symbol" and "allegory" is not absolute – but is a matter of degree – has sometimes been held to

---

[34] These Nietzschean qualities have been emphasized by Nicolas Berdyaev – see for example his *Slavery and Freedom* (New York: Scribner's, 1944) – but the orientation of his thinking nevertheless remains moralistic rather than mythic or revelatory.

[35] Compare Peacock, "Four ages of poetry."

undermine the kind of discussion which is being engaged in here.[36]
Owen Barfield gave the answer to this line of argument when –
replying to a critic who had proposed that "the faculty of fancy ... is
one of Coleridge's chimeras ... Fancy is nothing but a degree of
imagination" – he said: "Now this is only true in the sense that every
'chimera' in Coleridge's or any other brain is itself a 'degree' of
universal reality, and therefore does not differ 'in kind' from a polar-
bear or a toothbrush. The objection to the rarefied Eleatic standpoint,
which reduces all 'kinds' to 'degrees,' is not its falsity, but its inutility
... On the contrary, the distinction between Fancy and Imagination is
one which ought to be particularly emphasized in an age like ours"
[*Poetic Diction*, pp. 201–2].)

It is true, and by now agreed by almost all parties to the debate,
that myths cannot usefully be understood as descriptive hypotheses
about the origins and nature of the world; but it is also true that the
kinds of meaning or truth which myths embody cannot simply be de-
coded into abstract notions of responsibility, self-scrutiny or moral
commitment without undergoing an impoverishment exactly similar
to the loss of meaning which occurs when the substance of a novel or
a poem is reduced to a selection of general statements (what the
novelist or poet is "trying to say."). The kinds of meaning or truth
which myths embody are a part of, as well as the original basis of,
our ontological *vision* of the world, and if we are to come to terms
with the nature of these truths we shall need to allow ourselves to be
led in the direction of greater concreteness and imagistic plenitude
rather than in the direction of greater formality and abstraction. The
myths of our culture – which include those myths of other cultures
which are imaginatively accessible to us – contain, and can therefore
reveal, the fullest possible meaning of the world in which we live,
rather than merely the meanings of the kinds of desert landscape
which may appeal to those with (perhaps psychologically or politically compelling, but nevertheless religiously indefensible) reasons
for wanting to repudiate that world.

Not least among the philosophical problems which face the
modern theologian's move towards religious internalization is that it
is hard to see how on the internalized view of religious belief there
can be any such thing as a *religious* way of life or a *religious*
dimension of experience at all. The internalized account of religion,

---

[36] See for example Hazard Adams, in his otherwise richly suggestive study *Philosophy
of the Literary Symbolic* (Tallahassee: University Presses of Florida, 1983).

while being able to tell us certain – essentially ethical – things about what it calls "the religious requirement" or the need for behavioral authenticity, can in fact tell us nothing whatever about the true nature of the world itself or of religious *vision*. It can tell us nothing about the kinds of concepts or images in terms of which the world which we inhabit needs most authentically to be seen, and can therefore tell us nothing about what the notion of self-overcoming, or self-transcendence – which has been made central to the doctrine of internalization – can really amount to. The reason for this is that there is no way in which the self which is to be overcome or transcended can be defined in terms of its grasp, or lack of grasp, of a reality or truth (or ἀλήθεια) which our pursuit of self-transcendence might reveal to us. The doctrine of religious internalization simply gives us no theory or account of truth or reality at all. What it does instead (thereby assuring itself of an air of religiousness for those who cling to old-fashioned ideas about what religiousness consists in) is to take over, unexamined, certain traditional notions of spiritual self-improvement – among them the overcoming of acquisitiveness, the rejection of materialism, the mistrust of the flesh, the avoidance (in effect) of most of the available richness of human experience – and to take it for granted that the successful pursuit of these goals must be equivalent to spiritual progress. The philosophical root of the difficulty here is that the internalization doctrine can only base itself on a notion of a human self or subjectivity which is already *given by definition* (as it was for Kant or Kierkegaard); it can give us no notion at all of a self which must come into being (as it has to for much traditional mysticism, for poets such as Keats, or for philosophers such as Heidegger). The concepts of "religion" or of "transcendence" are in fact entirely meaningless when they are severed from the concepts of truth or vision, and in continuing to use these concepts the religious internalizer is borrowing the charisma of conceptual vestments to which he is no longer philosophically entitled. The world in which we live, on the religious internalizer's view, is as devoid of any inherent – or at any rate of any disclosable or revealable – meaning as it is for the most religiously sceptical Camusian-"absurdist" or Sartrean-existentialist.[37] Nothing at all, on such a view, can be said about what the world to which we belong

---

[37] See for example Albert Camus, *The Myth of Sisyphus*, trans. Justin O'Brien (London: Hamish Hamilton, 1955); Jean-Paul Sartre, *Being and Nothingness*, trans. H. Barnes (London: Methuen, 1957).

– and to which we are joined by such joining as may be possible for us – is really like.[38] Meaning can only be provided by what we choose or commit ourselves to *do*, so that all meaning – if there is to be any meaning at all – must in effect be man-created. (Nietzsche, not surprisingly, saw the claim to believe in God under such philosophical conditions as a form of moral idiocy.)

The Kantian–Kierkegaardian "voluntarist" tradition must therefore be abandoned as a blind alley for theology. Its blindness is almost literal, since it really only offers us a different version of the "absurdist" view of an inherently meaningless universe – or simply a different stance towards that same meaninglessness. For the Kantian–Kierkegaardian, there are no meanings to be *read* in the world, and the language of religion (principally of Christianity) is wrenched into new meanings to express a moral faith in the face of this apparent blankness. (The main defect of Kant's philosophy – as of Kierkegaard's, and also of Nietzsche's – from this point of view, is that the notion of "faith" needs to be built in to our account of human existence at the level of life itself, rather than having its basis only in the province of moral or religious behavior: every organism, in living life at all, is exemplifying a "faith," or some sub-human analogue of faith, that life is not senseless. Schiller begins to define this faith as it arises at the distinctively human level with his notion of the aesthetic.)[39] If there is to be such a separately identifiable discipline as theology at all, it can now coherently be based only on the recognition of the true nature of myth, and must be a matter of critical exploration of the principal mythic structures which the texts (in the widest sense) of our culture present us with. In this respect theology must be understood to be properly speaking an aspect, or a facet, of the discipline of artistic – and particularly of literary – criticism. From the mythographic standpoint the theologian has hitherto done little more than to conduct a defensive moral operation based on a narrow selection from among the available mythic texts – where the available mythic texts must in fact comprise the whole of our known mythology, including the whole of our poetry and literature (along with the more ordinary modes of awareness of

[38] The etymology of the word "religion," however obscure, would seem at least to suggest that to be religious means to concentrate more on the ways in which we are joined to the world than on the ways in which we are not.
[39] See *Aesthetic Education*, especially Twenty-Third Letter.

which these are an intensified expression).[40] If we are willing to
acknowledge the mythic origin and basis of all our more conscious
and rational modes of comprehension, then the move from a
descriptivist to an expressive understanding of myth may necessitate
the rehabilitation of substantial areas of myth which have never
received any special recognition or privileging within major religions
– as well as a more open-minded and heuristic choosing from among
those which have. Myths are born, and they also die. One of the most
powerful and dominant myths of Western culture is the (comparatively modern) Faust story, which – in its later versions where Faust is
saved rather than damned for his pursuit of experience – is in many
ways an exact inversion of Christian teachings. The myths of a
primal fall, and of a redemption through love, have an undiminished
appeal for the modern imagination – but usually in pagan rather
than in Christian forms. The great myths of sexual love, and of the
conflict of civic duty and erotic passion (again comparatively
modern, in such versions as *Antony and Cleopatra*, or *Carmen*) are
essentially pagan rather than Christian in their spirit. The myths of
Orpheus, or of Prometheus, which shape much of our modern
awareness, have no very persuasive analogies in Christian literature.
Not least of all, our modern preoccupation with the social role and
destiny of women has only the most fragile basis in any ancient
mythology: the archetypal story (as in *Cinderella*) of the woman who
dreams of being rescued or saved by a man is a part of our post-
medieval awareness – while the story of the woman who seeks to
define and to control her life in her own terms is perhaps as yet only
struggling to be born. All of these "anti"-Christian myths, along with
many others, and with the countless variations and proliferations to
which we find it harder to give any very definite names, make up an
essential part of the structure of our modern awareness.

We are now in fact at a cultural point of choice where religious
faith must go in one of two directions. Either (1) religious faith must
"de-mystify" itself altogether and must be altogether reborn as
ethics. It is this alternative – toiling in the wake of generations of
"humanism," and despite its adherence to certain familiar shreds of
religious vocabulary – that the doctrine of religious internalization is
in effect urging us to accept. Alternatively (2) religious faith, having
abandoned the idea of a descriptive relationship with reality, must

[40] Walter Kaufmann, in his *Critique of Religion and Philosophy* (London: Faber and
Faber, 1959), accuses theologians of "gerrymandering."

learn to see itself in terms of a symbolic-revelatory relationship with reality instead. It will then be obliged to look for whatever support it can find among the *actually revealed spiritual meanings* of the world. The first of these two alternatives must be inauthentic, since we are now in a philosophical position to see that "transcendence" is a necessary part of our human spiritual condition, because it is a necessary part of human existence itself. It follows from our necessary embodiment or incarnation in the world that we are *in* the world before we experience or understand the world, and that all our experience or knowledge is a partial disclosure or revelation out of a surrounding obscurity. Subjectivity must be seen as something which we *come into*, rather than as something which we are equipped with fully-fledged and by definition and independently of any questions about our apprehension of truth or reality. We are therefore left with the second alternative as the only possible authentic direction for the future development of our religious faith. As Christianity (to take the example of the religion which is most strongly institutionalized within our modern Western culture) becomes de-descriptivized in the direction of more expressive modes of interpretation, a pressure can be expected to be felt for other quite alien or – to Christianity – hostile mythic structures to be able to assert their claims. And this is indeed what we find. The crumbling back of Christianity into equality of disbelief with other myths in the modern world has been accompanied by a simultaneous up-grading of the status of myth as a mode of insight into human life. With the increasing, if still tacit, recognition of myth as the primal form both of perception and of language, and with the decline during the modern period of any general acceptance of philosophical *arguments* in support of the orthodox religions, the tendency to see imaginative literature and its "epiphanies" as special, sacred or sacralizing manifestations within a de-sacralized world – a tendency which began with the Romantic reaction against the mechanistic philosophies of the seventeenth and eighteenth centuries – has persisted and grown. As the Bible (for example) has come to be re-classified on many library shelves as "foreign poetry," it is to the poetry or literature of our own culture (and to what is naturally and undistortedly accessible to us from other cultures) that we have increasingly found ourselves looking for a *re-mythologizing* of our spiritual landscape. This cultural move towards re-mythologization is philosophically well-founded, because it is mainly poetry or literature (with a degree of help from the other arts, as well as from psychology, anthropology and the history of religion) which can enable us to discover *which* myths do in fact have a hold on our imagination.

4

The essential inward identity of poetry and religion – leaving aside the more superficial conceptual divergences which have grown up (and which have been institutionalized) on the basis of a misunderstanding of that identity – has been memorably if only half-comprehendingly registered by the poet and critic T. E. Hulme when he dismisses the greater part of the thought and literary theory of the Romantic tradition as "spilt religion." Hulme is arguing against Romanticism from what he regards as a "classical" view of the nature of life and literature, according to which our knowledge of truth, and of the nature of humanity, would be something to which we can have access quite independently of our transient experiential intuitions:

> One can define the classical quite clearly ... Man is an extraordinarily fixed and limited animal whose nature is absolutely constant...

> The classical view is absolutely identical with the normal religious attitude. I should put it this way: That part of the fixed nature of man is the belief in the Deity.[41]

What we must recognize instead, and in contrast to the view which Hulme himself expresses, is that the tradition of Romantic literary thought in fact largely succeeds in defining the essential nature of poetry itself (including many of the recommendations which Hulme himself makes in his opposition to unnecessary obscurity), and that *all* poetry, and not only the poetry of the Romantic tradition, is "spilt religion." More importantly (this being the truth implicit in all doctrines of religious "internalization" or "de-mythologization" – which themselves radically question the notion of the "fixed" nature of man), we need to recognize that poetry is religion *properly so spilt*. There can in fact be no wholly "classical" literature, in the sense that there can be no permanent and unchanging framework of comprehension to which we can have access quite independently of our

[41] T. E. Hulme, *Speculations* (London: Routledge and Kegan Paul, 1960), pp. 116–18.

temporally-based intuitions and mythic awareness. It is because this necessity went for so long unrecognized that we might now be justified in speaking of the entire pre-Romantic phase of our literary tradition as the "pre-history" of literature, and of literature as having come of age only with the Romantic recognition (here we are indebted to Schiller and Hegel) of its historical or temporally-based nature.

A philosophical view which recognizes the essential affinity of literature and religion – but which has no need of a notion of classical orthodoxy, and which defines the distinction between literature and religion directly in terms of their relationships to practical life – has been expressed by Paul Ricoeur:

> It is necessary that we must first lose contact with ordinary things in order maybe, thanks to this liberation of language, to redirect it once more towards some more deeply rooted forms of experience...
>
> I would say, in turn, that I see religious language as some kind of poetic language ... I should say that what makes the difference between poetry and religious kerygma[42] is that poetry opens ways for my imagination to try, ways of thinking, ways of seeing the world, under the rule of play – that is to say, I am not committed. I have only to open my imagination.
>
> Religious experience, whatever it may be ... adds at least three elements ... which add to this capacity of opening an element of commitment. Secondly [sic], the belonging to a certain community. And, thirdly, the attempt to connect that to a social, ethical, political stance.

Ricoeur nevertheless does not suggest why poetry must only ever be play, or why religion might not also sometimes be play; and as though to point up his distinction he goes on to argue that

> there is nothing like a poetical system to which each poet would claim to contribute. So the idea of contributing to a body of truth is completely alien to my mind.
>
> Even in fictional works, we could not say that a novel can be added to the other novels and that this constitutes a kind of ... body of fictional work ...[43]

---

[42] The Greek word κήρυγμα has connotations both of revelation and of rather imperious obligation.

[43] Paul Ricoeur, interviewed in *The Manhattan Review*, 2 (Summer 1982), 11–16. See also his *The Rule of Metaphor*, trans. Robert Czerny with Kathleen McLaughlin and John Costello (University of Toronto Press, 1977).

Despite the partial validity of this argument (the system to which, for example, a scientist might "claim to contribute" is after all very different from the system to which a poet might "claim to contribute"), Ricoeur has here over-emphasized the uniqueness of particular poetic works or visions at the expense of any recognition of the over-all unity of literature or of mythology – or therefore, on a deeper level, of the over-all unity of human nature itself.[44] The literary *tradition* to which most poets would be more than ready to "claim to contribute" is in fact nothing other than a particular historically- and culturally-based perspective on such an over-all unity. Ricoeur has defined his position in a way which excludes the possibility that poetry and religion might both encompass "play" (just as and for the same reason that all our conceptually-articulated language must be supposed to have its basis in certain forms of expressive gesture)[45] or that they might both stand in a close relationship to such demands as may be laid on us in our pursuit of authentic behavior within our ordinary lives. In our comparatively unsuperstitious modern culture, neither poetry nor religion will be likely to stand in any very simple relationship to action or "commitment" – which is not to say that their cultural influence, through their ability to change the very way in which we conceptualize our world, may not be profoundly moral.[46] (In the case of a mythology such as paganism the relationship between poetry and action may perhaps be relatively uncomplicated: the ideal will be an evident aspect of what we see, and our commitments will arise more or less naturally out of that vision. With an inherently more "improbable" mythology such as Christianity[47] we shall perhaps have a greater need for a "kerygmatic" notion of commitment and for explanations of where our obligations lie.) If there is to be a clear distinction between poetry and religion in a culture in which the nature of fictions has come to be properly

---

[44] For an almost opposite view of literature to Ricoeur's, in this respect, see Northrop Frye's *Anatomy of Criticism*.

[45] See above, chapter 2.

[46] When the poet Robert Frost was asked in the 1930s if he did not think that "art can be considered good only as it prompts to action" his answer was: "How soon?" See James M. Cox (ed.), *Robert Frost: A Collection of Critical Essays* (Englewood Cliffs NJ: Prentice-Hall, 1962), p. 18.

[47] "Why ... should the Hellenic world have broken with the creations of its own genius, so plastic, eloquent, and full of resource, to run after foreign gods and new doctrines that must naturally have been stumbling-blocks to its prejudices, and foolishness to its intelligence?" (George Santayana, *Interpretations of Poetry and Religion* [New York: Scribner's, 1900], p. 77).

understood, it will need to be a distinction in terms of ritual or – if there is to be such a thing in such a culture – "ecclesiastical practice,"[48] rather than in terms of moral commitment or obligation. The "play" of both poetry and religion alike, in such a culture, will not be a merely fanciful and truth-free sporting with images, but a play of the imagination which never wholly loses its awareness of the dimension in which the play of our imagination makes possible the disclosure of reality or truth (ἀλήθεια). We shall perhaps feel less need for the special and rather morally heavy notion of the "kerygmatic" if we recognize that all truth whatever must have its foundation in our concrete and empirical intuitions; and we shall perhaps be likely to "play" less whimsically or egoistically if we recognize that this play of our imagination is in fact the only opening on to reality that we can hope to have. (It follows from our necessarily embodied nature that "mind" or "spirit" can never be expected to come to a full and conceptually-definite self-knowledge – which would set poetry free to be mere fancy – but must always conduct a part of its operations in an area which, in Kant's phrase, "language ... can never get quite on level terms with or render completely intelligible" [Critique of Aesthetic Judgement, sec. 49]. It may also perhaps be useful to remind ourselves that our relationship with reality or truth is an active as well as a passive one, that language-using acts are themselves deeds which create history, and that religion is likely to be as much concerned with power as it is with idealism or moral goodness.)

A view of the relationship between poetry and religion not unlike that of Ricoeur was expressed rather earlier by George Santayana, when he proposed that poetry and religion "differ merely in the way in which they are attached to practical affairs,"[49] and that "[o]ur religion is the poetry in which we believe." Belief does indeed entail commitment –

> [t]he inspirations of religion demand fidelity and courageous response on our part. Faith brings us not only peace, not only the contemplation of ideal harmonies, but labour and the sword

– and this is true even for a pagan culture:

[48] This will of course mean any kind of public ceremony, rite, pageantry, or communal affirmation, rather than something as narrow or specific as the Christian notion of a church or of worship.

[49] Interpretations of Poetry and Religion, p. v.

Besides the gods whom we may plausibly regard as impersonations of natural forces, there existed others; the spirits of ancestors, the gods of the hearth, and the ideal patrons of war and the arts. Even the gods of Nature inspired reverence and secured a cultus only as they influenced the well-being of man ... The vividness and persistence of the figures of many of the gods came from the fact that they were associated with institutions and practices which controlled the conception of them and kept it young.

(pp. 26–27)

But for Santayana poetry and religion need to be seen as potentially identical in their nature, rather than as mutually exclusive, and as being "concentric" (p. 5) with all the other imaginative expressions of human nature, including reason:

[T]he rational poet's vision would have the same moral functions that myth was asked to fulfil ... [I]t would employ the same ideal faculties which myth used confusedly.[50]

Santayana's view leaves open the possibility that as we come to grasp the true nature of fictions – and as we recognize them to be expressive aspects of a single realm which is human nature – the distinction between "poetry in which we believe" and poetry in which we do not believe may become less sharp; also that "play" may itself become a more recognized aspect of religion, and that our present religious systems may come to be replaced by – or transformed into – something less narrowly imperious and more catholicly reflective of the real demands of authentic living.

5

The first decline of mythic awareness in the face of the progress of rational thought occurred in the ancient world with the decay of Hellenic paganism. This god-abandoned world was saved from its own directionlessness and lack of spiritual purpose by the rise of Christianity. A comparable mythic decline took place in the modern world in the face both of the rational thought-systems of seventeenth-century philosophy and science and of the manipulative or technological thought-habits which were their inseparable accompaniment. One of the most important differences between the modern and the ancient worlds may be that we have become too

[50] Santayana, *Reason in Art* (New York: Scribner's, 1905), p. 224.

unsuperstitious and careful in our modern thought-patterns to be able again to accept such a total and exclusive religious revelation as Christianity was, with its conspicuous omission or rejection of so many aspects of our religious instincts or of our imaginative ideals. This imaginative exclusiveness must itself have been a part of the reason for Christianity's modern decline; and it has now perhaps even begun to seem likely that Christianity was never imaginatively well-suited to the inquiring and open-minded temperament of the Hellenic world, and that after two millennia it is still the pagan religion of the ancients which makes up our deepest spiritual language. Santayana has suggested that

> [ancient mythology] remains still the mother-tongue of the imagination and, in spite of all revolutions and admixtures, is the ... language of art and poetry, which no other means of expression has superseded.
>
> (*Interpretations of Poetry and Religion*, p. 56)

A similar view is implied by Mircea Eliade when he argues that

> [t]he progressive de-sacralization of modern man has altered the content of his spiritual life without breaking the matrices of his imagination: a quantity of mythological litter still lingers in the ill-controlled zones of the mind

and goes on to propose that

> [t]hese degraded images present to us the only possible point of departure for the spiritual renewal of modern man. It is of the greatest importance ... to rediscover a whole mythology, if not a theology, still concealed in the most ordinary, everyday life of contemporary man ...[51]

The third great advent of spirituality to the Western world was Romanticism; and the religious scriptures that Romanticism brought with it are the rich, various and multi-faceted visions of imaginative literature. The new understanding of aesthetic experience and symbolism provided by such writers as Goethe, Schiller and Schelling – or in England by Blake, Coleridge and Shelley – laid a foundation for a view of poetry or imaginative literature as the most essential

---

[51] Mircea Eliade, *Images and Symbols*, trans. Philip Mairet (London: Harvill Press, 1961), p. 18. Jung, although his notion of a "collective unconscious" would entail the availability of all myths to all cultures, is committed to an essentially similar view.

mode of language and therefore as the primary mode of human ontological comprehension. The artistic practice of Romanticism was already moving well in advance of such philosophical ideas, and it is Romanticism as a spiritual movement which stands in the same relationship to modern rationality and to the decline of Christianity as Christianity stood in to ancient rationality and to the decline of paganism. From the point of view of its spiritual content Romanticism may seem to be a revival or liberation of long-buried imaginative dispositions which have their earliest basis in ancient myth, and therefore to be in its essence a form of neo-paganism. This is a view of it which would in fact very largely be justified. But Romanticism is also, like Christianity (and unlike paganism in its earlier forms), a vision which is inherently historical, and which points to the human possibility of becoming a better creature and a better spirit (or we may prefer to say, to the notion of "God" as manifest in the development of human history);[52] and because of its historicality, there is no limit to the range of literary or religious symbolism which the Romantic view of literature or of religion may allow us to embrace from any period or region of our culture. The once-unified – however "wild" – vision of Christianity[53] has in the modern world split apart into abstract science and moral allegory; and this splitting-apart must in fact in large measure be the result of Christianity's mythic implausibility and of the simultaneous pressures of abstract reason. But if it is in part the pressures of reason which have brought about religion's decline it is also only the false aspects of religion (above all its pretensions to compete in the realm of fact and understanding) that reason has been legitimately able to undermine.

The great and unprecedented strength which Romanticism – unlike either paganism or Christianity – can call upon in its re-spiritualizing of our cultural world is that reason itself is never again likely to exercise the same fascination or the same destructive power as it has succeeded in exercising in earlier centuries in relation to

[52] "Process theology" has begun to develop this notion, but has also remained largely tied to monotheistic conceptions and has not yet acknowledged the indispensability of the realm of myth as a basis for its ideas. When it does so, it will discover that the province of process theology and the province of literary criticism are substantially identical.

[53] "[T]he believer in any adequate and mature supernatural religion clings to it with such strange tenacity and regards it as his highest heritage, while the outsider, whose imagination speaks another language or is dumb altogether, wonders how so wild a fiction can take root in a reasonable mind" (Santayana, *Interpretations of Poetry and Religion*, p. 88).

religion or myth. In the Hellenic world, abstract reason was a novelty, and its powers seemed themselves to be almost as magical as those of the religious notions which it displaced; the rather more rapid rise and development of modern rationality was not altogether different in the relationship in which it stood to medieval Christianity. Leaving aside the possibility of a massive re-primitivization of world culture, we are unlikely again to be able to see reason in such an all-redeeming role, or therefore again to be able to expect reason entirely to displace or to replace our capacity for religious or mythic faith. We are now in a position to grasp – as neither Plato nor most of the subsequent mainstream of Western philosophy were yet in a position to grasp – that abstract reason is no less centered on ourselves and on our embodied and human nature than is the imagination from which it springs, or than are the imaginative fictional creations which we refer to variously as poetry or as religion. Reason is our imagination employed to make the best conceptual sense that we can of the whole of reality; but there are also imaginative fictions which invest that reality with a local habitation and a name,[54] and which link our phenomenal experience (which for Plato and for many of his successors was of small significance) directly to our vision of reality by means of symbolic or metaphorical relationships.

It was the absolute decay of paganism in the face of abstract reason which made possible its absolute supersession by Christianity; but we live now in a less absolute world, and we are unlikely again to experience that impassioned highlighting of particular images or symbols as the center for a cult and a pattern of ritual which made Christianity possible. With the better understanding of fictions and symbolism which is now available to us, it may at last be possible for us to set aside both the absoluteness of reason and the absoluteness of Christianity and to re-familiarize ourselves with those mythic agencies which have for so long been operative in the depths of our imagination, along with such newer spirits or presences as recent

---

[54] The poet's eye, in a fine frenzy rolling,
   Doth glance from heaven to earth, from earth to heaven;
   And as imagination bodies forth
   The forms of things unknown, the poet's pen
   Turns them to shapes, and gives to airy nothings
   A local habitation and a name.
                    (Shakespeare, *A Midsummer Night's Dream*, V, i, ll. 12–17.)
   Compare Kant, *Critique of Aesthetic Judgement*, sec. 49.

centuries may have added to their pantheon. The great absolute myths – of God, of the center, of eternity[55] – may perhaps do us no great spiritual harm in so far as they are ways of focusing our idealism; but in the modern world they are unlikely to do us any great spiritual good either, since they encourage us towards intolerance in our ideas or extremism in our behavior, and can give us little guidance in the great middle ground of action and commitment within which we live our actual reflective lives. The help that we need in this middle ground will be available to us above all from the fictions of literature – from those fictions which we feel to be idealistically credible or real, rather than from those which our better judgement enables us to see to be superficial, sentimental, frivolous or fantastic. All cultures possess myths which express absolute spiritual ideals, and most cultures possess myths which represent the actual earthly difficulties of attaining to such ideals. But in all cultures except that of the modern West, these myths are almost invariably more allegorical and abstract, as well as less relevant to our own culture from the point of view of their content, than the kind of flexibly realistic fictions which we now need. Santayana has remarked of the oriental mind – for example – that

> [it] has no middle; it oscillates between extremes and passes directly from sense to mysticism, and back again; it lacks virile understanding and intelligence creative of form.
>
> (*Interpretations of Poetry and Religion*, p. 96)

This is of course consistent with the fact that art and literature – which are what we now need for our spiritual regeneration – are taken less seriously in the East than in the West. It also explains why even so undogmatic a religion as Buddhism, alone and unsupported by any structure of mythic or aesthetic comprehension, must be an inadequate spiritual creed for the modern Western mind. To the extent that its tendency is negative with respect to all established modes of thought (in this it is the most quintessential and drastic of all religions), Buddhism is in practice inclined to emphasize a contentless mysticism rather than the fullness of lived experience, and to concentrate on getting us into a proper spiritual state for life's journey rather than on giving us any actual help along the road. Tolstoy, in the course of formulating his own view of the relationship

---

[55] See for example Eliade, *Images and Symbols, passim.*

between art and religious perception, suggested that the Buddhists, no less than certain other religious extremists, "have gone so far as to repudiate all art."[56]

As a general conclusion of the present argument it could perhaps be claimed that if we are now to accept the need for a re-mythologization of religion in terms of the myths or stories which are authentically accessible to our imagination, then the only religious *scriptures* we shall need (as distinct from such formal rules or codes as we may need for the regulation of our practical conduct) will be the poetry or literature to which our own culture gives us access. This may entail the abandonment of some of the less relevant – therefore less true – myths or stories of the traditional religions and their replacement by other myths or stories which lie culturally nearer to hand. (Matthew Arnold, in "The study of poetry,"[57] suggested that poetry was on the way to replacing religion as our main source of spiritual nourishment and that "[m]ore and more mankind will discover that we have to turn to poetry to interpret life for us, to console us, to sustain us." His efforts elsewhere to explain why this should be so, on the other hand, tend to be philosophically confused. Heidegger, in his later writings, gives a central place to poetry as the means to the sustaining or the restoration of our spiritual vision – but seems to hold an unreconstructedly priestly view, derived from his own meditations on Hölderlin, of who can count as a poet. Wallace Stevens thought that poetry must "take the place / Of empty heaven and its hymns,"[58] and proposed that "[a]fter one has abandoned a belief in God, poetry is that essence which takes its place as life's redemption."[59] The present argument shares this view and is concerned to provide it with a philosophical basis. Not all critics who have been influenced by Stevens have registered that in his later work he regards fictions as a discovering of order in the world rather than as an imposing of order on it – which is to say that they are essentially religious in their nature.) From a literary standpoint, we could sum up much of the present argument by saying that it is only by swallowing theology whole that literature can be restored to a faith in its own proper spiritual meanings. The destiny of a system

---

[56] Leo Tolstoy, *What is Art?*, trans. Aylmer Maude (London: Oxford University Press, 1930), p. 125.
[57] See Matthew Arnold, *Selected Prose* (London: Penguin, 1970), p. 340.
[58] Wallace Stevens, "The Man with the Blue Guitar."
[59] Stevens, *Opus Posthumous* (London: Faber and Faber, 1959), p. 158.

such as Christianity would in that case have to be allowed to rest on how far it was able to sustain or to regain its place within the free "fictional space" of the myths or stories which our culture makes accessible to us.[60]

The next advance of liberal theology may therefore be to acknowledge that we cannot rest any longer in the Kantian–Kierkegaardian voluntarist position – but to insist that we can instead rely on something which is very close to it and in part derived from it. The *embodied or incarnational* view of the human condition does not deny human moral or religious autonomy in the Kantian sense: it merely situates that autonomy within the processes of biological and cultural life, and sees such autonomy not as a matter of free choice within an inherently purpose-free universe (this being the Kantian–Kierkegaardian view, with which the early-Sartrean and "absurdist" views have much in common) but of authentic vision within a world which world-envisioning humanity itself inhabits, and which it can articulate only with a necessary obscurity and through symbolic or mythic modes of integration. Where the Kantian–Kierkegaardian view endorses, and even demands, an *in vacuo* commitment against all natural constraints (if nature makes us desire something, then that thing cannot *per se* be moral or religious[61] – a teaching which conveniently falls in with most traditional religion's hatred or rejection of the life of the body), the embodied or incarnational position allows us to understand our human transcendence less as a war with nature and more as a purification or harmonizing of our natural inclinations. Instead of fighting the beast within himself,

---

[60] That this fictional space is not properly speaking free, in so far as our awareness may always be open to ideological falsification, is a consideration which does not need to be dealt with in this context. Our consciousness may indeed be falsified, but our aesthetic awareness nevertheless remains our only starting-point for arriving at truth, and there is nothing of general human benefit to be gained by pretending otherwise. As a first move, we can perhaps try to comprehend the traditional religious appeal to scriptural authority as itself a form of ideological falsification. (Blake remarked in *The Marriage of Heaven and Hell*: "thus began Priesthood ... Choosing forms of worship from poetic tales," and devoted much of the rest of his writing to this question. His insights have been developed more systematically by Marxism, by Nietzsche, and by the ideology-theorists of the Frankfurt school.)

[61] Nietzsche remarked rather severely of this phase of Kant's thinking that "Kant became an idiot." "What destroys more quickly than to work, to think, to feel without inner necessity, without a deep personal choice, without *joy*? as an automaton of 'duty'?" (*The Antichrist*, trans. R. J. Hollingdale [London: Penguin Books, 1968], sec. 11).

man can set out to become an animal at a higher level.[62] On this view, although there is indeed a human nature, human nature becomes something which needs to be explored, rather than something which we can (either impressionistically, or on the basis of an antiquated scriptural authority) simply decide to think the worst of. A religious dialogue with Romantic, Marxist, or other historically-grounded philosophies of nature might on this basis at last begin to become imaginable.

[62] This is of course a notion which is familiar in the poetry or philosophy of many "prophetic" writers (for example Nietzsche or Lawrence).

6

TOWARDS A TRUE
POST-MODERNISM

I require of you only to look.

ST. TERESA OF ÁVILA

1

Despite the unwillingness of post-structuralist theorists themselves to recognize the fact, the most central of the doctrines of post-structuralism – above all that the significations of our human signs are *relational*, and that there is no "self" except as a part of *structure* – can in the end be seen to be disguised (we might perhaps do better to say travestied) versions of certain very traditional religious notions. The first of these doctrines, if we view it from only a slightly more traditional angle, means that the world is One. The second – if we are to be allowed to retain any concept of a "self" at all – means that we are members one of another. Through its elimination, for linguistic purposes, of the subject–object view of human life which is basic to post-Cartesian "humanism," post-structuralism opens the way to a truly aesthetic comprehension both of language and of imaginative literature. By taking the focus of attention away from the author and by placing it on the words themselves – an emphasis which is in fact already central to Romantic philosophy since the time of Schiller's *Aesthetic Education* – post-structuralism provides us with a new way of abstracting our treatments of expressive language from the instrumental or manipulative functions of the practical world. In the realm of poetry or literary fictions it is indeed, as Heidegger says, "language that speaks," and not man [as conscious *ego*] himself.[1]

---

[1] See above, chapter 4, n. 31.

That post-structuralism provides us with no "self" with which to exercise our expressiveness – a self not in the sense of a conscious *ego*, but of any pre-conscious structure of care or concern – must be regarded as a culturally disastrous but perhaps still corrigible defect. The choice which now faces the theorists of post-structuralism is that of either joining in the enterprise of helping to explore or to map the *living* structures of truth within our culture (the living physiology of literature or criticism, rather than the ahistorical and dead anatomy of it); or if they persist in their pursuit of the merely "ludic" charm[2] with which post-structuralism has so far been associated, of coming to seem at best a rather whimsical cultural diversion and at worst yet another stage in the history of humanity's reality-rejecting pride or hubris.[3]

There is a need, in the present de-sacralized state of our culture, for a truly essential or revelatory poetry or literature. Such a literature need not involve an elevation of Arnoldian "high seriousness" *above* the ludic: in Schiller's sense of the ludic, all art is play. But it will nevertheless need to be an art which goes beyond the ludic in its currently mainly trivial interpretations. An essential literature of the kind which is now most culturally needed will in effect be what Schiller called a "naive" poetry rather than what he called a "sentimental" poetry;[4] but this is only to say that a truly aesthetic poetry is more profound and more culturally regenerative than a partly manipulative poetry, even if both – like symbol and allegory, or like imagination and fancy – comprise only different degrees of creativity or expressiveness. Such a literature will not be play for its own sake, or because play is the only thing we can now do; but nor will it – as for example allegory does – lend itself easily to moral de-coding and therefore to a practical over-riding of its aesthetic power. It will give few footholds for these and other varieties of philistine misinterpretation. In prose fiction this will perhaps mean a renewal of the kind of poetic integration which modernists have sought and admired in novels since *Madame Bovary*: a re-commitment to the "airplane" novel which must fly, as opposed to the "train" novel

---

[2] Or Barthes might say, orgastic "absorption."

[3] To explore the living structures of truth within a culture is of course likely to mean the uncovering of profound ideological conflicts. Since these are in fact the source of our political thinking rather than simply consequences of it, we should perhaps not be too quick to translate them into already-familiar political terms.

[4] See Schiller, "On simple and sentimental poetry" in *Works* vol. 6 (London: George Bell and Sons, 1910).

which has an engine at the front and which can haul an indefinite number of coaches.[5] In verse – where the problems are less severe, since poets have usually been instinctively drawn towards the poetic – it may involve nothing more than a re-subscription to the aesthetic principles by which Romanticism defined itself against the literary manipulativeness of earlier centuries (making Shakespeare an honorary Romantic in the process), and to which the strongest modern verse traditions – not least those of modernism itself – have adhered ever since. If such a literature is to be called naive, on the other hand, it will not be naive in the most usual sense of that word, since it will be written out of an educated, sophisticated and historically aware sensibility – but one which is prepared to rely on its unconscious creative imagination to make the best use of its education or sophistication, rather than allowing them to assume a controlling function on the page.[6] Such a sensibility first came clearly into the light with the Romantic movement, was the most central and vigorous growth-point of modernism, and continues to survive through the later twentieth century (however much it may also have become choked by various ranker kinds of literary vegetation).

The modernist movement in literature explored the nature of literary meaning and meaningfulness in a variety of iconoclastic and sometimes deliberately anarchic technical ways. Its most central concern, even so, was to find or to re-assert the basis of human existential meaning in what Romanticism had called the poetic symbol (itself necessarily mythic) and what modernism itself variously called the Symbol or the Image.[7] Modernism's central function, and the real achievement of its technical explorations, was to remind us once again of the aesthetic nature of fictions. For this

5 This useful piece of semiology was invented by the novelist David Garnett. We might now add to it the "fairground" novel, to accommodate some of what is currently called "post-modernist" fiction.

6 Ideas like these may help us to understand Tolstoy's requirement (which has sometimes been held to be contradictory) that art should be comprehensible to ordinary people and yet should also convey a deep and complex vision. The artist must *know* everything, yet must *be* simple.

7 "The artist seeks out the luminous detail and presents it," said Ezra Pound. "His work remains the permanent basis [perhaps we should here read "permanently the basis"] of psychology and metaphysics" (*The New Age*, 7 December 1911). Artists, he astutely discerned, are the antennae of the race. See also Frank Kermode's illuminating discussion of Symbol and Image in literary modernism in *Romantic Image* (London: Routledge and Kegan Paul, 1957).

purpose it was necessary to fight over again the battle with artistic representationalism (and therefore also with didacticism, self-expressivism, and every other kind of manipulativeness) which had been the main concern of Romantic aesthetics. A novelist like Flaubert may have been an arch-Romantic by virtue of his concern with the poetic organization of his fictions, but he could easily be mistaken for a representationalist as a result of his naturalistic concern with their surface detail. Much of the prose fiction of the nineteenth century was content to do its job without making any systematic effort to transcend the status of the "large loose baggy monsters" which Henry James diagnosed some of the more acclaimed novels of the nineteenth century to be.[8] One of literary modernism's most effective ways of breaking with the looseness or bagginess of the nineteenth-century novel (as well as of some of the looser and baggier kinds of nineteenth-century verse) was by drawing attention to the fictionality of fictions. That the truth of art is not representational, and that it resides instead in the power of art to inscribe new imaginative unities rather than to manipulate already-familiar descriptive counters, can be more easily seen when the truth of art is presented by non-naturalistic methods. The technical innovations of modernism – its renderings of the stream of con- sciousness, its systematic derangements of the senses, its narratorial shifts of time and of viewpoint, its frequent aggressions against its own medium – are all ways of breaking with the world's appearances and of finding deeper meanings behind the "common sense" spatio-temporal framework of superficial representation. That this can also be done by a process of selection – as with the Flaubertian novel or the Imagist poem – is centrally important for literary philosophy; but the need for modernism arose partly from the fact that by these methods alone it cannot so easily be seen that this is what is being done.

One of the main theoretical by-products of modernism's technical virtuosity was the widely-accepted view that art need not be in any sense "realist." When coupled with the concepts of semiology or linguistic structuralism, this was effortlessly transformed into the view that there is no such thing as "realist" for art to be. In this way the literary movement which is now called "post-modernism" was enabled to take on a high degree of literary-theoretical respectability

[8] See Henry James, preface to *The Tragic Muse* (New York: Charles Scribner's Sons, 1910), p. x.

and thereby to acquire an entire new generation of practitioners and adherents. That "realism" is an incoherent and delusive notion is in fact the founding principle of so-called "post-modernist" literature. What this delusive philosophical premise obscures is the fact that a genuine realism of the imagination has always been – and has widely been recognized to have been – a defining characteristic of literature whether before, during, or after the modernist period. The most important distinction that we now need to hold on to – and it is one which cuts across almost all questions of technical method – is the distinction between writing which is art because it attains reality, and writing which is not art because it does not attain reality – whether (1) because it fails to, or (2) because it claims that no such attaining is possible.[9] A true post-modernism can now be defined only in terms of a head-on rejection of the nihilism which would reduce literature to the status of a game with itself, or with language, on the illusory ground that there is "nothing outside the text" for it to relate to.

2

Poetry or imaginative literature is our most fundamental mode of inscription of reality, and it is imaginative or imagistic concreteness that we need for this purpose, rather than the abstractions either of the intellect or of the traditional systems of religious symbolism. Blake was right when he said that the artist paints "not Man in General, but most minutely in particular" (*Complete Writings*, p. 465), and that – as contrasted with true imagination or vision – "Fable and Allegory are a totally distinct & inferior kind of Poetry" (p. 604). Coleridge was right for similar reasons when he claimed that "[f]ormal similes" are not to be excluded from poetry, but that they do not suit the highest kind of poetry.[10] For a true post-modernist sensibility, the kind of nature poetry which uses animals as emblems of human qualities will seem secondary to the kind of nature poetry which recognizes that animals are literarily interesting in their own right. (Blake's own allegories, which include poems about animals, should perhaps best be understood as his rather eccentric way of doing philosophy.) When once we have recognized that the concretely experiential – which means the local and the embodied – is our primary means of access to reality, we shall also

[9] (1) can of course easily enough be rationalized into (2).
[10] See his letter to William Sotheby of 10 September 1802.

recognize that the value of allegory or of a literature which depends essentially on a structure of formal simile must be mainly philosophical or satirical.[11] One of our most effective forms of modern satire is science fiction, and it depends for its effectiveness not on the imaginative credibility of its "future" world, but on being tacitly de-allegorizable into a commentary on our present world – on which it gains a purchase by borrowing from it a key range of psychological habits or mythic structures.

The centrality to modern literature of lyric poetry, or of any writing which works imaginatively on words with its bare hands to convey a "felt" experience, is a consequence of this necessary primacy of embodied and located awareness.[12] The poetic lyric is what Northrop Frye has called "the genre which most shows the hypothetical core of literature" (*Anatomy of Criticism*, pp. 271–72), and it shows this core because its very nature is to be a poetry of mood, and because mood is our primary way of being open to the world. In a discussion of Heidegger's conception of "being in the world," Walter Biemel points out that

> [w]hat was commonly overlooked or misunderstood – indeed actually suppressed – in the [rationalistic] view of man ... is the immediately revelatory function of attunement. Let us take a simple example. We become acquainted with a man. Our first reaction is determined by the attunement or mood ... which his presence near us evokes. This general feeling may undergo changes in the course of a longer time spent in his company, or it may alter suddenly. But this does not diminish the significance of moods as a primary mode of being open. The revelatory character of dispositions is the exciting thing about this phenomenon, which cannot be grasped, however, so long as moods are understood merely as a kind of "psychical coloring" constituting the "irrational" part of the psyche.[13]

The poetic lyric may be strikingly non-naturalistic, as when T. S. Eliot writes that "[e]very street lamp that I pass / Beats like a

[11] Jonathan Culler nails himself irretrievably to the wrong mast when he writes that the poetic symbol "is a natural sign in which [signifier] and [signified] are indissolubly fused, not an arbitrary or conventional sign in which they are linked by human authority or habit. Allegory, on the other hand ... is the mode which recognizes the impossibility of fusing the empirical and the eternal and thus demystifies the symbolic relation ... " (*Structuralist Poetics*, pp. 229–30). For Culler and other post-structuralists, all mystery is mystification.

[12] See also above, chapter 3.

[13] Walter Biemel, *Martin Heidegger*, trans. J. L. Mehta (London: Routledge and Kegan Paul, 1977), p. 47.

fatalistic drum," or when he experiences as "[h]is soul stretched tight across the skies / That fade behind a city block" what to a more naturalistic mode of perception might seem only to be the striations of a city sunset.[14] A lyric may reach into more reflective moods, as in poems like Gray's "Elegy in a Country Churchyard" or Wordsworth's "Tintern Abbey," or in such briefer meditations as Rilke's "Herbsttag" ("Autumn Day"):

> Herr: es ist Zeit. Der Sommer war sehr groß.
> Leg deinen Schatten auf die Sonnenuhren,
> und auf den Fluren laß die Winde los.
>
> Befiehl den letzten Früchten voll zu sein;
> gib ihnen noch zwei südlichere Tage,
> dränge sie zur Vollendung hin und jage
> die letzte Süße in den schweren Wein.
>
> Wer jetzt kein Haus hat, baut sich keines mehr.
> Wer jetzt allein ist, wird es lange bleiben,
> wird wachen, lesen, lange Briefe schreiben
> und wird in den Alleen hin und her
> unruhig wandern, wenn die Blätter treiben.

> Lord, it is time. The summer was too long.
> Lay now thy shadows over the sundials,
> and on the meadows let the winds blow strong.
>
> Bid the last fruit to ripen on the vine;
> allow them still two friendly southern days
> to bring them to perfection and to force
> the final sweetness in the heavy wine.
>
> Who has no house now will not build him one.
> Who is alone now will be long alone,
> will waken, read, and write long letters
> and through the barren pathways up and down
> restlessly wander when dead leaves are blown.[15]

The lyric may become almost detached from particular location, as in a poem like Mallarmé's "Brise Marine" ("Sea Breeze") where the

---

[14] T. S. Eliot, "Rhapsody on a Windy Night," and "Preludes."
[15] Translation by C. F. MacIntyre, from *Rilke: Selected Poems* (Berkeley: University of California Press, 1962), p. 39.

only sensible answer to the question "Where are we?" is perhaps that we are in a poem:

> La chair est triste, hélas! et j'ai lu tous les livres.
> Fuir! là-bas fuir! Je sens que les oiseaux sont ivres
> D'être parmi l'écume inconnue et les cieux!
> Rien, ni les vieux jardins reflétés par les yeux
> Ne retiendra ce coeur qui dans la mer se trempe
> Ô nuits! ni la clarté déserte de ma lampe
> Sur le vide papier que la blancheur défend,
> Et ni la jeune femme allaitant son enfant.
> Je partirai! ...

The flesh is sad, alas! and I have read all the books. To escape! To escape far away! I feel that birds are drunk to be among unknown foam and skies! Nothing – not old gardens reflected in the eyes – will keep back this heart soaking itself in the sea, O nights! nor the desolate light of my lamp on the empty paper, defended by its own whiteness, nor the young wife feeding her child. I shall depart! ...[16]

What the varieties of the lyric all have in common is that they are a poetry of mood, and that they must inter-relate ultimately with more ordinary and naturalistic modes of awareness: if we are to be able to experience a street lamp beating like a fatalistic drum, we must also know in more ordinary and naturalistic ways what a street lamp and a drum are. The lyric itself will in turn "feed back" into everyday life and alter the nature of our naturalistic perception. The lyric of the descriptively naturalistic surface is the Imagist poem, which – if we extend it beyond its particular lyrical "instant of time" – is continuous with the first-person naturalistic story or novel.

The mood-based and personal quality of the lyric encompasses the greater part of what has been called "confessional" poetry.[17] The autobiographical nature of much confessional poetry is in fact literarily irrelevant to it (although the poet may of course find it more emotionally trustworthy, as well as easier, to use his life as material): as far as its nature as poetry is concerned, it could all equally well

---

[16] Prose translation by Anthony Hartley, from *Mallarmé*, in the Penguin Poets series (London: Penguin, 1965), p. 29. Some of Blake's earlier lyrics, which are often called "Symbolist," might perhaps be seen as poems of this kind.

[17] The term "confessional poetry" was invented by M. L. Rosenthal. See for example his review of Robert Lowell's *Life Studies*, "Poetry as confession" (*Nation*, 189: 21 March 1959, pp. 154–55); also *The New Poets* (New York: Oxford University Press, 1967) and *The Modern Poetic Sequence* (New York: Oxford University Press, 1983).

have been made up. The importance of the confessional poem is that it is the quintessential poem of experience – of personal experience from a lived-in and concrete situation. Discussing the "confessionality" of Robert Lowell's *Life Studies* poems, Gabriel Pearson has pointed out that "in explicitly treating his life as materials, he was not making his poetry more personal but depersonalising his own life ..." There is a particular need for this kind of regeneration of public or mythic meaning out of private experience in the present state of our culture:

> Lowell's verse assumes that ... we are all [now] private men and that this is a fact of the utmost public urgency. His verse explores a condition in which public worlds have to be built and sustained out of the rubble of purely personal existence.[18]

This is perhaps the insight which Yeats experienced rather earlier in his poem "The Circus Animals' Desertion," where – finding that his more abstract symbolic inventions had abandoned him – he decided

> Now that my ladder's gone,
> I must lie down where all the ladders start,
> In the foul rag-and-bone shop of the heart.

Δ – striving for impersonality

hence enough Keats.

(In this particular poem he does not go very far towards explaining why the heart's rag-and-bone shop should be foul.) A traditional sub-category of the lyric is the love poem, and in its modern versions this too recognizes the problematic nature of the relationship between the private and the public – in this case the problematic relationship between "love" (so neatly abstracted by Elizabethan and other early lyricists) and the wider world of culture and society. From Arnold's "Dover Beach," through the passionate possessiveness of Browning's love lyrics, to the aggressively "innocent" postures of a poet such as E. E. Cummings, there is little modern love poetry (there is little enough modern love poetry in any case) which does not reflect a more immediate or less immediate social threat. Personal love-dramas of the kind which provide the focus of such political novels as *Anna Karenina* or *Dr. Zhivago* or *Nineteen Eighty-Four* are the ordinary everyday business of love poetry. (In *Howards End* E. M. Forster noted that the only organic bond in the cosmopolitan and capitalist society of the future would be personal love, and com-

the presence of feeling? thought?

[18] Pearson, "Robert Lowell," *The Review*, No. 20 (1969), p. 5.

mented: "May love be equal to the task.")[19] Personal love both substitutes for, and symbolizes, the organic community which modern society does not provide us with.

Beyond the lyric of immediate experiencing there is the lyric which reaches farther into society or politics from a "confessional" foundation. (Robert Lowell's "For the Union Dead" is a poem of this kind.) Dramatic poetry, or the poetry of masks or of imagined *personae*, on the other hand, is a version of the lyric which tries on principle to emancipate itself from the poet's "empirical" self. It was fear of the worldlily autobiographical which led such poets as Yeats and Eliot to strive for impersonality, just as it was fear of the debased ordinary world which led "Symbolist" poets to insist that "as for living, our servants can do that for us,"[20] that "the earth has no alternative but to become invisible – *in* us,"[21] or that "Je est un autre."[22] Yet what matters in poetic achievement is not the closeness or otherwise of the poem's *persona* to "the bundle of accident and incoherence that sits down to breakfast,"[23] but whether or not the incoherences of sitting down to breakfast can be wrought into a truly imagined experience. (For literature to remain fully alive, someone somewhere will always have to be writing about sitting down to breakfast.) The need in modern verse for a "poetry of experience" – of experience by a possible person, at whatever distance from the poet's "own" self – has been persuasively argued for by Robert Langbaum in his study of nineteenth-century English verse *The Poetry of Experience*. The "historically unique purpose" of Romanticism, he suggests, was not to reject intellectual or abstract meanings "but to renew them by empirical means."

> Much could be learned from the isolation of a poetry of experience. It would reveal for the first time, in addition to the distinctively romantic sensibility and subject matter which we already know, a distinctively romantic form in poetry – a form of which the potentials are realized in the so-called reactions against romantic poetry, in the dramatic monologues of the Victorians and the symbolist poems of the moderns. Such a form, furthermore, if it were treated as a way of meaning, a

[19] *Howards End* (London: Penguin, 1975), p. 257.
[20] The aphorism of Villiers de l'Isle Adam's character Axel, which Mallarmé admired and endorsed.
[21] Rilke, letter to Witold von Hulewicz of 13 November 1925.
[22] Arthur Rimbaud, letter to Paul Demeny of 15 May 1871.
[23] Yeats, "A general introduction for my work" in *Essays and Introductions* (London: Macmillan, 1961), p. 509.

way of establishing the validity of a poetic statement, would become the best index of a distinctively modern tradition.[24]

From the dramatic monologue, or the verse of different kinds of experiencing "I," it is a straightforward step to the prose fiction of the multi-character novel. In the traditional multi-character novel the disparate viewpoints of the characters are themselves elements of the novelist's central vision or "poem." The single-character or existentialist novel, on the other hand, or the "romance" in which the story is strongly subjected to the author's symbolism or imagery at the expense of multiple character development, is closer to the verse lyric with its single center of vision. The reasons for the modern primacy of the "confessional" lyric are also the reasons why so much modern prose fiction has tended towards the autobiographical. The move towards a literature of experience represents a fundamental shift of sensibility, because it represents the recognition that concrete experience – and with it the literature of concrete experience – is our most essential means of access to reality. This is the culmination of literary Romanticism and the self-conscious replacement of the "prehistoric" phase of literary art by literary art proper. None of these considerations is an argument for naturalism (that there are arts, such as music, which virtually cannot be naturalistic is a reminder of the limits of naturalism); yet naturalism must remain an open option for prose fiction just as the Imagist poem must remain an open option for verse.[25] Contemporary narratology has usefully shown the degrees or stages which may intervene between a seemingly descriptive or "low-mimetic" naturalism and the most complexly ludic or self-referring kinds of meta-literature. It has not given much recognition to the fact that for the latter to have any meaning for us (other than a merely destructive or "anti-art" meaning) we must also possess the former. The poetic lyric, and with it the novel of "empirically renewed"[26] vision, are the "core" of literature because they create,

---

[24] Robert Langbaum, *The Poetry of Experience* (London: Chatto and Windus, 1972), pp. 22, 36.

[25] If we abstract, as we must, from meter and rhyme as the defining characteristics of verse, it is not even clear that the distinction between verse and prose is any longer very important. The middle ground between verse and prose fiction has become increasingly occupied, and a substantial amount of good modern verse could as well be (and if it will satisfy hostile critics, might just as well be) categorized as prose. Almost all "found" poetry, or as-it-might-be-found poetry, is necessarily of this kind.

[26] See Langbaum, *The Poetry of Experience*, p. 22.

or re-create, myth. Other more abstract, or more stylized, or more intellectual, or more allegorical forms of literature, by contrast, make *use* of myth; or as Blake expressed the point in *The Marriage of Heaven and Hell*, "devour" it:

> The Giants who formed this world into its sensual existence, and now seem to live in it in chains, are in truth the causes of its life & the sources of all activity; but the chains are the cunning of weak and tame minds which have power to resist energy ...
>
> Thus one portion of being is the Prolific, the other the Devouring: to the Devourer it seems as if the producer was in his chains; but it is not so, he only takes portions of existence and fancies that the whole.

(Complete Writings, p. 155)

Both of these procedures are necessary poles of literature and of human existence, but the first also contains and "renews" the second (the struggle to regenerate myth and to redeem abstractions is the struggle of Los to build "the stubborn structure of the Language, acting against / Albion's melancholy"),[27] and to be entirely given over to the second will be to have fallen into a sleep, or a death, of vision.

3

That there has been a "breakdown of meaning" in modern culture and that this has been reflected (or ought to be reflected, or is necessarily reflected) in modern literature has been a commonplace of twentieth-century literary discussion, but only comparatively recently has it begun to be suggested that this breakdown is in effect the discovery of a necessary truth, and that the idea that language relates to and expresses – whether more adequately or less adequately – an apprehension of the nature of reality is simply a philosophical illusion.

A general weakening of confidence in language and in linguistically-based meaning as a whole is in fact an aspect of the post-Romantic philosophical sensibility of the past century and a half which has been called existentialism. Faced with an objectified world which seems to be inadequately intelligible to our intuitive awareness, the experiencing agent becomes conscious of his discontinuity

[27] "Jerusalem" in *Complete Writings*, p. 668.

from that world and its categories, and (at the limit) questions whether any categories or language whatever can be adequate to the true nature of human experiencing. This crisis of language and meaning is properly speaking a crisis of religious belief: it is a late result of our loss of the mythically-unified world of ideas and values which was once underwritten by organized religion, and in this respect we can see ourselves as on the last arc of a trajectory which began with the Middle Ages. As far as literature is concerned, the importance of this phase can of course be exaggerated: the greatest literature has always called the whole world in question and has always worried about the difficulty of saying what we mean. A certain obscurity – a disparity between our intuitive apprehensions and the categories of our already-existing language – is the necessary condition of all poetry and the very element in which it works. Towards the end of the nineteenth century, on the other hand, this anxiety about meaning sometimes came to seem dangerously absolute, and any attempt whatever at poetic expression to seem to lie under some kind of metaphysical threat. This apparent breakdown of the ordinary expressiveness of language dominated the work of a poet like Rimbaud, and his response to it was to surrender to the experiential disorder deliberately and systematically. Mallarmé, by contrast, sought to purge language of its worldly meanings altogether and to move towards a poetry of pure structure which had no reference beyond itself. A poet such as T. S. Eliot acknowledged the problem in a more urbane way when he spoke of an "intolerable wrestle / With words and meanings" or of a "raid on the inarticulate / With shabby equipment always deteriorating."[28] (Awarenesses of the shortcomings of poetic imagery in the face of a rebarbative actual world can in fact be traced back in the history of English verse through the Victorian poets and to such early Romantics as Shelley and Keats. It is already almost taken as a datum by the forefathers of modern Symbolism, the German *Frühromantik* poets such as Novalis in his *Heinrich von Ofterdingen*. Modern American poets, following Whitman and Rimbaud, have often moved in the contrary direction and embraced the contingent richness of experience at the expense of any real attempt at symbolic ordering.) This kind of crisis of meaning, or intensified linguistic self-consciousness, has become built into our modern sensibility, and to such an extent pervades our

[28] "East Coker," II, V, ll. 70–71 and ll. 179–80.

ordinary awareness of the world that the writer who denies it or ignores it courts a middle-brow second-rateness and ephemerality. The relationship between this "crisis of meaning" and the modern literary preoccupation with violence and emotional extremity – as we can see in the case of a writer such as Dostoevsky – is also very close. "When action involves choosing between worlds, not moving in a single world," Iris Murdoch has argued,

> loving and valuing, which were once the rhythm of our lives, become problems. Emotions, which were the aura of what we treasured, when what we treasured was what we unreflectively did, now glow feverishly like distant *feux follets*, or have the imminent glare of a volcanic threat.[29]

Modern violence and evil are (as Blake recognized) in part generated by a repressive civilization which denies form to our instincts and therefore turns us over to unchanneled emotion. It is for literature to try to make sense of this condition by revealing possibilities within us which transcend the existing order. Since a heightened linguistic awareness is a part of our modern sensibility, it will not be surprising if a great deal of modern literature seems to be less concerned with experience itself and more concerned with the nature of experiencing. But even with this newly-intensified concern with the nature of linguistic meaning, the defining objective of literature continues to be realism: its function is to express what it truly feels like to be alive – which includes, at whatever level of explicitness, a measure of self-consciousness about the nature of linguistically-vehicled experience or of truth. (Too much such self-consciousness might perhaps fairly be taken to be a symptom of spiritual disorder.)

The question of "realism" in literature very largely cuts across the question of modes or genres. The most descriptively naturalistic poem or novel can fail to be real, while the most fiercely experimental poem or novel can be dedicated to truth. Representationality had always threatened to close over the nineteenth-century novel, and the reactions of experimental novelists such as James, Conrad, Joyce or Virginia Woolf against the descriptive "realism" of their contemporaries or predecessors were attempts to find ways of achieving a more imaginative capturing of reality. In the case of such modernist writers as these, a technical preoccupation with story-telling and with the nature of fictions expresses a mode of vision: it conveys an

---

[29] Iris Murdoch, *Sartre* (London: Fontana, 1967), p. 47.

experiencing of uncertainty or of ambiguity or of the relativity of truth, rather than merely a modish preoccupation with the devices of writing. Frederick R. Karl has suggested of Conrad that

> his work on *Chance* indicated he was attempting to grapple with Bergson's warnings, close to his own sense of things, that the logical mind created continuity where none really existed; ... and that, besides this mechanistic impulse, there was another which tried to understand vital phenomena. Conrad's way of handling this discrepancy between the logical and intuitive was by means of a narrative frame (the logical sequencing) which distanced the fragile inner core that palpitates according to a mode of existence unknown to the Powells, Marlows, and Fynes [narrating characters within Conrad's own narrative], who hover on the outside.[30]

Virginia Woolf, in a famous manifesto on behalf of attempts by novelists like Joyce and herself to capture this "fragile inner core" more directly, argued that

> the form of fiction most in vogue [in 1919] more often misses than secures the thing we seek. Whether we call it life or spirit, truth or reality, this, the essential thing, has moved off, or on, and refuses to be contained any longer in such ill-fitting vestments as we provide ... Life is not a series of gig-lamps symmetrically arranged; life is a luminous halo, a semi-transparent envelope surrounding us from the beginning of consciousness to the end. Is it not the task of the novelist to convey this ... spirit ... with as little mixture of the alien and external as possible?[31]

The presence of a built-in "fictionality-awareness" in English verse as far back as early Romanticism has been pointed out by Gabriel Pearson in a discussion of Keats's "Ode to a Nightingale":

> The content of a romantic poem ... is ultimately the experiencing self ... [T]he poet tries to watch himself observing the world, tries to catch himself in the act of experiencing ... In Keats's "Ode to a Nightingale," the poet begins with his state of mind. This state is modulated through ever widening circles of involvement with the bird's song which is at the same time the poem he is writing. The circles become so wide that for a moment they seem to embrace the whole of worthwhile human

[30] Frederick R. Karl, *Joseph Conrad, the Three Lives* (London: Faber and Faber, 1979), p. 743.
[31] "Modern fiction" in *Collected Essays*, vol. 2 (London: Hogarth Press, 1966), pp. 105–6.

experience: emperor, clown, the sad heart of Ruth, faery lands forlorn ...

But it is a dynamic generation of circles rather than a simple curve away into the world and back. The area covered is still held in dynamic tension even when the poem has been tolled back to Keats.[32]

A great deal of post-Romantic and especially modernist writing has been explicitly or implicitly concerned with what it feels like to be a writer. (Almost everything written by Virginia Woolf, for example, might be read from a certain point of view as being "about" the experience of writing fiction.) To the extent that it opens up the questionability of descriptive truth, of viewpoint, of time-sequence, and of many other presuppositions of our ordinary practical living, modernist writing is a new and more profound exploration of questions which had already been raised by *The Tempest* or by *Tristram Shandy* but which the "mirroring" or representational conception of literature had largely suppressed or re-obscured. But this modernist "revolution" has also long ago become a phase of our literary history; and now that its smoke has cleared we can see that in its aftermath there is already a tradition of literature which – instead of continuing to worry about the nature of meaning – simply gets on with the definitional literary function of finding meaning. The "highbrow" literature of modernism parted company with a popular literature which was uninterested in modernism's methodological experimentation; but it is now in a position to re-unite itself with that literature by carrying its self-consciousness not in the technical hyper-sophistication of its writerly surfaces but in the imaginative bloodstream of its experiential content.

A true post-modernist art will also be a post-"highbrow" art, and a true post-modernist literature (if we must continue to use such a term at all) will be a literature which goes on from the "fictionality-awareness" of modernism to the actual finding of revelatory fictions. What has recently and fashionably come to be known as "post-modernism," meanwhile, very rarely does this at all. In the movement to which the term "post-modernism" is now (approvingly or otherwise) most commonly applied, such writings as exist in which the concern for truth or reality has been preserved have become

---

[32] "Romanticism and contemporary poetry," *New Left Review*, No. 16 (1962), pp. 50–51. Even earlier than Keats, Blake had remarked that "We are led to Believe in a Lie / When we see [With *del.*] not Thro' the Eye" ("Auguries of Innocence," *Complete Writings*, p. 431).

indistinguishably submerged among writings in which such a concern has been playfully (or defiantly, or self-congratulatorily, or wistfully) dismissed as a pre-Saussurian delusion. The prevailing "post-modernist" atmosphere of fictional sporting while the onto-theological cat is away has been well summed up by Raymond Tallis when he points out that

> [m]any "serious" novelists, in whose work formal experimentation is not especially evident, now include goblins, unfortunates who are twice-born or undergo innumerable incarnations, creatures with magic powers and other such implausibilia in their cast of characters ... A story that suspends disbelief or is open to interpretation at least in a quasi-realistic sense has failed to be sufficiently advanced. In order to guard against this, truly modern fiction will signpost its own artefactual – and advanced – state by referring to itself, contradicting itself, breaking out into a delirium of puns or fading into white spaces where the reader can reflect on the status of the fictive ... There is a famous and much commented-on opening paragraph in Alain Robbe-Grillet's *In the Labyrinth*. The first sentence announces that it is raining and the second that the sun is shining. This has been interpreted by critics to be an attack on our assumptions about the relation between language and reality.

The vacuity of such a critical stance is neatly shown by Tallis when he goes on to remark:

> It would seem that, in order to tear the mimetic contract to shreds and to subject the referential function of language to a searching examination, all I have to do is write the following sentence:

THIS IS NOT A WRITTEN SENTENCE.[33]

A "post-modernist" poet who talks a great deal about meaning-within-poetry (and even meaning-within-*his*-poetry) within his poetry is John Ashbery; and in at least one of his poems he succeeds in creating something of an *experience* out of the loss of more traditional modes of literary experiencing:

> I am coming out of one way to behave
> Into a plowed cornfield. On my left, gulls,
> On an inland vacation. They seem to mind the way
>   I write ...

33 Raymond Tallis, "Not Saussure," *PN Review*, 14, No. 2 (1987), 24.

What is writing?
Well, in my case, it's getting down on paper
Not thoughts, exactly, but ideas, maybe:
Ideas about thoughts. Thoughts is too grand a word.
Ideas is better, though not precisely what I mean.
Someday I'll explain. Not today though.

I feel as though someone had made me a vest
Which I was wearing out of doors into the countryside ...[34]

At the back of this (a long way at the back of it) we can hear a winsomely "post-modernist" echo of the communicative despair of the "I should have been a pair of ragged claws" of T. S. Eliot's "The Love Song of J. Alfred Prufrock," or even of Kafka's "Metamorphosis." Elsewhere in Ashbery's verse, on the other hand, there are poetic images to be found, but they float in and out of the writing – mentioned, as philosophers might say, rather than used ("All things seem mention of themselves," Ashbery himself confesses at one point)[35] – and are never allowed any fictional time or space in which to develop their potential significances. To write directly about, or to be intensely aware of, the activity of writing poetry must of course – in its own little corner – always be a valid thing to do; but since the human activity of writing poetry is only an insignificantly small ingredient of the world as a whole, the hypertrophying of this concern into an entire mode of awareness must be poetically very impoverishing. Even where such a reflexive awareness goes with a sustained presentation of poetic images – as for example in the case of the English "metaphysical" poets of the seventeenth century – the reflexiveness must always tend to draw our attention towards the writer's performance rather than towards his subject matter, and must always be open to some version of Dr. Johnson's charge against the metaphysicals that "their thoughts are often new, but seldom natural," or that they "wrote rather as beholders than partakers of human nature."[36] For the most part, the persistent emphasis of

[34] John Ashbery, "Ode to Bill" in *Self-Portrait in a Convex Mirror* (New York: Viking Press, 1975).

[35] "Grand Galop" in *Self-Portrait in a Convex Mirror*.

[36] *Lives of the English Poets*, vol. 1, pp. 13–14. All of Johnson's charges apply to British poetry's recent "Martian" school of showy simile-mongering. (A true poetry of "defamiliarization" would mean a cleansing of the doors of perception, not a rendering of the earth Martian.) Cleverness and sophistication have become diseases of contemporary – especially British – poetry, and no poem which is simple, sensuous and passionate is nowadays likely to win a major poetry competition. Partly as a result, few poems which have these qualities are now being written. Kierkegaard

"post-modernist" writing on its own fictionality must achieve (if nothing worse, and even where it appears within a realistic framework) the same effect as, say, Trollope's repeated insistence in his novels that he is only "making believe" and that he can make the story come out any way the reader prefers: the main result is to discourage us from taking any of these fictions very seriously. The most convincing way of "naturalizing" some of the more common forms of "post-modernist" literary self-preoccupation is probably to naturalize them as the experience – if they can be naturalized as experience at all – of very clever, very insecure, very neurotic, or very young writers (but above all of writers). More ultimately they can perhaps be seen as the most recent literary symptoms of what F. R. Leavis called the "technologico-Benthamite" state of our culture (the *Frühromantik*-Symbolist movement was an earlier and relatively benign phase of this collapse of faith in the spiritual meanings of the world in which we actually live our lives).

"Only the sick man feels his limbs," said Oswald Spengler, in a phrase which summarized his account of the spiritual decadence of the entire later phase of Western culture;[37] and among earlier critics of literary modernism there were already many who had begun to see the exaggerated modern preoccupation with the nature of literary meaning as a state of affairs which called for diagnosis rather than for justification. In *The Withered Branch*, D. S. Savage regarded the cumulative linguistic involution of a writer such as Joyce in his progress towards *Finnegans Wake* as

> a symptom of the disintegration of the self-subsistent ego, turned in upon itself through the rejection of meaning consequent upon [an] initial failure of belief.[38]

In a study of some of our more celebrated modernist literature Georg Lukács saw this kind of "failure of belief," and the rejection of any humanly apprehensible meaning in reality, as central to the work of artists such as Joyce, Kafka and Beckett. Beckett's *Molloy*, he suggests, "is perhaps the *ne plus ultra* of this development."

once remarked perceptively that "[i]rony is an abnormal growth; like the abnormally enlarged liver of the Strasbourg goose it ends by killing the individual" (*The Journals of Kierkegaard 1834–1854*, ed. and trans. Alexander Dru [London: Fontana, 1958], p. 58).

[37] Oswald Spengler, *The Decline of the West*, ed. Helmut Werner, trans. C. F. Atkinson (London: Allen and Unwin, 1961), p. 186.

[38] D. S. Savage, *The Withered Branch* (London: Eyre and Spottiswoode, 1950), p. 198.

In Beckett's novel we have the same vision twice over. He presents us with an image of the utmost human degradation – an idiot's vegetative existence. Then, as help is imminent from a mysterious unspecified source, the rescuer himself sinks into idiocy. The story is told through the parallel streams of consciousness of the idiot and of his rescuer.[39]

A diagnosis of the later, more theoretical and "post-modernist" continuations of these developments would need to see them as having their roots in the anti-spiritual *laïque* tradition of French thought and as having been nourished, especially in America, by our preoccupation – endemic to an atomized or "individualized" society – with the nature and roles of the "self," but simultaneous inability – almost inevitable in an atomized or "individualized" society – to know or to have any faith in what that "self" really feels. With these moves towards a spiritually disabling self-consciousness there goes the now almost universal tendency in intellectual and academic circles to value literary criticism or literary theory on a level with, or even above, literary art itself, along with the many other symptoms in contemporary intellectual and academic life of a disbelief in reality and of a general "megalomania of the signifier."[40] At their best, our actual "post-modernist" fictions are overwhelmingly ironic in their mode, and the most literarily valuable results of this widespread cultural condition of inability to know what it is that we feel have been some brilliant satires, not least in America; but we cannot keep the plumber on as cook.

A general fascination with meta-poeticality and literary reflexiveness is a characteristic of almost all of the most celebrated literary art of the twentieth century. From one point of view we can see this as a part of the self-scrutinizing and self-dismantling process on which Western art has been engaged in its winding-down from the more abstractly based "great" art of earlier centuries. The focusing of our literary awareness on the immediate and concrete rather than on the distant and abstract, and at the same time the focusing of our awareness on our literary comprehension itself, is an integral part of the post-Romantic process whereby literature has gradually emancipated itself from its "classical" pre-history; but when this process is

---

[39] Georg Lukács, *The Meaning of Contemporary Realism*, trans. John and Necke Mander (London: Merlin Press, 1963), pp. 31–32.

[40] This useful phrase was coined by Perry Anderson. See his *In the Tracks of Historical Materialism* (London: Verso Books, 1983), p. 45.

carried to the point where our capacity for the apprehension of reality itself is abolished, its value is immediately destroyed. Weighed in the aesthetic balance – which must also mean the moral balance – the sophisticated and reality-rejecting hesitations of modern meta-poeticality must in the end be more destructive than any mere naiveté or sentimentality (naiveté or sentimentality can at any rate always be educated), since they strike at the very roots of our existential courage itself. The greater part of our modernist and "post-modernist" temporizing about the nature of art and artistic experience may be traceable to an existential inability to acknowledge or to accept (even though we intuitively sense it) the necessary relativity of the human condition, along with the corollary that instead of keeping a place open for the kinds of old-fashioned viewpoint-free morality and comprehension which (as we know on some level) we can no longer aspire to, we must commit ourselves instead to finding actual spiritual meanings from the standpoint of the embodied and located cultural situations which we contingently occupy. In the preface to the second edition of his *Poetic Diction*, Owen Barfield suggests that what poetry or literature must find on the other side of all reflection of its own alienated condition is "the creative imagination latent within the word itself [sc. within words themselves, which must also mean within the world itself]" (p. 37). To achieve this would mean the creation of a poetry or literature which accepts the necessary relativity of our condition (relativity does not have to be "mere") and which stays loyal to its origins in the ordinary experiential world where all our ladders start. It would be a poetry in which we could trust our imagination, for the good reason that – by calling it to higher duties than it had yet been called to, and by building our critical and meta-literary awareness into the unconscious depths of it – we had at last forged for ourselves an imagination which we could trust. There must be a place, as there must always be a place, for a literature which expresses our current spiritual condition – which may at the present time be one of jumpiness, neurosis, despair, immaturity, or of a sense of the world in bits and pieces. Literature which – like *The Waste Land* – expresses this "alienated" spiritual and cultural condition can be authentically revelatory. But because to experience the world in this way is to experience it mainly through a disability (there is another art which shows this to be so: to set against Dostoevsky there is also Tolstoy), there must always be the possibility of a literature which reaches beyond this disability to a greater wholeness and which aims to cure our spiritual condition rather than merely to express it. The one-armed poet does not content himself with a one-armed vision, and to try to transcend our spiritual disabilities must be the higher aim because it is to attempt to go beyond our contingent limitations – beyond our spiritual limitations, beyond our cultural limitations, beyond our living among the echoes of older literature, beyond our loss of existential nerve – in order to re-connect with the most central meanings of human life. There will always be room for a literature of the first kind, just as there will always be room for a literature which criticizes our lives, or which amuses us, or which tells us things we did not know, or which politically activates us. (In Virginia Woolf's phrase, "[t]here are seasons when it is more important to have boots than to have watches").[41] But at the center of our distinctively human needs there remains the need for a literature of the second kind: for a literature of "the imagination latent within words themselves," of a certain lyrical intensity, of a cutting through verbal mannerisms to an elemental directness, of a standing by what (from where we stand) we see to be how things are, of a certain firmness of diction and of tone. The other purposes of literature can be achieved in other ways, but if the poet abandons his job in order to do other people's jobs, there will be no one left for us to turn to who can do his.

4

Important questions of ideology and social power arise in all discussion of art. Whose conception of poetry is to count as poetry? *Is* literature – in the sense in which our culture virtually obliges us to construe it – a bourgeois concept? There is a need for the writer, as well as for the reader, to have an understanding of this ideological dimension and to build such an understanding into his literary imagination itself. If he does not do so, he will leave more work for his readers or critics to do, as well as more false trails and possibilities of misprision. Hierophantic postures – like those of Yeats, for example – will no longer serve.

A true post-modernist literature must have an awareness of ideological questions and of history – but it must have this aware-

[41] "Mr. Bennett and Mrs. Brown" in *Collected Essays*, vol. 1, p. 326.

ness, and its engagement with reason generally, in its bloodstream and not in its head. The true post-modernist will understand and "deconstruct" his own situation not intellectually but at the sources of his own creativity. He will (1) educate himself, and (2) trust to his unconscious mind to make imaginative use of that education.

How can the post-modernist writer be sure that his text has escaped from ideology – deconstructed itself – as far as possible? The answer is that he cannot.[42] But there are no other, greater ontological certainties available to us. Beyond all ideological distortions and falsifications which may infect our work, poetry or literature remains the most reliable access to reality that we can have. The poet "is a sage; / A humanist, physician to all men" (Keats). The purpose of art lies in its value for life (from this point of view the "Symbolist" movement is a spiritual dead-end) and the purpose of life "is life itself" (Goethe). These familiar "humanist" conclusions take on a new weight when we recognize that poetry replaces religion, or that (scripturally speaking) it *is* religion.

If art nourishes sensibility and keeps our sensuous apprehension alive, it can do so only within the material conditions which prevail at any time. The social or political problems of changing these conditions will not be directly affected by art. Yet enlightened social or political action is possible only on the basis of true vision. (Since we must comprehend Fascism before we can hope to eradicate it, the art of Wagner may be more illuminating to us here than the theories of Brecht.)

Is art *necessary* to human life? Could life alone, under certain conditions, be sufficient? The necessity of art in Western culture is not a metaphysical one but a relative and cultural one: art is necessary (1) as a counter to dogmatic belief, and (2) as a counter to the culture's prevailing technological mentality. In a more onto-logical or spiritual world, both of these needs would be less insistent. As Schiller and the subsequent liberal-humanist tradition clearly perceived, our need is for an art which can engage with, and thereby redeem, the mechanized and de-sacralized world of practical life. In this redemption of the practical, our most urgent literary need may be for an art which is comprehensible. The notion that in order to cope with a difficult world modern art must be difficult (T. S. Eliot)

---

[42] Hans-Georg Gadamer has argued similarly about the necessary effort of the historian to overcome the "tyranny of his own hidden prejudices." See his *Truth and Method* (New York: Seabury Press, 1975), especially pp. 236, 237, 269.

has never been seriously questioned; yet it seems much more likely that the reverse is in fact the case.

5

In superseding religious observances and rituals which no longer have a meaning for us, a new religious awareness must be drawn towards ordinary life and ordinary experience. In this respect the tradition of Taoism and of Zen Buddhism, with its philosophy of the sacredness of ordinary life, must be helpful to us – not least if we are able to set it free from its as-yet-undeconstructed historical limitations and dogmatisms.[43] The authentic religion of the future can only be: authentic living. Its scriptures can only be: poetry. This need not mean a religion of passivity or of docility: art, or religion, is a way into life, not a way out of it. Most traditional religions have rejected the carnal. (In the teachings of Nietzsche's Zarathustra there is dance and play; the orientals mostly sit.) The religion of the future will be a religion of full experiencing. All truth is carnal, and that Energy is from the Body is the true meaning of the Word made flesh.

6

All reality is aesthetic. Shakespeare saw this in *The Tempest* when at the end of the play he declined to allow the dramatic illusion to collapse. He also saw that the bad lords remain, and that Prospero must run his dukedom. Art and religion do not solve our practical problems: they only enable us to see the world truly. The poets have only interpreted the world. The point remains: to change it.

[43] My final acknowledgement must be to Robert M. Pirsig's once-acclaimed but now (it seems) almost forgotten fictional masterpiece *Zen and the Art of Motorcycle Maintenance* (London: Bodley Head, 1974). Much of what I have argued in the present book is only an intellectual elaboration of Pirsig's fine insights.

APPENDIX:
ROMANTICISM AND POETICS

> Man thinks, feels, and lives within language alone...But
> he senses and knows that language is only a means for
> him; that there is an invisible realm outside it in which he
> seeks to feel at home and that it is for this reason that he
> needs the aid of language.
>
> WILHELM VON HUMBOLDT

1

Kant's main purpose in his *Critique of Pure Reason* was to show that
our theoretical knowledge must necessarily be restricted to the
operation of our conceptual understanding within the realm of actual
or possible empirical experience. Any awareness we might have of a
unifying "whole" which lies within or behind empirical experience
belongs to the realm of reason, and cannot in any way be established
by means of empirical experience or conceptual argument. Our
understanding alone cannot prove that the natural world will go on
behaving in ways that conform to our intelligence; nor can it prove
that that world will go on behaving in ways that bear any relation to
our moral or spiritual interests. To go on being able to *live* in such a
world, on the other hand (and this is the main premise of Kant's
moral philosophy, as in his *Critique of Practical Reason*), we must in
fact make certain assumptions about the essential nature of the
universe "as a whole." We must assume, or act "as if," the natural
order around us will not in fact break down; and we must assume, or
act "as if," the moral duties that we believe to be laid upon us can also
in practice be carried out. The world of nature and the world of
freedom are quite separate realms, and – although we have no
justification for supposing them to be *incompatible* – our belief that

they are compatible can never be more than a working moral assumption.[1] Given this necessary separation between nature and freedom, on the other hand, we are almost bound to remain puzzled about how their actual compatibility within our experience is possible, and about the real basis on which this compatibility rests.[2]

In his introduction to the *Critique of Judgement* Kant sketches out his view of how a basis for the harmonious interplay between nature and freedom might in fact be found. It is in the realm of our aesthetic and teleological judgement – in our awareness of the sublime and the beautiful in nature and art, and of the forms which make up organic life – that the true ground of the unity between nature and freedom must be sought. In the course of his discussion of the nature of "aesthetic judgement," Kant makes various suggestions, and in a theoretically quite unprejudiced way, about what appear to him to be some of the more obvious aspects of our perception of beauty. The perception of beauty is a feeling of pleasure which is unrelated to practical interest. It depends on some kind of perception of purposiveness. It makes an implied claim to universality, but while having nothing to do with (for example) intellectual classification. Kant recognizes – and in doing so lays the foundation for most of the aesthetic thinking that follows him – that it is only if a basis can be found in this very experience itself for the unification of sense or nature on the one hand with reason or freedom on the other that any such kind of experience can be possible at all.[3]

Kant nevertheless speaks of our perception of beauty as a judgement of taste, and thereby emphasizes its subjectivity. Beauty, he suggests, is the effect of an harmonious "interplay" between our understanding and our imagination, and our awareness of beauty is neither intellectual nor related to desire (he is arguing here against both the rationalism of Leibniz and the sensationism of Hume). "The beautiful," he says, "is that which, without a concept [meaning that it cannot be brought under any particular concept, and thereby assimilated to understanding or desire], pleases universally" (*Critique of Aesthetic Judgement*, sec. 9). This emphasis on the "disinterested-

---

[1] In Kant's special parlance, the idea of our "freedom" can only be a "regulative" rather than a "constitutive" notion. See for example *Critique of Pure Reason*, B. 222–23, B. 296, B. 536–95, B. 670–96.
[2] It is to this problem that Kant begins to address himself in his *Critique of Judgement*. (The *Critique of Judgement* is sub-divided into the *Critique of Aesthetic Judgement* and the *Critique of Teleological Judgement*.)
[3] See *Critique of Judgement*, Introduction.

ness" of beauty, to which Kant tries to give a systematic formulation, is in fact the cornerstone of our entire modern notion of the "aesthetic," both in nature and in art. The "taste" by which we perceive beauty is, in Kant's view, entirely subjective, but can nevertheless claim universal validity because of its dependence on the harmonious interplay between certain important human faculties. At a later point in the *Critique of Judgement*, on the other hand, Kant seems to be trying to go beyond this view of the aesthetic as merely subjective, and he introduces the notion – never to be further elaborated by Kant himself – of the aesthetic imagination as involving some kind of apprehension of reality and as in some way "reaching beyond" the realm of empirical experience. An aesthetic idea, he proposes, is

> that representation of the imagination which induces much thought, yet without the possibility of any definite thought whatever, i.e. *concept*, being adequate to it, and which language, consequently, can never get quite on level terms with or render completely intelligible...

> Such representations of the imagination may be termed ideas. This is partly because they at least strain after something lying out beyond the confines of experience...[4]

This more ambitious view of the aesthetic and of "aesthetic ideas" seems to be related to the notion of the "symbol" which Kant introduces – though only briefly and fragmentarily (he remarks that "[h]itherto this function has been but little analysed, worthy as it is of deeper study. Still this is not the place to dwell upon it") – at yet another point in his argument. The symbol is an analogical rather than a direct mode of representation:

> [A] monarchical state is represented as a living body when it is governed by constitutional laws, but as a mere machine (like a hand-mill) when it is governed by an individual absolute will; but in both cases the representation is merely *symbolic*.

(sec. 59)

It remained for Kant's Romantic successors to explore the inter-relations between these not very clearly connected ideas and to

---

[4] Ideas, for Kant, belong to the faculty of reason, and are the notions which (contrarily to the terminology of the empiricists) are the farthest removed from sense perception. See also above, pp. 26, 35–37, 138.

develop them into the only coherent tradition of philosophical aesthetics that we now possess.

2

The first use of the term "aesthetic" in its modern sense was made by A. G. Baumgarten in his treatise *Aesthetica* (1750), but it was Kant who, by insisting on the disinterestedness of our awareness of beauty and on its independence of any immediately theoretical or practical interests, laid the most essential foundation of modern aesthetics. Hegel remarked of this aspect of Kant's achievement that Kant had uttered "the first reasonable thing [ever] said about beauty."[5] But the tradition of Romantic aesthetics that in many ways derived from Kant's *Critique of Judgement* found his position to be limited and unconvincing in two important respects. The first of these was the Kantian emphasis on the "subjectivity" of our aesthetic awareness and on its dependence on our subjective "taste." This, given the kind of metaphysics laid down by Kant himself in his *Critique of Pure Reason*, meant that beauty cannot at the same time be seen as "objective" or as in any way revelatory of the nature of reality. The second limitation lay in Kant's account of our experiencing of beauty as arising merely from an interplay of certain human faculties (the "imagination" and the "understanding"). This seemed to have the effect of restricting beauty to being an almost accidental occurrence and of cutting it off from any possibility of systematic comprehension or systematic pursuit. (Kant's own aesthetics are notoriously almost entirely devoid of any detailed concrete content.)

It was Schiller who, in the years immediately following the publication of the *Critique of Judgement* (1790), and abandoning his own literary work for several years in order to pursue philosophy, pressed much harder against the first of these two limitations than Kant himself had done with his tentative hints about the aesthetic imagination as in some way "reaching beyond" our ordinary experience. Schiller set himself to formulate a view of art and of aesthetic experience which would unify the realms of the natural and the spiritual (in Kantian terms, of "sense" and "freedom") and which would thereby also point the way to an escape from the second Kantian limitation – the apparently entirely accidental nature of our

---

[5] G. W. F. Hegel, *Lectures on the History of Philosophy*, trans. E. S. Haldane and F. H. Simon (London: Routledge and Kegan Paul, 1896, repr. 1968), vol. 3, p. 469.

experiencing of beauty. In a series of philosophical articles, as w
in the letters which eventually became his *On the Aesthetic Educati...
of Man*, Schiller tried to work his way free from the notion of beauty
as no more than a subjective matter of "taste," and to establish a
basis for his conviction – obviously partly derived from his own
experience as a creative artist – that if "sense" and "freedom" can
sometimes be experienced as in harmony with each other, then there
must be some respects more ultimate than merely accidental
occurrence whereby they essentially *are* in harmony with each other.
The fact of our enjoyment of beauty or aesthetic harmony, both in art
and in life, is for Schiller a sufficient ground for finding Kant's mutual
delimitation of the realms of nature and freedom unsatisfying. The
very existence of beauty argues that we must go beyond the
separation of these realms and must look for a third principle which
will account for the facts of their experienceable harmony. This third
principle Schiller finds in our capacity to take a contemplative –
neither theoretical nor practical – interest in the mere appearance, or
"semblance" (*Schein*), of certain things around us. In his *Critique of
Aesthetic Judgement* Kant had remarked of poetry that it "plays with
semblance, which it produces at will, but not as an instrument of
deception; for its avowed pursuit is merely one of play" (sec. 53).
Schiller seizes on these ideas and assigns a central place in his theory
(and ultimately in his entire view of human nature) to this
contemplative and playful activity. It is our impulse, or drive, to take
an interest in "semblance," as well as the expressive satisfaction that
our exercising of this drive gives us, that constitutes the third term
that Schiller believes to be missing from the Kantian opposition of
"sense" and "freedom."

Schiller distinguishes clearly between "aesthetic semblance" and
the kind of semblance which belongs to the "realm of actuality and
truth." Aesthetic semblance is

> semblance...which we love just because it is semblance, and not
> because we take it to be something better. Only the first is play,
> whereas the latter is mere deception [*Betrug*]. To attach value to
> semblance of the first kind can never be prejudicial to truth, because
> one is never in danger of substituting it for truth...To despise it, is to
> despise the fine arts altogether, the very essence of which is semblance.[6]

---

[6] *On the Aesthetic Education of Man*, Twenty-Sixth Letter, para. 5. "Truth," as Schiller
uses it here, means descriptive truth with respect to the circumstances of the actual
empirical world.

Among the qualities that define our aesthetic contemplation are its "honesty" and its "autonomy" with respect to the circumstances of the actual world.

> Only inasmuch as it is honest (expressly renounces all claims to reality), and only inasmuch as it is autonomous (dispenses with all support from reality), is semblance aesthetic. From the moment it is dishonest, and simulates reality, or from the moment it is impure, and has need of reality to make its effect, it is nothing but a base instrument for material ends, and affords no evidence whatever of any freedom of the spirit.

Schiller points out that "[t]his does not, of course, imply that an object in which we discover aesthetic semblance must be devoid of reality." "Semblance" is a characteristic not only of the arts, but of any "real" phenomenon of life when viewed under its aesthetic aspect:

> all that is required is that our judgement of it should take no account of that reality; for inasmuch as it does take account of it, it is not an aesthetic judgement. The beauty of a living woman will please us as well, or even a little better, than a mere painting of one equally beautiful; but inasmuch as the living beauty pleases better than the painted, she is no longer pleasing us as autonomous semblance...

> (*Aesthetic Education*, Twenty-Sixth Letter, para. 11)

To this impulse to experience "aesthetic semblance," as distinct from the kinds of interest we may have in the world as it "really" (it might be better to say "actually") is, Schiller gives the name "play-drive" (*Spieltrieb*). It is a fundamental aspect of our apprehension of the world that the sensory experience we seek out (Schiller speaks of a "sense-drive" [*sinnliche Trieb*]), and to which we have an impulse to give form (*Formtrieb*), is at certain times able to take on form quite effortlessly. At such times there is a kind of "living form" already manifesting itself in our experience, and this is only another name for what we ordinarily call beauty.[7]

> Beauty...is indeed an object for us, because reflection is the condition of our having any sensation of it; but it is at the same time a state of the perceiving subject, because feeling is a condition of our having any perception of it. Thus beauty is indeed form, because we contemplate it; but it is at the same time life, because we feel it.

> (Twenty-Fifth Letter, para. 5)

[7] See *Aesthetic Education*, especially Twelfth Letter and Fifteenth Letter.

In our perception of the beautiful object or state of affairs, the entire concrete or sensory content which is present is taken up within the form in question. This is quite unlike our classification of experience "under a concept,"[8] where only certain of the object's sensory properties are relevant to the concept which is being applied. The separateness of content and form is therefore overcome (*aufgehoben*)[9] in something which is qualitatively entirely new. Our exercise of this third capacity is – as Schiller knows from his own experience as a poet – beyond the reach of effort or will, and can therefore properly be designated as a kind of "play."

In his development of his two interdependent key notions of "aesthetic semblance" and the "play-drive" Schiller moves aesthetic theory dramatically beyond the point where Kant had left it in his *Critique of Aesthetic Judgement*. In our exercise of the play-drive, the two sides of our nature which Kant defines in contrast to each other are united in a way which seems less like mere accident and more like a true, if intermittent, expression of a harmony within our nature and the nature of the world. For Schiller, it is only when man has learned to value "aesthetic semblance" that he becomes truly human at all. In one of his best-known philosophical propositions he declares:

> [M]an only plays when he is in the fullest sense of the word a human being, and he is only fully a human being when he plays.

> (Fifteenth Letter, para. 9)

The claim that Schiller is making here amounts to a profound reversal of the view of art (as – precisely because of its playful aspect – a danger to our moral seriousness) which had prevailed within Western philosophy since the time of Plato. It also amounts to a radical undermining of the Kantian conception of morality as a matter of "duty for duty's sake,"[10] where duty is itself defined in contrast to any naturally given inclinations or desires. Through his notions of semblance and the play-drive, Schiller offers us a view of human

---

[8] Compare Kant, *Critique of Aesthetic Judgement*, sec. 9.

[9] *Aesthetic Education*, Eighteenth Letter, para. 4. ("Since, however, both conditions remain everlastingly opposed to each other, there is no way of uniting them except by destroying them [*als in dem sie aufgehoben werden*].") This notion of preservation through destruction was later much used by Hegel, who may have derived his use of it from Schiller. Hegel saw Schiller's work as an important stage between Kant's *Critique of Aesthetic Judgement* and his own account of aesthetics.

[10] The expression is Hegel's. See *Aesthetics*, trans. T. M. Knox (Oxford: Clarendon Press, 1975), vol. 1, p. 61.

nature, and therefore of morality, in which man is at his highest only in his exercising of his capacity for aesthetic experience, and in which morality is therefore potentially reconcilable with our natural self-expression rather than in a state of permanent tension with it. This leads him to speculate about the establishment of such a harmony on a more than transient basis in human society – as it in some respects at one time existed in the ancient world.[11] In Schiller's fusion of "sense" and "freedom" in the concept of "aesthetic semblance" we have the basis for a connection between art (and also our awareness of beauty in life itself) and what have traditionally been thought of as more "religious" modes of contemplation or experience.[12] Where artistic theory itself is concerned, we also have a basis for later Romantic views of art as a receptive or contemplative mode of apprehension of reality (as in Keats's notions of "negative capability," with its profound affinities with the *via negativa* of theology, or of the poet as "camelion").[13] With such ideas as these we have moved a long way beyond Kant's repeated insistence on the merely "subjective" nature of our experience of beauty.

The most important and interesting problems in aesthetics, for Schiller, relate not so much to the transition from "beauty" to "truth" as to the question of how it is that humanity finds its way to aesthetic awareness in the first place:

> There can, in a single word, no longer be any question of how [man] is to pass from Beauty to Truth, since this latter is potentially contained in the former, but only a question of how he is to clear a way for himself from common reality to aesthetic reality, from mere life-serving feelings to feelings of beauty.
>
> (Twenty-Fifth Letter, para. 7)

[11] It is from his reflections on the difference between the art of antiquity and the art of modernity – the first theoretical recognition that such a difference existed – that Schiller derives his contrast between "naive" and "sentimental" poetry. (See his essay "On Simple and Sentimental Poetry," trans. anon., in *Works* [London: George Bell and Sons, 1910], vol. 6.) Much in "post-modernist" literature could be seen as a wild extrapolation of Schiller's notion of the "sentimental."

[12] Compare, for example, the Zen Buddhist idea of the "third eye" with Schiller's "third thing" or "third principle," as different versions of our faculty for contemplating existing things not in virtue of their actual existence but of their essential form or nature. Schiller sees the fully developed "aesthetic state" as one in which we could go about our ordinary business, but with a changed spiritual attitude towards it (Twenty-Seventh Letter). This idea is closely paralleled in Buddhist teaching.

[13] "In the aesthetic state, then, man is Nought..." (Twenty-First Letter, para. 4). Compare Keats, letter of 21–27 Dec. 1817 to George and Tom Keats, and letter of 27 October 1818 to Richard Woodhouse.

Since the operations of reason are involved in the aesthetic faculty itself – albeit in an entirely concrete way – it is possible to claim that it is at the unarticulated level where the transition occurs between vital activity and aesthetic activity that man's moral development has its true origin.[14] The aesthetic is, for Schiller, a radical function of the whole psyche, and lies at the very basis of our humanity. This is the reason why art may be the richest source of our cultural nourishment, and the best cure for all our spiritual ills.[15] He therefore begins to sketch an anthropology which would place our apprehension of aesthetic semblance or beauty at the source of all our other distinctively human qualities – but is prevented from going very far with this by his lack of any concept of nature, or of life, which would provide him with the purposive ideas that he needs.[16] What is unavailable, for Schiller, is any account of the metaphysical basis on which a more than merely accidental unity of nature and the human spirit might coherently rest. This would in effect mean a view of nature, or of life – such as underlies our higher human faculties, and out of which our aesthetic faculty is born – as itself in some way tending towards the spiritual.[17] (This would be in contrast with the Kantian view, with which poets such as Schiller and Goethe determinedly struggled, of our only "objective" experience being of nature as mechanical – a merely phenomenal awareness of a reality in itself inaccessible to us.) What Schiller needs is a conception of nature or of life as inherently a force, or realm of forces, which can be directly apprehended by us in our experience of the phenomena themselves. Even Kant had been pulled in this direction when he said that "nature gives the rule to art" (*Critique of Aesthetic Judgement*, sec. 46) – since only a spiritually-tending nature could ever give such a rule – but it remained for later thinkers to give systematic form to the concepts which were needed.

Two of the criticisms which have been made of Schiller's concept of "play" may be worth mentioning in this context. First, it has been

---

[14] Compare Blake's view on the same question, as in *The Marriage of Heaven and Hell*: "Energy is the only life, and is from the Body; and Reason is the bound or outward circumference of Energy." One of the things Blake is repudiating here is the notion of reason as coming to us – from where? – already fully-fledged at the human level.

[15] See *Aesthetic Education, passim*. Compare, for example, Keats's "sure a poet is a sage; / A humanist, physician to all men" ("The Fall of Hyperion," lines 189–90).

[16] See *Aesthetic Education*, Nineteenth Letter, Twenty-Third Letter *et seq*. Schiller's discussion here in some ways anticipates Heidegger's articulation of the notion of *Dasein*.

[17] See also above, especially the discussion of the relationships between gesture, myth and the birth of language.

suggested that the presence of "play" is neither a necessary nor a sufficient condition for the presence of the "aesthetic." There is play which – as in many kinds of amusement – has no real expressive content; and there are kinds of aesthetic expression – as in the case of craftsmanly work – which are not "play" in the ordinary and un-Schillerian sense of that word. Secondly – in effect an emphasis on one aspect of this first criticism – it has been claimed that the concept of "play" may undermine certain aspects of the seriousness of art or of aesthetic experience and in particular may undermine any view of it as a revelation of reality, or as related to those kinds of revelations of reality which have been called "religious."[18] "Play" might therefore seem to be a metaphysically distorting concept on which to base any theory of art, since "play" – being usually contrasted in our own culture with work or labor – may all too easily evoke suggestions of art or aesthetic activity as being merely an escape or relaxation. Even with these reservations, nevertheless – which seem in the end to be mainly verbal – Schiller's key ideas represent a major advance in the conceptualization of aesthetic questions. What "play" and the "aesthetic" most significantly have in common is that they involve some kind or degree of symbolic, or analogical, relationship to life itself.[19]

3

It was probably Goethe who, despite his deeply ingrained resistance to almost every kind of abstract thought, did the most to prepare the ground for the "spiritualizing" of nature which became a common tendency among later Romantic writers. For this reason alone he may have been the greatest single source of inspiration behind the aesthetic and philosophical theories of Romanticism. Goethe's conception of nature as a living force was in part intellectually derived from Herder (as well as less directly from Hamann, Vico, and Spinoza), but his embodiment of this conception in every aspect of his work as a poet, an aesthetic theorist, and a scientist constituted an all-

[18] This was the reaction of Friedrich Hölderlin, for example. Schiller himself deals rather loftily with this objection in the course of putting forward "play" as his master-concept. See Fifteenth Letter, para. 7 et seq.

[19] Much larger claims for the importance of Schiller's insights than have been made here may turn out to be justified. It may very well be that some of the most important metaphysical advances in the whole of modern philosophy were first sketched out by this practicing poet.

pervasive influence on the age in which he wrote. From a philosophical point of view, there is every reason to agree with the
estimation of Goethe by one twentieth-century literary theorist as the
"uncrowned king of Romantics."[20]

Goethe's main theoretical difficulty, even though he was in no
conceptual position to recognize it as such, was created for him by the
empiricist and Kantian reliance on the notion of a fundamental
opposition between "subject" and "object" as definitional to the
nature of human experiencing. This opposition gave rise to such
problems in aesthetic theory – which both Goethe and Schiller sensed
to be unreal problems – as whether the human capacity for the
recognition of beauty should be considered a "subjective" or an
"objective" matter. The entire natural bent of Goethe's thinking was
towards a break with this dichotomy, and in his early and ground-
breaking essay on Gothic architecture he had already begun to argue
for a view of beauty in art as a matter both of feeling and at the same
time of the organization of the subsidiary parts or elements of the
beautiful object into a typical or "characteristic" whole:

> Now this characteristic art is the only true art. When it acts on what
> lies around it from inward, single, individual, independent feeling,
> indifferent to and ignorant of everything else that is alien to it, then
> whether born of rude savagery or of cultivated sensibility, it is whole
> and living...The more that the soul rises to the feeling of those
> relationships which alone are beautiful and timeless...so much the
> happier is the artist.[21]

Of Kant's three Critiques only the *Critique of Judgement* made any
favorable impression on Goethe, and his reaction to it was to take
over Kant's subjective ("as if," or "regulative") treatments of the
purposiveness of beauty or organic life and to interpret them as
constitutive accounts of reality. For Goethe, art and science (which he
scarcely distinguished from each other) have a common relationship
to the typical or "characteristic," and are at the same time both a
revelation of reality and also an expression of the human spirit.[22]

[20] See Barfield, *Romanticism Comes of Age*, p. 16.
[21] Goethe, "Von Deutscher Baukunst," in *Gedenkausgabe der Werke, Briefe und
Gespräche*, ed. Ernst Beutler (Zurich: Artemis-Verlag, 1954), vol. 13, pp. 24–25.
This essay, published when he was twenty-four and before the appearance of Kant's
Critiques, shows Goethe already struggling against an inherited and inadequate
critical vocabulary.
[22] His scientific studies of the metamorphoses of plants derive from this notion.
Schiller remarked of Goethe's plant studies that they were "ideal" (in the Kantian
sense) rather than empirical.

Human genius or creativity is itself a natural process continuous with the natural life of all organisms. In his rejection of the fundamental status of the subject–object distinction Goethe anticipates the tra- dition of evolutionary thought from Schelling to Hegel, through Bergson to Heidegger,[23] which sees the categories of subject and object as derivative from a more primary order of life (or nature, or Being) in which both are unified. The dominant conception in all of Goethe's thought is the idea of nature, or life, as a universal current or force of which man is only a part – even if he is also in some respects its highest expression.[24]

Goethe's famous distinction between "allegory" and "symbol" in literature is in some ways a direct expression of this general philosophy of life or nature. The distinction nevertheless seems to have been articulated by Goethe on an entirely intuitive basis and without any dependence on pre-existing theoretical formulations. Later thinkers – for example Schelling, followed by Coleridge – arrived at the same distinction by more abstract routes, and in differing versions it has provided a foundation for the widely held view in post-Romantic literary theory that the "particular" in some sense *contains* the "universal" rather than merely being either an illustration of a general truth or (as in neo-Platonist theory) an immanent pointer to an inaccessible realm of ideas.[25] In what seems to have been his earliest formulation of the allegory/symbol antithesis Goethe distinguishes *inter alia* between an "idealistic" art which is nonetheless particular and sensuous, and a kind of art which is an "attempt to embody the highest abstractions in a sensory mode of representation." In the former, the artistic subjects may become "symbols" through their elicitation of human feeling and be "deeply significant by virtue of their participation in the ideal, which always carries a universality with it." In the latter, on the other hand, "among which we include all allegory," the abstract method can only "destroy the interest of the representation itself and drive the spirit back into itself...and take away from its eyes what is actually

[23] Derrida, with his "middle voice" concept of "*différance*," has also partly affiliated himself to this tradition.

[24] When Margarete in Goethe's *Faust* asks Faust if he believes in God, he answers her with ecstatic talk about life and love.

[25] This view could be traced all the way from Goethe to the often-echoed poetic tag of William Carlos Williams that there are "no ideas but in things" (see his poem "A Sort of Song"). The main theoretical influence behind Williams's view is probably Emerson.

represented."[26] Goethe makes other attempts to express this distinction, but the best known of them is probably the formulation in his *Maxims* of 1822:

> It makes a great difference whether the poet seeks the particular for the universal or beholds the universal in the particular. From the first procedure originates allegory, where the particular is considered only as an illustration, as an example of the universal. The latter, however, is properly the nature of poetry: it expresses something particular without thinking of the universal or pointing to it. Whoever grasps this particular in a living way will simultaneously receive the universal too, without even becoming aware of it – or realize it only later.[27]

At another point he remarks that

> the true "symbol" is present where the particular represents the universal, not as dream and shadow, but as a living and immediate revelation of the inscrutable.[28]

Goethe does not seem to be suggesting that allegory is not in its own way a valid form of art; only that it is a dependent and spiritually inferior form of art which cannot itself illuminate the essential relationship to reality on which art depends. With Goethe, almost as much as with his more obviously religious-minded contemporary Blake, we are dealing with a quasi-religious conviction which would be impossible to reduce to any pattern of intellectual influence or belief. The most essential function of literature, for Goethe, is to *manifest* a reality in, or on the level of, experience itself, rather than to point to a realm beyond (or behind, or above, or beneath) appearances to which we can only have an indirect and problematical access.[29] What Goethe is trying to find adequate critical terms to express is the notion (which was developed further by Hegel, but which had in fact

---

[26] Über die Gegenstände der Bildenden Kunst," in *Gedenkausgabe der Werke*, vol. 13, pp. 124–25.

[27] Maxim 279. See *The Permanent Goethe*. See also above, p. 53.

[28] *Maximen*, no. 314, in *Gedenkausgabe der Werke*, vol. 9, p. 532. When Goethe speaks of a "revelation of the inscrutable" (*Offenbarung des Unerforschlichen*) he means the same as Kant means when he speaks of the artist as "transgressing the limits of experience" (*Critique of Aesthetic Judgement*, sec. 49). Both the inscrutability and the transgression are with respect only to the limits of the Kantian "understanding."

[29] There are anticipations here of such modern notions of immanent universality as, for example, Hopkins's 'inscape," or the "intellectual and emotional complex" of Imagism. One of Goethe's problems is that the already available and much-used term "idea," whether in its Platonic, Plotinian or Kantian uses, suggests an *other*worldliness or inaccessibility which is precisely what he is trying to overcome.

already been sketched out by Vico) of the "concrete," or "imaginative," "universal." For Goethe, the manifestation of reason *in* concrete experience is (just as it was for Schiller) a radical notion not only for our comprehension of the nature of art, but also for our comprehension of the essential nature of human life itself.

Goethe's allegory/symbol distinction implies an opposition between radically "poetic" and more superficially "logical" relations within literature, and his main intellectual source for this opposition may have been Herder's exploration of the same opposition within the very nature of language itself.[30] A more remote ancestor of this notion, *via* Hamann and Herder, was Vico.[31] It is to Vico that the credit belongs for the first clear expression of a distinction between "poetic logic" or "poetic wisdom" and what we should now call "conceptual logic" (or simply "logic"), as well as for the suggestion that in the childhood of the world all men were poets and that language is "originally" poetry. The earliest wisdom, for Vico, was

> a metaphysics not rational and abstract like that of learned men now, but felt and imagined as that of the first men must have been, who, without power of ratiocination, were all robust sense and vigorous imagination.[32]

In the modern world, Vico argues,

> when we wish to give utterance to our understanding of spiritual things, we must seek aid from our imagination to explain them and, like painters, form images of them. But these theological poets, unable to make use of the understanding, did the opposite and more sublime thing: they attributed senses and passions...to bodies, and to bodies as vast as sky, sea, and earth. Later, as these vast imaginations shrank and the power of abstraction grew, the personifications were reduced to diminutive signs.

> *(The New Science*, p. 128)

What these primitive perceptual unities express is a primal mode of comprehension of reality which has not yet been split apart into (as later thinking would see it) a conceptual or abstract meaning and a

---

[30] Goethe came strongly under Herder's personal influence during the most impressionable years of his intellectual life.

[31] Goethe was given a copy of Vico's *New Science* in 1787 but seems not to have done much more than to glance at it. See Isaiah Berlin, *Vico and Herder* (London: Hogarth Press, 1976), pp. 90–91.

[32] *The New Science of Giambattista Vico*, trans. T. G. Bergin and M. H. Fisch (Ithaca: Cornell University Press, 1968), p. 116.

concrete – but merely allegorical – image or illustration. Unities of this kind are what Vico calls "imaginative universals," and are essentially the same thing as Goethe tried to define through his notion of "symbol."[33]

Vico's thought was not generally known to German writers of the eighteenth century, but the notion of the priority of the "poetic" over the "logical" dimension within language itself was given an independent elaboration by Herder.[34] In his essay *On the Origin of Language*, Herder concerns himself with the problem of the true nature of linguistic consciousness and of the part that it plays in human life. Traditional theory from Greek times down to the French Enlightenment had taken for granted the notion of words or statements as standing in some kind of relation of "correspondence" with things or states of affairs in the world, but Herder addresses himself instead to the question of how it is that such a relationship of reference or correspondence can be possible. In doing so, he raises (even though he does not himself answer) the question of how it is that a transition can occur from the kind of awareness or consciousness which is characteristic of non-language-using creatures to the kind of linguistically based consciousness which is a distinctive (and even the main distinctive) characteristic of human beings. Confronted with established theories either of the divine origin of language,[35] or else of its contractual status as a deliberately framed human invention,[36] Herder rejects both alternatives and tries to explore instead some of the relationships between linguistic and pre-linguistic modes of consciousness. Herder recognizes that a certain form or analogue of language exists even at the animal level,[37] and he therefore sets himself to define the distinctive nature of linguistic consciousness as it exists at the human level proper. Language, he

[33] Isaiah Berlin remarks that "Vico supposed that [primitive] men used similes, images and metaphors much as people, to this day, use flags, or uniforms, or Fascist salutes, to convey something directly; this is a use of sign which it would today seem unnatural to call either metaphorical or literal" (*Vico and Herder*, p. 46).

[34] Herder did in fact read Vico, but seems to have developed his main ideas before doing so. Some of Vico's ideas may have come to Herder through Hamann. See Berlin, pp. 76n., 91, 147.

[35] This view was common from Greek times down to Hamann, and was of course the orthodox Christian view. In doubting it, Herder (who was a Lutheran minister) was taking risks in terms of religious orthodoxy.

[36] As, for example, in the theories of Hobbes, Rousseau, or Condillac.

[37] "Schon als Thier hat der Mensch Sprache." See Herder, *Sämtliche Werke*, ed. B. Suphan *et al.* (Berlin: Weidmannsche Buchhandlung, 1877–1913), vol. 5, p. 5.

suggests, when understood from this standpoint, must be seen as a mode of expression (rather than as a matter of conventionally established relationships between signs and things signified), and what distinguishes the human mode of consciousness which goes with linguistic forms of expression is the capacity for "reflection" (*Besonnenheit*), a term which Herder seems to choose partly in order to avoid the (for his purposes) misleading connotations of the philosophical concept of "reason." Man alone possesses this reflective power; it is the complex resultant of all his faculties, rather than merely one faculty among others, and it is in this capacity for reflection that human freedom also has its source.[38] It is language which makes this distinctively human – we might call it "fully experiential," or experientially "focussed" – mode of awareness of reality possible.[39] Unlike the instincts of animals, the human powers involved in reflection are capable of growth and development, and human language is both the product and also the guide of this process of reflective thought.[40] Thought, being necessarily linguistic, can take place only as an expressive activity and in a behavioral medium, and must necessarily be physically embodied, located, and concrete.[41] In his dispute with the notion of language as essentially a logical or referential framework rather than an evolving mode of expression, Herder many times echoes Hamann's insistence (which may in turn derive from Vico) that poetry is the mother tongue of the human species.[42]

[38] "Es ist die ganze Einrichtung aller Menschlichen Kräfte: die ganze Haushaltung seiner sinnlichen und erkennenden, seiner erkennenden und wollenden Natur; oder vielmehr – Es ist die Einzige positive Kraft des Denkens, die mit einer gewissen Organization des Körpers verbunden bei den Menschen so heißt, wie sie bei den Thieren Kunstfähigkeit wird: die bei ihm Freiheit heißt, und bei den Thieren instinkt wird" (*Sämtliche Werke*, vol. 5, pp. 28–29). There are obvious affinities between this notion and Schiller's concept of the aesthetic.

[39] There is a parallel here with Kant's proof of the dependence of objective experience on conceptual language, but Herder, unlike Kant, is concerned with the way in which this mode of apprehension arises, as well as with its connection with freedom (which Kant sees only in "regulative" or "as if" terms and leaves unexplained).

[40] "Durch die Sprache lernen wir bestimmt denken, und bei bestimmten und lebhaften Gedanken suchen wir deutliche und lebendige Worte" (*Sämtliche Werke*, vol. 1, p. 147). In seeing language-using activities as "forms of life," Herder anticipates Wittgenstein's re-orientation of modern views of language towards this notion.

[41] The pluralistic and anti-universalistic nature of all of Herder's thinking rests on this idea. Herder can be seen as a philosophical forefather of the cultural and ethnic pluralisms which dominate the present age wherever universalist philosophies (such as Marxism, for example) have gone into decline.

[42] "Poesie ist die Muttersprache des Menschengeschlechts." See J. G. Hamann,

For Herder, human thought is inseparable from human language, and different human languages, along with the different cultural forms of life to which they belong, must be seen as different – and for Herder (in contrast to the universalism of the Enlightenment) perhaps equally valid – ways of being human. The idea of the inseparability of thought and language was developed further by Wilhelm von Humboldt, who strikingly anticipates many modern discussions of poetic creativity when he says:

> Man thinks, feels, and lives within language alone...But he senses and knows that language is only a means for him; that there is an invisible realm outside it in which he seeks to feel at home and that it is for this reason that he needs the aid of language. The most commonplace observation and the profoundest thought, both lament the inadequacy of language, both look upon that other realm as a distant country toward which only language leads – and it never really. All higher forms of speech are a wrestling with this thought, in which sometimes our power, sometimes our longing, is more keenly felt.[43]

On this Herderian and Humboldtian view it becomes possible both to give a full recognition to the "behavioral" aspect of language but also at the same time to raise questions about the *adequacy* of our concepts or linguistic "forms of life" to the previously unarticulated awarenesses which we make use of them to express.[44] In addition to this, if language, as well as being a means of referring to items in the world, is also a means of human expression and of more developed apprehension of reality, then it becomes natural and inevitable to see language as continuous with the activities and phenomena which the aesthetic theorists of the later eighteenth century were beginning to comprehend as art and aesthetic experience. In this respect the

Sämtliche Werke, ed. J. Nadler (Vienna: Verlag Herder, 1949), vol. 2, p. 197. Wittgenstein, in his *Philosophical Investigations*, criticizes the "correspondence" theory of language-acquisition in a way that closely resembles Herder's. He too, consistently with his opposition to philosophical theories, does not offer a theory of his own.

[43] See *Humanist Without Portfolio: An Anthology of the Writings of Wilhelm von Humboldt*, trans. Marianne Cowan (Detroit: Wayne State University Press, 1963), p. 246. Compare Humboldt's "invisible realm outside" with Kant's "transgressing the limits of experience." This notion of an "extra-linguistic" dimension of language is what post-structuralist thinkers prevent us from discussing when they say that "there is nothing outside the text."

[44] The possibility also opens up of a "hermeneutic" questioning of one set of cultural values in terms of another – a notion which Herder's own straightforward pluralism (perhaps too direct a reaction against the Enlightenment's idea of progress) is not really equipped to deal with.

views of language of Herder and Humboldt converge with those of writers such as Goethe and Schiller, who were concerned to understand art as a mode of human expression rather than as a mode of representation or of imitation. Since art and language are on this view regarded as human nature's – or life's – highest manifestations, they are also necessarily brought closer to the concerns of traditional religion.[45]

The first thinker to deal systematically with the opposition between the "poetic" and the "logical" dimensions of human experience was Vico, but the notion is presented in his writings in an historical or chronological form. For Vico, human thought originates in poetry and myth, and before we can understand more developed forms of thinking we must first of all understand the more primitive ways of comprehending reality which poetry and myth embody. This we can hope to achieve by an effort of systematic imagination (Vico perhaps over-estimates the ease with which such an effort can become successful). In defiance of the prevailing intellectual climate of his age he insists that primitive poetry or myth is not "allegorized" reason, and is not therefore open to being discounted or dismissed by any standards with which reason has independently provided us. The poetic symbol, or trope, is a mode of awareness which cannot be reduced to something else. Yet Vico also believes (and it is a view which must in the end be seen as positivistic) that this precedence of the poetic over the logical aspect of language is only an historical one. History moves in cycles (this is perhaps the best-known and the least plausible of all Vico's doctrines), and the poetic stage of consciousness is succeeded by an "heroic" or dogmatic stage, which is followed by a critical or rational stage, after which comes a return to chaos and perhaps the beginning of a new cycle. Poetic language therefore precedes logical language in evolutionary terms, but not metaphysically in terms of the necessary conditions which underlie the very kind of human life or existence which we now possess. Vico was not drawn towards formulating a view of language as (regardless of whatever systematic or abstract developments it may have undergone) radically and in its very nature poetic or mythic – which would mean that (in Shelley's words) "if no new poets should arise-...language will be dead to all the nobler purposes of human

---

[45] This was an aspect which interested Schelling and Hegel more than it interested Goethe or Schiller – who, we might say, were religiously more radical (the same is even true in some respects of Herder).

intercourse"[46] – or even perhaps to the purposes of human intercourse as such.

4

Vico's account stops short of any view of language as dependent for its survival on a continuing interplay between a process of universalizing abstraction and a process of poetic or mythic "reconcretizing" of what has been abstracted. This is a view which seems always to have been implicit in the ideas of Goethe, and for which the Herderian conception of language as a mode of expression based in more primitive modes of apprehension provides a theoretical basis. If language is rooted in concrete life, then the various systematically abstracted uses of language must always be secondary with respect to the primary involvement in the current of life which is its aspect as myth or poetry. A view of language as an open-endedly creative manifestation of human life in this sense was given an explicit, if not very theoretical, formulation by both Blake and Shelley. Where Vico saw the relationship between myth and abstraction chronologically, Blake and Shelley were in their different ways concerned to establish a view of living language as dependent on a permanent interplay between its poetic and its logically structured aspects.[47] Similar ideas were developed more systematically by both Schelling and Hegel, but they were also made to lead in the end to a re-closing of the very gap, or "transcendence," within which human creativity has been shown to operate.

The earlier work of Schelling is an attempt to provide a metaphysical basis both for Schiller's view of the harmonizing which occurs between nature and freedom in aesthetic experience and also for Kant's (in his own terminology merely "regulative") view of the purposiveness of beauty and of organic life. In his *System of Transcendental Idealism* Schelling offers a conception of reality as a universal life-process (such as had already been unsystematically believed in by Goethe) in which human creativity brings to completion the unconscious purposiveness which is already present

[46] Shelley, *Defence of Poetry*, pp. 102–03.
[47] The theories of language of Blake and Shelley are discussed below. Echoes of their ideas can be found in modern poetic theorists such as Ezra Pound, as when he claims that "[t]he artist seeks out the luminous detail and presents it...His work remains the permanent basis of psychology and metaphysics." See above, p. 149.

in nature. In art and aesthetic experience, Schelling suggests, the conscious and free activity of the human spirit comes together with the unconscious life of nature which operates in the depths of the human mind and which is the source of artistic inspiration. The artist, Schelling claims,

> is driven to production involuntarily, and even against an inner resistance (hence the sayings of the ancients: 'pati Deum,' etc.; hence above all the notion of inspiration by means of another's breath)...No matter how purposeful he is, the artist, with respect to that which is genuinely objective in his production, seems to be under the influence of a power which separates him from all other men and forces him to express or represent things that he himself does not fully comprehend...[48]

More than any other Romantic theorist, Schelling makes central to his view of art the notions both of its dependence on inspiration and also of its unconscious origin. Because at this stage of his thought he still sees art as the highest possible form of unity or harmony between the conscious and the unconscious, he can claim that

> [t]he ideal world of art and the real world of objects are...products of one and the same activity...The objective world is only the primitive, still unconscious poetry of mind; the universal organon of philosophy – and the keystone of its entire arch – is the philosophy of art.
>
> (*Werke*, vol. 2, p. 349)

In this way Schelling answers the question that seemed to have been posed by Kant about the ultimate reconcilability of nature and freedom. Human freedom does not conflict with nature but is rooted in the very life-process which in its unconscious form is nature itself. Human imagination creates both nature and art, and it is for this reason that the objective world is the "unconscious poetry of mind."[49]

Art, which for Schelling is the expression of the highest form of imagination, is a process which actually *creates* the unity of subjectivity and objectivity (or in Goethean or Schillerian terms, of concrete particularity and universal meaning), and it is from the direction of this general metaphysical theory that Schelling arrives at

[48] F. W. J. Schelling, *Schellings Werke*, ed. Manfred Schroter (Munich: Beck und Oldenbourg, 1927–59), vol. 2, p. 617.

[49] Coleridge's distinction between the "primary" and the "secondary" imagination seems to derive more or less directly from his religious discomfort with this Schellingian view. See also above, p. 70.

his conceptions of the nature of artistic symbolism. On the basis of a discussion of the contrast between ancient and modern modes of artistic signification (another Schillerian theme) Schelling formulates his own version of the distinction between "symbol" and "allegory." In his *Philosophy of Art*, he sees the artistic "symbol" as not merely signifying, but also as simultaneously being what it signifies:

> The synthesis...in which neither the universal signifies the particular, nor the particular the universal, but where both are absolutely one, is the symbolic.
>
> (*Werke*, vol. 3, p. 427)

He relates this concept of the "symbol" to a discussion of the nature of ancient or primitive myth. In the ancient world, Schelling believes, the spiritual or ideal significance of an object or person was limited to what could (in some sense) be directly apprehended through a perceptual experiencing of that object or person. In the modern world, on the other hand, and not least in the world-view of Christianity, the spiritual or ideal significance of an object or person (as for example of Jesus) is made to extend far beyond the realm of the perceptible – but at the same time to take on a narrowed and highly specific range of moral purport. In the first case we are dealing with something more like "symbol," while in the second case we are dealing with the kind of incomplete symbolism which at its extreme becomes "allegory." Mythology is central to art, for Schelling, precisely because of its involvement in this most essential mode of apprehension which is the artistic "symbol." An artist of sufficient power – he mentions Shakespeare – can create his own mythology, and the kind of mythology which is artificially imported from earlier or other cultures can only be an empty formalism. "Symbol," therefore, and myth in the sense of the myth which adequately presents its own meaning, are for Schelling essentially the same thing.[50]

Schelling's views on myth, at this stage of his thinking, are paralleled by those of Friedrich Schlegel, who worked on the same questions for a number of years, and who suggests for example that

> [in the ancient world] mythology and poetry are one and inseparable. All poems of antiquity join one to the other, till from ever increasing

[50] See *Werke*, vol. 3, pp. 463–65 and *passim*.

masses and members the whole is formed…Ancient poetry is a single, indivisible, and perfect poem.[51]

The modern poet, by contrast, suffers from the division between subjectivity and objectivity which goes with the development of conceptual understanding, and the effect has been a progression (or regression) from a living and concrete use of myth to a kind of generalized pantheism or to a merely allegorical use of mythic figures. The modern poet must therefore create new mythic entities out of his own experience. For both Schelling and Schlegel, "symbol" and the fully presentational kind of myth are fundamentally identical, and art, which is essentially based in the articulation of such primal apprehensions of reality, is the highest possible mode of human awareness. According to Schelling's view in his *Philosophy of Art*, the disappearance of the gods, or of God, from immanent presence in the objectified modern world is open to redemption through the artist's activity of creating new myth out of the materials around him. (Later, Schelling comes to see this artistic process merely as a stage on the way towards an apprehension of God which will transcend all particular artistic presentations. In this eventual down-grading of art he is followed by Hegel, for whom the Schellingian life-force or Absolute is interpreted as the progress of a world-mind or spirit through which – at the end of the evolutionary process by which thought articulates itself out of nature – a full conceptual clarity will be achieved, so that the symbolic presentations of both art and religion will ultimately be surpassed in the rationality of philosophy.)

Many of Schelling's most important ideas were also embraced by Coleridge as a part of his reaction against the empiricist or associationist philosophy of Locke and Hartley. Coleridge's formulation of the allegory/symbol distinction closely resembles Goethe's,[52] and his well-known contrast between "fancy" and "imagination" as qualities in poetic writing directly reflects the contrast between the mental philosophies of associationism and of German idealism.[53] Coleridge's treatment of myth diverges from Schelling's to the extent that his literary theory as a whole stands under the constraint of his

[51] Friedrich von Schlegel. *Dialogue on Poetry and Literary Aphorisms*. trans. E. Behler and R. Struc (University Park, Penn. and London: Pennsylvania State University Press, 1968), p. 82.

[52] See *The Statesman's Manual*, in *Collected Works*, vol. 6, p. 30.

[53] For Coleridge's definitions of "imagination" and "fancy" as mental faculties see *Biographia Literaria*, vol. 1, pp. 304–05. See also above, p. 70.

prior commitment to the truths of the Christian religion. In invoking the notion of the Bible as an original Word or reality Coleridge is enabled to make a more effective transition to the discussion of particular literary texts than any other Romantic theorist made, but it also follows from his commitment to Christianity that he is unable entirely to accept the Schellingian view of myth and of the human imagination. According to this view, the artistic imagination not only explains the coherence of the particular poem or art-work, but is also itself the origin and guarantee of all our comprehension of reality. This was more than Coleridge wanted, since it not only made nature a creation of the human imagination,[54] but also gave no special privileged status to the biblical mythology which for Coleridge was revealed truth. It may be for this reason that Coleridge eventually fell silent on the question of the imagination. For him poetry and religion are the same – but there is only one religion. True symbol or poetry is a revelation of reason – whereas allegory is man-made – and must necessarily confirm Christian faith.[55]

5

Almost all of the ideas of the German Romantic philosophers about the nature of myth or literary symbolism were anticipated or independently elaborated – albeit in mythic or literary-symbolic rather than in discursively philosophical ways – by Blake. For Blake, the religious implications of idealism which later created problems of orthodoxy for Coleridge were incorporated directly into his poetic system without any attempt to preserve a notion of a Deity independent of human activity. "The Eternal Body of Man is the Imagination, that is, God himself," Blake proposes. "It manifests itself in his Works of Art."[56] Poetry, he suggests in his nearest approach to an explicit definition of it, is

> Allegory address'd to the Intellectual powers, while it is altogether hidden from the Corporeal Understanding...

> (*Complete Writings*, p. 825)

The concept of "intellectual" or "mental" powers, here as elsewhere

---

[54] Coleridge's unease with this notion is shown in his account of the human "primary" imagination as a "repetition" in human terms of divine creativity. Coleridge in many respects remains more of a neo-Platonist than an idealist.

[55] See, for example, *The Statesman's Manual*, Appendix C.

[56] Blake, *Complete Writings*, p. 776.

in Blake, is interchangeable with the concept of human "imagination" (for which he also uses the term "fancy" as a synonym), or "vision." The "corporeal understanding," by contrast with this, belongs to the realm of sense perception (in some respects it resembles the "understanding" of Kant or of empiricism), and is connected by Blake with the mode of life or response which is mere "nature" as opposed to human creative imagination or spirit.[57] His use of "allegory" in this particular context, on the other hand, is uncharacteristic, and seems to equate allegory with any kind of successful fictional or story-telling activity. More often, Blake uses "allegory" in a pejorative way to mean a symbolically disguised process of generalization or abstraction – a process to be contrasted with the truest and deepest kind of literary imagination, which is to be found in an awareness of concrete particulars. (Here he of course parallels the Goethean allegory/symbol distinction and the notions of concrete universality of Vico and Schelling.) "Ideas cannot be Given but in their minutely Appropriate Words" (p. 596), he insists, and the artist paints "not Man in General, but most minutely in Particular" (p. 465). In comparison with this, "[t]o Generalize is to be an Idiot" (p. 451). By contrast with true vision or imagination,

> Fable or Allegory are a totally distinct & inferior kind of Poetry. Vision or Imagination is a Representation of what Eternally Exists, Really & Unchangeably. Fable or Allegory is Form'd by the daughters of Memory. (p. 604)

"Memory," for Blake, is the province of the merely psychological and associative kind of mental activity which Coleridge labels as "fancy."

Almost the entire history of Western thought since Descartes is impugned by Blake's insistence on the spiritual reality of "vision" or "imagination" as contrasted with the spiritual unreality of "memory" or the "corporeal understanding." The corporeal understanding is an awareness which arises through the splitting-up of a primal and visionary mode of apprehension into subjectivity and objectivity – with the consequent establishment of a separate "material" world set over and against the newly defined and independent "self." For Blake, this state of affairs is a sleep of vision, and arises from the abstraction of a certain limited way of seeing into an entire

---

[57] He can therefore declare that "There is no Natural Religion," and can berate Wordsworth for what he sees as his pantheistic tendencies. See *Complete Writings*, pp. 97, 782–84.

framework of false – because incomplete and partial (though perhaps also spiritually undemanding) – consciousness.[58] True reality is vision, or poetry, or the creative faculty itself. In *The Marriage of Heaven and Hell* Blake gives us an anthropological sketch which embodies much of what he claims elsewhere about the nature of imagination or vision:

> The ancient poets animated all sensible objects with Gods or Geniuses, calling them by the names and adorning them with the properties of woods, rivers, mountains, lakes, cities, nations, and whatever their enlarged & numerous senses could perceive.
>
> And particularly they studied the genius of each city and country, placing it under its mental deity;
>
> Till a system was form'd, which some took advantage of, & enslav'd the vulgar by attempting to realize or abstract the mental deities from their objects: thus began Priesthood;
>
> Choosing forms of worship from poetic tales.
>
> And at length they pronounc'd that the Gods had order'd such things.
>
> Thus men forgot that All deities reside in the human breast.
>
> (p. 153)

Blake's invocation of the "ancient poets" recalls similar ideas in Vico, and also looks forwards to Shelley's claims in his *Defence of Poetry* about the originally poetic nature of all abstractly systematized language. For Blake, the systematizings of religion and the systematizings of abstract knowledge are both, and for similar reasons, deadenings of an original visionary mode of perception. It would be in the spirit of all of Blake's writings to see the prophets of abstract knowledge as priests (and enslavers of the vulgar) along with the priests of all other systematized religions.

Blake presents his account of the decline of poetry in *The Marriage of Heaven and Hell* in what seems to be an historical form, but he makes clear in his treatments of the same issue elsewhere that his idea cannot merely be seen as a "positive" hypothesis about the history of consciousness. Many of Blake's earlier mythic or "prophetic" poems deal with oppositions between the forces of youth and age, revolution and tyranny, change and fixity – some of these concerns obviously deriving from his response to contemporary political revolutions – and these inter-related oppositions are usually embodied in his partly

---

[58] There are obvious parallels here with the thought of modern existentialist philosophers such as Heidegger.

invented but partly traditional mythic figures Orc and Urizen. In his later work, by contrast, these oppositions become subsidiary to a concern with the radically creative capacity which must underlie all such conflicts (Blake's view of the history of consciousness resembles Vico's, but his hope for a transcending of its conflicts has affinities with Schelling) and which Blake principally embodies in his mythic character Los or Urthona. Los, the divine blacksmith, is Blake's equivalent of the creative Demiurge of Plato's *Timaeus* (we could also say that he expresses a shift from "Promethean" to "Orphean" concerns in Blake's poetry), and his principal work is to build the eternal city of Golgonooza, which when completed will be man's final state in which his vision has transcended his mere nature (and which will therefore also be the City of God or New Jerusalem). All genuinely imaginative or creative acts or artistic achievements contribute to the building of Golgonooza. The notably "allegorical" fictional edifice in which these stories feature is *inter alia* Blake's way of telling us that original language, or what we might call "myth" or "symbol" (though Blake himself never uses these words), is a presupposition of every kind of abstraction or imaginative fixity. Los is the human creativity which – constantly re-enacting the work of the "ancient poets" – is the continually dissolving and re-creating force of the imagination.[59]

Blake is in fact the first literary theorist or thinker to move beyond the merely historical version of the idea of the primacy of myth to this "solvent" notion of the nature of human imagination or vision. If we translate his views out of his own terminology into a more modern parlance we could say that the precedence of myth over abstraction (or over any fixed symbolism, or over discursive referential thought in general) is a necessary truth about the nature of language. In this relationship between the two poles of language – even though both poles are necessary to human existence as we know it – the pole of

---

[59] Blake's view of poetry as foundational to reality, and of there being no reality independently of human vision, could be seen as anticipating some of the main findings of modern philosophy (as for example in the work of Thomas Kuhn and others on the nature of scientific paradigms). Blake, nevertheless, does more than merely displace or replace "epistemology" or the "theory of knowledge" as the central concern of human thought. In making such a shift, he transfers our focus of attention to the nature of human imagination or vision, which most anti-epistemological or pragmatically-minded modern philosophers do not do. The modern idea of philosophy as a "kind of writing" (as in the work of Derrida or of Richard Rorty) is unsupported by any philosophical account of what writing itself really is. See also above, pp. 40, 50.

myth or symbol is the primary one, because the referential dimension of language can never entirely replace or displace its creative dimension. In terms of poetic theory, the Blakean view means that myth or symbol must be seen as *containing* allegory as a special case and not vice versa. Where religion is concerned, the centrality of the human myth-creating activity means that all deities are necessarily in the human breast. Blake's special treatment of Jesus results directly from his interpretation of him as fully visionary or imaginative man as such. Jesus is important not historically, but as a present possibility of imaginative perfection ("Jesus was all virtue, and acted from impulse, not from rules").[60] God, likewise, and to complete the religious framework, is not an independent entity or First Cause but human imagination as such. (In these ideas Blake leaves most of modern theology toiling behind him, although there are affinities between his ideas and those of his near-contemporary Schleiermacher.)

One of the most important aspects of Blake's account of poetry and imagination is his commitment to a view of literary symbolism in which the symbol does not negotiate with any other realm "beyond" the ordinary world, but instead finds its transcendent meaning or universality *in* the particularity of our concrete experience. (The Kantian "transgressing of the limits of experience," we might say, does not for Blake go with any notion of another, inaccessible reality "beyond" our ordinary existence.) Blake's own philosophical ground for this emphasis is his recognition of the dependence of all human thought and awareness on human *embodiment*. "Energy is the only life, and is from the Body; and Reason is the bound or outward circumference of Energy" (p. 149). Like Goethe, and like Keats after him – and despite his own tendency to express his ideas allegorically in his verse – Blake has an instinctive poetic faith in the reality of immediate experience, and it is alien to him to think of the world we live in as merely a "shadow" (to use Goethe's term) of some other reality. Blake's views are therefore diametrically opposed to all forms of Platonism. There is only one reality, which is open to our immediate experiencing, and there can be nothing else for that one reality to be subordinated to. Blake's emphasis on the metaphysical primacy of

---

[60] *Complete Writings*, p. 158. It would be too much to expect Blake to have dispensed with the mythic centrality of Jesus, but his re-interpretation of him in fact brings Jesus very close to Nietzsche's conception of Zarathustra and of the over-man (*Übermensch*).

embodiment – perhaps already implicit in Herder and Goethe – anticipates the modern philosophies of embodiment and of "being-in-the-world" of, for example, Heidegger and Merleau-Ponty. We are *in* the world before we understand the world, and all existence is temporal. No perception or understanding can escape from temporality except in the task of aesthetic re-creation which is the real meaning of eternity.

6

A rather more argumentative and less poetically indirect attempt to establish the "originally" poetic nature of language and also the necessary priority of poetry over instrumental and scientific kinds of language-using was made by Shelley in his *Defence of Poetry*. Shelley's notions of "the youth of the world," where "men dance and sing and imitate natural objects, observing in these actions, as in all others, a certain rhythm or order," and of an "infancy of society" where "every author is necessarily a poet, because language itself is poetry," recall the anthropological ideas of both Vico and Blake – but Shelley also goes beyond mere anthropological hypothesis to a rather more philosophical account than Blake's (as in his notions of Prolific and Devourer, or in the myth of Los) of the necessary primacy of poetry as the underlying creative principle of all language. The language of poetry or of poets, he tells us,

> is vitally metaphorical; that is, it marks the before unapprehended relations of things and perpetuates their apprehension, until words, which represent them, become through time, signs for portions or classes of thought, instead of pictures of integral thoughts; and then, if no new poets should arise to create afresh the associations which have been thus disorganized, language will be dead to all the nobler purposes of human intercourse.[61]

This famous claim amounts in effect to an assertion of the metaphysical necessity of the poetic principle of language as the continuing underlying basis of all human existence. There is the principle of τὸ λογίζειν, which is the capacity of language to form general concepts of objects in the external world, and there is the principle of τὸ ποιεῖν, which is the poetic capacity of language to restore to the objects of the external world the emotional significance which they have lost

---

[61] *Defence of Poetry*, pp. 102–03. See also above, p. 55.

through the process of objectification. Implicit in this view is the notion of an original unity of emotional and descriptive meaning which was sustained by our primitive and as-yet-unbroken mythic awareness, but which in the world of subjectivity and objectivity needs to be regained through an at least partly conscious process of metaphorical reconstruction. The original unity of the world which was directly perceived by the "ancient poets" must be re-created by modern poets by means of individualized poetic activity.

When he goes on to discuss poetry in its narrower and more literary sense, Shelley – and here he echoes Schiller in his *Aesthetic Education of Man* – argues for the greater social and educational value of poetry or literature as contrasted with the value of more directly practical or moral kinds of thinking:

> The exertions of Locke, Hume, Gibbon, Voltaire, Rousseau,[62] and their disciples, in favour of oppressed and deluded humanity, are entitled to the gratitude of mankind...But it exceeds all imagination to conceive what would have been the moral condition of the world if neither Dante, Petrarch, Boccaccio, Chaucer, Shakspeare, Calderon, Lord Bacon, nor Milton, had ever existed; if Raphael and Michael Angelo had never been born; if the Hebrew poetry had never been translated; if a revival of the study of Greek literature had never taken place; if no monuments of ancient sculpture had been handed down to us; and if the poetry of the religion of the ancient world had been extinguished together with its belief. The human mind could never, except by the intervention of these excitements, have been awakened to the invention of the grosser sciences, and that application of analytical reasoning to the aberrations of society, which it is now attempted to exalt over the direct expression of the inventive and creative faculty itself. (pp. 133–34)

Like Blake, Shelley is asserting the priority of the poetic faculty over the "grosser sciences," and like Schiller he is also offering us a practical assessment of the relative place and importance of these functions within human life. If "utility" is to be the basic criterion of value, then the "utility" of poetry must be wider and deeper than that of all other, more obviously useful-seeming activities. In bringing his discussion down from the apocalyptic levels of much Romantic theorizing, Shelley opens the way for more realistic explorations of

[62] "Although Rousseau has been thus classed, he was essentially a poet. The others, even Voltaire, were mere reasoners" (Shelley's footnote).

the actual and possible place of creative activity within human society. As far as its effect on personal "morality" is concerned, poetry or literature is for Shelley moral not by means of precepts but through its power of opening the "self" to new perceptions and possibilities (Shelley's essay is one of the great Romantic statements of this point of view):

> The whole objection...of the immorality of poetry rests upon a misconception of the manner in which poetry acts to produce the moral improvement of man...The great secret of morals is love; or a going out of our own nature, and an identification of ourselves with the beautiful which exists in thought, action, or person, not our own...The great instrument of moral good is the imagination.
>
> (p. 111)

Natural science is for Shelley also only a branch of poetry and subsidiary to it: in the modern world science has outgrown poetry – although this does not mean that it must always necessarily be at odds with it:

> The cultivation of poetry is never more to be desired than at periods when, from an excess of the selfish and calculating principle, the accumulation of the materials of external life exceed the quantity of the power of assimilating them to the internal laws of human nature...
>
> Poetry is indeed something divine. It is at once the centre and circumference of knowledge; it is that which comprehends all science, and that to which all science must be referred.   (p. 136)

All forms of abstraction depend on our acquisition of "signs for portions or classes of thought" (or what Kant called "concepts of objects"), and human awareness itself has its basis not in the "objective" mode of consciousness but in the integrated (mythic) awareness of ancient poetry and in the capacity of modern poetry to re-create that awareness within the analytical framework of the modern understanding.

In taking seriously both the poetic faculty itself and also the actual conditions within which that faculty is obliged to operate, Shelley's *Defence of Poetry*, like Schiller's *Aesthetic Education of Man*, points forward to the nineteenth- and twentieth-century tradition of realistic concern with the place of imaginative activity within the institutions of practical life. Shelley himself, like Coleridge (who also addresses these issues through his notion of the "clerisy"), tends towards a neo-Platonist view of the poetic "symbol," and can speak of poetry as "lay[ing] bare...the spirit of [the world's] forms" or of "the unchangeable forms of human nature" (pp. 108, 139) in a way which suggests the subservience of our secular or this-worldly culture to some higher or "religious" order. A more down-to-earth view of the nature of poetic activity and of its place in the temporal world can be found in both Wordsworth and Keats. Wordsworth, speaking always out of his efforts to comprehend his own imaginative experience rather than from a priori theoretical considerations, sees it as a fact of the human condition that "[t]here are in our existence spots of time" through which our minds can be "nourished and invisibly repaired,"[63] and argues that an imaginative perception of "incidents and situations from common life" has a redemptive power to "counteract" the spiritual distortions of a mechanistic age – which may otherwise reduce the human mind "to a state of almost savage torpor."[64] (When he fully embraces Christianity, on the other hand, Wordsworth subordinates such notions to Christian teaching and begins to reconstruct his imaginative autobiography, as in his later emendations of The Prelude.)

More radical than Wordsworth both in his determination to arrive at valid philosophical ideas on the basis of his own intuitions, and also in his ingrained resistance to all kinds of institutionalized moral or religious doctrines, is Keats. One of Keats's earliest philosophical concepts is that of "the truth of imagination" which exists alongside the truth of correspondence and "consequitive reasoning."[65] This is in effect his attempt to register the same notion of "ontological truth" as the German Romantic theorists had developed in their rein-terpretations of Kant's "subjective" concept of beauty. It is in this sense that the urn in Keats's "Ode on a Grecian Urn" can tell the poem's reader that "Beauty is truth, truth beauty."[66] This conception of a wholly aesthetically based mode of truth is in turn Keats's reason for "hat[ing] poetry that has a palpable design upon us."[67] When he

---

[63] William Wordsworth, The Prelude, book XII, ll. 208–15.
[64] Preface to Lyrical Ballads (1802).
[65] Keats, letter to Benjamin Bailey of 22 Nov. 1817.
[66] This identification has in effect already been made by Schiller. "There can, in a single word, no longer be any question of how [man] is to pass from Beauty to Truth, since this latter is potentially contained in the former" (Aesthetic Education, Twenty-Fifth Letter, para. 7).
[67] Letter to John Hamilton Reynolds of 3 Feb. 1818.

carries this notion of a purely aesthetic awareness into the realm of our actual experience, Keats arrives at his concept of "negative capability," which is the ability, within the constraints and necessities of practical life, to lay oneself open to the unpracticalities of beauty or of ontological truth:

> [S]everal things dovetailed in my mind, & at once it struck me, what quality went to form a Man of Achievement especially in Literature & which Shakespeare possessed so enormously – I mean *Negative Capability*, that is when man is capable of being in uncertainties, Mysteries, doubts, without any irritable reaching after fact & reason...[68]

Keats's commitment to life within the ordinary world is evident in his claim that negative capability goes "to form a Man of Achievement." A year or so later he develops the full religious (or anti-religious) counterpart to his concept of negative capability in his view of the world as a "vale of Soul-making" (in this he anticipates some of the ideas of Nietzsche and of the modern psychology of personal growth and "integration"):

> The common cognomen of this world among the misguided and superstitious is "a vale of tears" from which we are to be redeemed by a certain arbitrary interposition of God and taken to Heaven – What a little circumscribe[d] straightened notion! Call the world if you Please "The vale of Soul-making"...There may be intelligences or sparks of the divinity in millions – but they are not Souls till they acquire identities, till each one is personally itself...[H]ow then are souls to be made?...How, but by the medium of a world like this? This point I sincerely wish to consider because I think it a grander system of salvation than the christian religion...As various as the Lives of Men are – so various become their souls...This appears to me a faint sketch of a system of Salvation which does not affront our reason and humanity...[69]

In sketching out these interdependent notions of "negative capability" and of the "vale of Soul-making" Keats in fact arrives at a radically modern version of the traditional theological *via negativa* – but with the important difference that for Keats the idea is severed from every kind of religious doctrine and from every kind of privileging of particular myths.[70] Like Goethe, Keats regarded belief in the Bible and in Christianity as "misguided and superstitious," and himself

[68] Letter to George and Tom Keats of 21–27 Dec. 1817.
[69] Letter to George and Georgiana Keats of 14 Feb. – 3 May 1819.
[70] See also above, p. 129.

called upon pagan mythology whenever it suited his poetic purposes. The creations of art, for Keats, are an undoctrinal "friend to man,"[71] and the poet "is a sage; / A humanist, physician to all men."[72] His view of poetry or literature as our primary source of spiritual nourishment would have been strongly endorsed by both Goethe and Schiller.

7

The highest Romantic hopes for a unification of freedom and worldly necessity were linked with the political hopes of the French Revolution, and were often expressed as notions of a world set free from all man-made oppressions, or of a benignly consummatory "end" to history. These aspirations were associated by many Romantic thinkers with the idea of the centrality of art to human life as such. When these high aspirations began to recede in the face of post-Revolutionary political developments, they opened the way to more realistic treatments of the actual and possible functions of art within the existing world. For less imperious and absolute-minded Romantics (such as Goethe or Keats) both before and after the Revolution, art must always be seen as having its place *within* human life – and actual social institutions therefore as needing to be confronted directly in institutional terms as well as indirectly through the solvent processes of the imagination. (Goethe's contempt for the kind of Romantic art that turns away from the world is well known, as well as sometimes unjust. The early German Romantic poets in many ways anticipated the unworldliness of French Symbolism and of later forms of "aesthetic" escapism.) Imaginative transcendence, we might say, is from this point of view a necessary dimension of human existence; but equally necessary to human existence as we know it is the practical or instrumental function of our various contingently changing human institutions. Imaginative transcendence has its place *within* existing institutions, and is the always-present means to their transformation towards a greater degree of reality – a process which we cannot usefully think of as having any "end" or consummation. Questions about the nature of art or imagination must therefore lead *inter alia* to questions about the nature of aesthetic or imaginative education. This necessity was

[71] "Ode on a Grecian Urn," l. 48.
[72] "The Fall of Hyperion," ll. 189–90.

clearly recognized and explored by Schiller even before the higher aspirations of the Romantic movement had begun to take shape. This more realistic mode of Romantic thinking also points towards the "disillusioned" Romanticism of Victorian poetry, towards the great realistic achievements of the nineteenth-century novel (culminating perhaps in such large-scale explorations of "romantic failure" as *Middlemarch* or *Anna Karenina*), as well as towards the world-repudiating aestheticism and formalism of many of the writers of the 1890s and of modernism. It is at this point that other and less spiritual dimensions of literature begin to claim our attention both theoretically and in artistic practice, and that the history of literary Romanticism might (albeit mistakenly) be supposed to have come to an end.

INDEX